FROMMER'S

SANTA FE, TAOS, AND ALBUQUERQUE

JOHN GOTTBERG

□

1989–1990

Published by Prentice Hall Trade Division
A Division of Simon & Schuster, Inc.
Gulf + Western Building
One Gulf + Western Plaza
New York, New York 10023

ISBN 0-13-791096-7
ISSN 0899-2789

Manufactured in the United States of America
Text Design: Levavi & Levavi, Inc.

*Although every effort was made to ensure the accuracy
of price information appearing in this book,
it should be kept in mind that prices
can and do fluctuate in the course of time.*

CONTENTS

MAPS

INFLATION ALERT: I don't have to tell you that costs will rise regardless of the level of inflation. For that reason it is quite possible that prices may be slightly higher at a given establishment when you read this book than they were at the time this information was collected. Be that as it may, I feel sure these selections will still represent the best travel bargains in Santa Fe, Taos, Albuquerque, and their environs.

CHAPTER I

INTRODUCING NEW MEXICO

□ □ □

Santa Fe—there's no other place like it. The longest continually occupied capital city in the United States, founded by Spanish colonists a full decade before the Pilgrims set foot on Plymouth Rock, it is caught in a time warp between the 17th and 21st centuries, between traditional Indian and Hispanic cultures and the modern onslaught of tourism.

Here in the purified air of New Mexico's state capital, 7,000 feet up in the pastel foothills of the Sangre de Cristo Mountains, Native Americans sit cross-legged hawking their wares to eager shoppers beneath the portico of the 380-year-old Palace of the Governors. As a visitor, you're just as likely to share a park bench with a turquoise-adorned San Ildefonso Indian or a Stetson-hatted Hispanic rancher as with a tourist from Dallas or Atlanta or New York, in town to patronize posh art galleries or to take in the famed Santa Fe Opera. It's no accident that locals call their town "The City Different."

A carefully considered plan to preserve and perpetuate pre-20th-century architecture has made downtown Santa Fe look like an adobe enclave. Much of the rest of this city of 54,000 has followed suit. For miles in all directions, flat-topped, earth-colored homes, many of them valued in the millions of dollars, speckle the hills amid sparse piñon and mesquite forests. Most of the construction is actually stuccoed concrete: A standing joke in Santa Fe art circles is that the city sanctions the use of 42 shades of brown.

Santa Fe is the center of the fast-growing northern New Mexico tourist region, an area that also includes Taos, a one-time frontier town now famed worldwide as an art colony; Albuquerque, a booming high-tech metropolis of half a million people; the 19 surviving settlements and numerous ruins of the centuries-old Pueblo Indian culture; and a spectacular outdoors appealing to wilderness lovers of all ages and fitness levels with its outstanding skiing, backpacking, fishing, hunting, rafting, and other pursuits.

THE LAY OF THE LAND

Forget any preconceptions about the New Mexico "desert." It can be hot in the summer, certainly; but it's cold in the winter and on spring and fall nights. Santa Fe is at 7,000 feet elevation, Taos at 6,950. Albuquerque is in the "lowlands" at 5,300 feet.

The most notable physical features of northern New Mexico are the Sangre de Cristo (Blood of Christ) Mountains and the Rio Grande (Big River). The Sangre de Cristos, with their summit at 13,161-foot Wheeler Peak just north of Taos, are the southern extremity of the Rockies. The Rio Grande flows through a deep north-south cut dividing the mountains from the mesa country to the west. Albuquerque is on the Rio Grande; both Santa Fe and Taos are within 25 miles east on tributary streams.

New Mexico is classified as having a "semi-arid subtropical" climate. That means there's lots of sun; precipitation is light and relative humidity is low. But because of the elevation differences, temperatures at Santa Fe and Taos are often 10° cooler than at Albuquerque. At 7,000 feet you can expect midsummer highs to be in the 80s, with lows in the 50s. Spring and fall highs run in the 60s, with lows in the 30s. Typical midwinter day temperatures are in the low 40s, and overnight lows are in the teens.

Average annual precipitation ranges from 8 inches at Albuquerque to 12 inches at Taos and 14 at Santa Fe, most of it coming in July and August as afternoon thunderstorms. Snowfall is common from November through March, and sometimes as late as May, though it seldom lasts long. Santa Fe averages 32 inches total annual snowfall. At the high-mountain ski resorts, as much as 300 inches (25 feet) may fall in a season—and stay.

Visitors should be aware of the elevation for two reasons. The first is clothing: don't come at any time of year, even in the middle of summer, without at least a warm sweater and rain gear. The second is health: don't push yourself too hard during the first few days after your arrival. The air here is thinner, the sun more direct. You should expect to sunburn more easily and stop to catch your breath more frequently.

A BIT OF HISTORY

INDIANS AND SPANIARDS: The native residents of the upper Rio Grande Valley, the Pueblo Indians, are believed to be descendants of the Anasazi, who lived from the 9th to the 13th century in the Four Corners region, where the states of New Mexico, Arizona, Colorado, and Utah meet. The Anasazi built spectacular structures such as those recalled by ruins at Chaco Canyon and Mesa Verde. It isn't known for certain why they abandoned their homes (some archeologists suggest drought; others, social unrest), but by the time the first Spanish arrived in the 1500s they were long gone and the Pueblo culture was well established throughout northern and western New Mexico.

A distinguishing and unifying mark of the otherwise diverse Anasazi and Pueblo cultures was architectural style. Both built condominium-style communities of stone and mud adobe bricks, three and four stories high. Focused around central plazas, these villages incorporated circular spiritual chambers called *kivas*. The Indians were primitive farmers who used the waters of the Rio Grande and its tributaries to irrigate fields of corn, beans, and squash, and in their spare time created elaborate works of pottery.

The Spanish ventured into the upper Rio Grande after their conquest of Mexico's Aztecs in 1519–1521. In 1540 Francisco Vasquez de Coronado led an expedition in search of the fabled Seven Cities of Cibola, unwittingly introducing horses and sheep to the region. Neither Coronado nor a succession of wealth-thirsty conquistadors could locate the legendary cities of gold, so the Spanish turned their attention to suppressing the natives, first with Christianity and later with government.

Franciscan priests attempted to turn the Indians into model Hispanic peasants. Their churches became the focal points of every pueblo, with Catholic schools an essential adjunct. By 1625 there were an estimated 50 churches in the valley. (Two of the pueblo missions, at Isleta and Acoma, are still in use today.) But the Indians weren't enthused about doing "God's work"— building new adobe missions, tilling fields for the Spanish, and weaving garments for export to Mexico—so soldiers came north to back the padres in extracting labor. For all practical purposes, the Indians were slaves.

Santa Fe was founded in 1610 as the seat of Spanish government in the upper Rio Grande. Governor Don Pedro de Peralta named the settlement La Villa Real de la Santa Fe de San Francisco de Asis, the Royal City of the Holy Faith of St. Francis of Assisi. His capitol, the Palace of the Governors, has been continuously occupied as a public building ever since by Spanish, Mexicans, Americans, and for 12 years (1680–1692) by the Pueblo Indians. Today it is a major museum.

The Pueblo occupation signaled the culmination of decades of resentment against the Spanish colonials. Between the late 16th and mid-17th centuries, the number of pueblo villages had shrunk by half. Rebellions in the 1630s at Taos and Jemez left village priests dead, but were savagely repressed. In 1680 a unified Pueblo rebellion, orchestrated from Taos, succeeded in driving all Spanish from the upper Rio Grande. Forced to retreat to Mexico, it was 12 years before the colonists could reconquer Santa Fe. Bloody battles continued for the next several years, but by the turn of the 18th century Nuevo Mexico was firmly in Spanish hands.

It remained so until Mexican independence in 1821. The most notable event in the intervening years was the departure in the mid-1700s of the Franciscans, exasperated after being unable to wipe out all vestiges of traditional Pueblo religion in eight generations.

ARRIVAL OF THE ANGLOS: The first Anglos (non-Hispanic Caucasians) to linger in the upper Rio Grande Valley were mountain men: itinerant hunters, trappers, and traders. Trailblazers of the United States' westward expansion, they began entering New Mexico in the first decade of the 19th century. Many married into native or Hispanic families. Perhaps the best known was Kit Carson, a sometimes federal agent, sometimes Indian scout, whose legend is inextricably interwoven with that of early Taos. Said Carson: "No man who has seen the women, heard the bells, or smelled the piñon smoke of Taos will ever be able to leave." The home in which he settled and lived for 40 years, until his death in 1868, is now a museum.

Wagon trains and eastern merchants followed Carson and the other pathfinders. Santa Fe, Taos, and Albuquerque, already major trading and commercial centers at the end of the Chihuahua Trail (the Camino Real from Veracruz, Mexico, 1,000 miles south), likewise became the western terminuses of the new Santa Fe Trail (from Independence, Missouri, 800 miles east).

Even though independent Mexico granted Pueblo Indians full citizenship and abandoned the restrictive trade laws of their former Spanish rulers, the 25 years of direct rule from Mexico City were not peaceful in the upper Rio Grande. Instead they were marked by continual rebellions against severe taxation, especially in Taos. Neither did things quiet down immediately when the United States assumed control during the Mexican War. Soon after Gen. Stephen Kearney occupied Santa Fe (in a bloodless takeover) on orders of President James Polk in 1846, an 1847 revolt in Taos resulted in the slaying of the new governor of New Mexico, Charles Bent. The Treaty of Guadalupe Hidalgo officially transferred title to New Mexico, along with Texas, Arizona, and California, to the United States in 1848.

As settlers moved west, the U.S. built Fort Union, 90 miles east of Santa Fe, in 1851 to guard against Apache, Kiowa, and Comanche raids from the eastern plains. Fort Union played a key role 11 years later as the bastion of federal troops against a growing Confederate threat to the southern Rockies region. The Union prevailed in an important battle in 1862 at Glorieta, only about 20 miles east of Santa Fe.

THE PRIEST AND THE BISHOP: Perhaps the two most notable personalities of 19th-century New Mexico were priests. Father José Martinez (1793–1867) was one of the first native-born priests to serve his people. Ordained in Durango, Mexico, he took over the Taos parish and rocked the Catholic boat by abolishing the enforced church tithe because it was a hardship on poor parishioners, publishing the first newspaper in the territory (in 1835), and fighting large land takeovers by Anglos after the U.S. annexed the territory.

On all of these issues he ran at Loggerheads with Bishop Jean Baptiste Lamy (1814–1888), a Frenchman appointed in 1851 to direct the first independent New Mexico diocese. Lamy, the basis for Willa Cather's novel *Death Comes for the Archbishop,* served the diocese for 37 years. He didn't take kindly to Martinez's independent streak, and after repeated conflicts, excommunicated the maverick priest in 1857. But Martinez kept preaching. He formed a breakaway church and continued as northern New Mexico's spiritual leader until his death.

Lamy did much for New Mexico, especially in the areas of education and architecture. Santa Fe's Romanesque Cathedral of St. Francis and the nearby Gothic-style Loretto Chapel, for instance, were constructed under his aegis. But he never willingly accepted other viewpoints. Martinez, on the other hand, embraced the folk tradition, including the craft of *santero* (religious icon) carving and a tolerance of the Penitentes, a flagellant sect which flourished after the departure of the Franciscans in the mid-18th century.

With the advent of the Atchison, Topeka & Santa Fe Rail Road in 1879, New Mexico began to boom. Albuquerque in particular blossomed in the wake of a series of major gold strikes in the Madrid Valley, close to ancient Indian turquoise mines. By the time the gold lodes began to shrink in the 1890s, cattle and sheep ranching had become well entrenched. The territory's growth culminated in statehood in 1912.

Territorial Gov. Lew Wallace (served 1878–1881) helped inspire the interest in arts which today is symbolic of life in northern New Mexico. Wallace penned the great biblical novel *Ben Hur* while occupying the Palace of the Governors. In the 1890s the Taos art colony was launched by Ernest Blumenschein, Bert Phillips, and Joseph Sharp; it boomed in the decade following World

War I when Mabel Dodge Luhan, D. H. Lawrence, Georgia O'Keeffe, Willa Cather, and many others visited or established residence in the area.

During World War II the federal government purchased an isolated boys' camp west of Santa Fe and turned it into the Los Alamos National Laboratory, where the Manhattan Project and other top-secret atomic experiments were developed and perfected. Today Albuquerque is among the nation's leaders in defense contracts and high technology.

Tourism is No. 1 in the Santa Fe and Taos economies today. In Santa Fe, the biggest throngs collect for the acclaimed eight-week opera season (July-August), the annual Indian Market (third weekend of August), and the Fiesta de Santa Fe (weekend following Labor Day). Top events in Taos are the Spring Arts Celebration, highlighting contemporary fine and performing arts for three weeks beginning Memorial Day weekend, and the Fall Arts Festival, focusing on traditional fine arts the last week of September and first week of October.

GETTING THERE

BY AIR: The gateway to Santa Fe, Taos, and other northern New Mexico communities is burgeoning Albuquerque. **Albuquerque International Airport** (tel. 505/842-4366), undergoing a major expansion and renovation in 1988–1990, is the lone port serving national and international flights into the state.

Airlines serving Albuquerque include America West (tel. toll free 800/247-5692), American (tel. 505/242-9464, or toll free 800/433-7300), Continental (tel. 505/842-8220, or toll free 800/525-0280), Delta (tel. toll free 800/221-1212), USAir (tel. 505/243-8461, or toll free 800/435-9772), Southwest (tel. 505/831-1221), TWA (tel. 505/842-4404, or toll free 800/221-2000), and United (tel. 505/242-1411).

Albuquerque is approximately 670 air miles from Dallas, 800 from Los Angeles, 1,350 from Chicago, and 2,000 from New York.

Visitors can make connections to Santa Fe, Taos, Farmington, Gallup, Roswell, Las Cruces, Hobbs, Clovis, Alamogordo, Carlsbad, and Silver City, New Mexico, and Durango, Colorado, and in winter to such ski resorts as Angel Fire, Red River, and Rio Costilla, from Albuquerque via Mesa Airlines (tel. toll free 800/637-2247).

BY BUS: Because Santa Fe is only 58 miles northeast of Albuquerque via Interstate 40, most visitors travel by bus directly from the Albuquerque airport. **Shuttlejack** buses (tel. 505/243-3244 in Albuquerque or 982-4311 in Santa Fe, or toll free 800/452-2665 outside New Mexico) make the 75-minute run between the airport and Santa Fe hotels eight times daily each way, from 5 a.m. to 10:15 p.m. (cost is $15, payable to the driver). Two other bus services shuttle between Albuquerque, Santa Fe, and Taos (cost is $30): **Moreno Valley Transit** (tel. 505/377-3737) and **Faust's Transportation** (tel. 505/758-3410, or toll free 800/345-3738).

The public bus depot in Albuquerque (tel. 505/471-0008) is located on 2nd Street at Silver Avenue. **Greyhound/Trailways** and **Texas, New Mexico & Oklahoma (TNM&O)** all run regular service (usually twice a day) between Albuquerque, Santa Fe, and Taos. Fares run about $9 to Santa Fe, $18 to Taos. But because bus stations in Santa Fe and Taos are several miles south of the city centers, additional taxi or shuttle service is needed to get to most accommodations, and most travelers find it more convenient to pay a few extra dollars for an airport-to-hotel shuttle.

BY TRAIN: The National Railroad Passenger Corporation **Amtrak** (tel. 505/842-9650, or toll free 800/421-8320) links Albuquerque with the frontier village of Lamy, 14 miles southeast of Santa Fe, en route to Chicago. Trains depart daily at 1:40 p.m., arriving in Lamy at 2:45 p.m., with a shuttle van (tel. 505/982-8829) leaving for Santa Fe 45 minutes later. The fare is $15.50 for the train ride, plus $9 additional for the shuttle. The southbound Lamy–Albuquerque train leaves daily at 2:48 p.m. There is no rail service to Taos.

BY CAR: The most convenient way to get around the Santa Fe region is by private car. Auto and RV rentals are widely available for those who arrive without their own transportation, either at the Albuquerque airport or at locations around each city. I have received particularly good rates and service from **Avis Rent-a-Car** at the airport (tel. 505/842-4080 in Albuquerque, 505/982-4361 in Santa Fe, or toll free 800/331-1212) and from **Rich Ford Rent-a-Car**, 8601 Lomas Blvd. NE, Albuquerque (tel. 505/299-9251 in Albuquerque, 505/758-9501 at the Taos airport).

If you're arriving by car from elsewhere in North America, Albuquerque is the crossroads of two major interstate highways. **I-40** runs from Wilmington, N.C. (1,870 miles east) to Barstow, Calif. (580 miles west). **I-25** extends from Buffalo, Wyo. (850 miles north) to El Paso, Texas (265 miles south). I-25 skims past Santa Fe's southern city limits. To reach Taos, you'll have to leave I-25 at Santa Fe and travel north 74 miles via **U.S. 84/285** and **N.M. 68,** or exit from I-25 9 miles south of Raton, near the Colorado border, and proceed southwest 100 miles on **U.S. 64.**

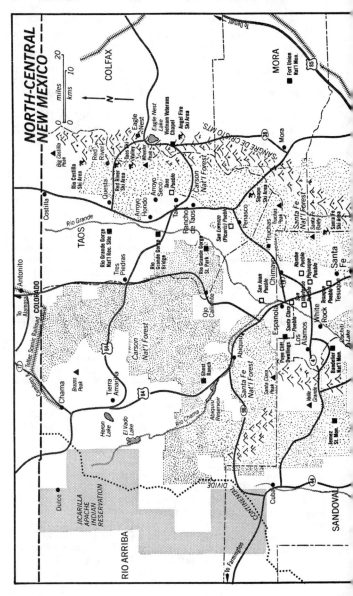

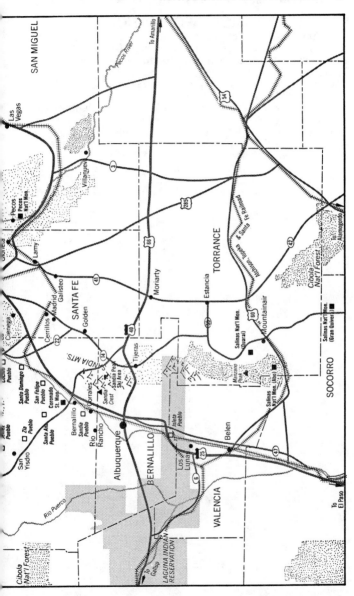

TOURIST INFORMATION

Numerous agencies can assist with your trip planning. The state body responsible for tourism is the **New Mexico Economic Development and Tourism Department,** whose Tourism and Travel Division is housed in the Joseph M. Montoya Building, 1100 St. Francis Dr., Santa Fe, NM 87503 (tel. 505/827-0291, or toll free 800/545-2040).

Other important contacts are the **Santa Fe Convention and Visitors Bureau,** Sweeney Center, Marcy and Grant Streets (P.O. Box 909), Santa Fe, NM 87504 (tel. 505/984-6760, or toll free 800/528-5369); the **Taos County Chamber of Commerce,** S. Santa Fe Road (P.O. Drawer I), Taos, NM 87571 (tel. 505/758-3873, or toll free 800/732-8267); and the **Albuquerque Convention and Visitors Bureau,** 625 Silver St. SW, Suite 210 (P.O. Box 26866), Albuquerque, NM 87125 (tel. 505/243-3696, or toll free 800/284-2282).

CHAPTER II

GETTING TO KNOW SANTA FE

☐ ☐ ☐

Part of the charm of Santa Fe is that it's so easy to get around. Like most cities of Hispanic origin, it was built around a park-like central plaza, with its centuries-old adobe buildings and churches lining the narrow streets. Many of them now house restaurants and art galleries, and the venerable Palace of the Governors, the oldest public building in continuous use in the United States, is the flagship of the Museum of New Mexico system.

ORIENTATION

Santa Fe is situated high and dry at 7,000 feet elevation, at the foot of the rugged Sangre de Cristo Mountains. Santa Fe Baldy rises to more than 12,600 feet a mere 12 miles northeast of the Plaza. The city's downtown straddles the **Santa Fe River,** a tiny tributary of the Rio Grande that is little more than a trickle for much of the year. North is the Española valley (a beautiful view of which is afforded from the Santa Fe Opera grounds) and beyond that, the village of Taos, 66 miles distant. South are ancient Indian turquoise mines in the Cerrillos Hills; southwest is metropolitan Albuquerque, 58 miles away. To the west, across the Caja del Rio Plateau, is the Rio Grande, and beyond that, the 11,000-foot Jemez Mountains and Valle Grande, an ancient and massive volcanic calderon. Indian pueblos dot the entire Rio Grande Valley an hour's drive in any direction.

The limits of downtown Santa Fe are demarcated on three sides by the horseshoe-shaped **Paseo de Peralta,** and on the west by **St. Francis Drive,** otherwise known as U.S. 84/285. **The Alameda** follows the north shore of the Santa Fe River through downtown, with the State Capitol and other federal buildings on the south side of the stream, and most buildings of historic and tourist interest on the north, east of Guadalupe Street.

The **Plaza** is Santa Fe's universally accepted point of orientation. Its four diagonal walkways meet at a central fountain, around which a strange and wonderful assortment of people, of all ages, nationalities, and lifestyles, can be found at nearly any hour of the day or night.

If you stand in the center of the Plaza looking north, you're gazing directly at the Palace of the Governors. In front of you is Palace Avenue; behind you, San Francisco Street. To your left is Lincoln Avenue and to your right **Washington Avenue,** which divides downtown avenues into "East" and "West." St. Francis Cathedral is the massive Romanesque structure a block east down San Francisco Street. The Alameda is two full blocks behind you.

Streaking diagonally to the southwest from the downtown area, beginning opposite the state office buildings on Galisteo Avenue, is **Cerrillos Road.** Once the main north-south highway connecting New Mexico's state capital with its largest city, it is now a six-mile-long motel and fast-food "strip." **St. Francis Road,** which crosses Cerrillos Road three blocks south of Guadalupe Street, is a far less pretentious byway now connecting Santa Fe with the I-25 freeway four miles south of downtown. The **Old Pecos Trail,** on the east side of the city, also joins downtown and the freeway. **St. Michael's Drive** interconnects the three arterials.

THE ABC'S OF SANTA FE

Here are quick answers to some of the questions most frequently asked by visitors.

AIRPORT: The **Santa Fe Municipal Airport** (tel. 471-0828) is just outside the southwest city limits, on Airport Road off Cerrillos Road. Inquire with **Mesa Airlines** (tel. toll free 800/637-2247) about commuter service. Charter services include **Post Aviation** (tel. 471-2525) and **Santa Fe Aviation** (tel. 741-6533).

ARCHITECTURE: Traditional southwestern homes are built of adobe—sun-dried clay bricks mixed with grasses for strength—with a network of *vigas* (large beams) and *latillas* (smaller crossbeams) supporting the roof. In modern Santa Fe, few true adobe homes remain; a majority, it seems, are imitation adobe.

But the imitations are effective. Strict buildings codes have been enforced by the city's Historic Design Review Board since the 1950s, requiring that all new structures within the circumference of the Paseo de Peralta conform to one of two revival styles: Pueblo, reflecting the mud-dabbed adobe look of Pueblo Indians

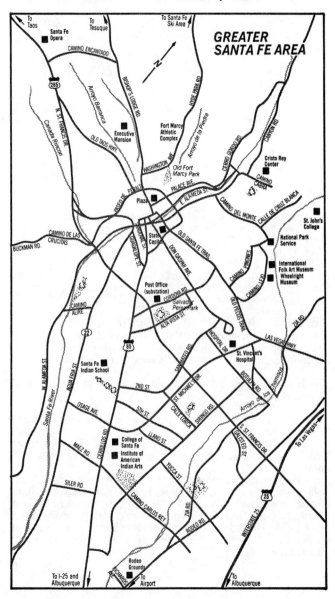

and early Spanish colonists; or Territorial, which came into vogue in the 19th century when railroads could carry in bricks, large logs, and other building materials.

Much of the rest of the city has conformed to the example set by downtown. Now for miles in all directions, flat-topped, earth-colored homes—some valued in the millions of dollars—speckle the hills amid sparse piñon and mesquite forests. In 1988 citywide standards were established to assure good taste in architecture in new developments and restrict the use of neon, large signs, and the like.

ART GALLERIES: Santa Fe is the third-largest art market in the United States. There are more than 125 art galleries in the city, principally in the downtown and Canyon Road areas. (For more information, see Chapter VI).

AUTOMOBILE RENTALS: All the national rental-car companies have branches in Santa Fe, and several local firms also exist. You might try **Adopt-a-Car,** 3570 Cerrillos Rd. (tel. 473-3189); **Avis,** Garrett's Friendship Desert Inn (tel. 982-4361, or toll free 800/331-1212); **Budget,** 1946 Cerrillos Rd. (tel. 984-8028, or toll free 800/527-0700); **Hertz,** 855 Cerrillos Rd. (tel. 982-1844, or toll free 800/654-3131); or **Thrifty,** 750 N. St. Francis Dr. (tel. 988-7484, or toll free 800/367-2277).

AUTOMOBILE REPAIRS: Centrally located and established, **Payne's Auto Center** is at 950 Cordova Rd. (tel. 983-8614). Many other garages, including import specialists, are listed in the telephone directory. For **AAA towing service,** call 982-4633.

BABYSITTING: Try the **Santa Fe Kid Connection,** 1015 Valerie Circle (tel. 471-3100).

BANKS: Hours vary somewhat, but most banks are open from 9 a.m. to 3 p.m. Monday through Thursday and 9 a.m. to 6 p.m. on Friday. A few are also open Saturday morning. Drive-up windows may be open later. Most branches have cash machines available 24 hours.

Full services are provided by the **Bank of Santa Fe,** with four offices (tel. 984-0500); **Banquest/First National Bank of Santa Fe,** with eight offices (tel. 984-7400); **First Interstate Bank of Santa Fe** (tel. 982-3671); **Sunwest Bank,** with three offices (tel. 471-1234); **United New Mexico Bank at Santa Fe,** with two offices (tel. 984-8500); and **Western Bank Santa Fe,** with two offices (tel. 982-6000).

BARBERS AND BEAUTY SALONS: You can get your hair cut in the Inn at Loretto, the La Fonda Hotel, or numerous other locations throughout the city. Santa Fe's **Supercuts** franchise is at 1936 Cerrillos Rd. (tel. 988-7559).

BOOKSTORES AND NEWSSTANDS: The **Los Llanos Bookstore,** 500 Montezuma St. (tel. 982-9542), has the most extensive selection in Santa Fe. Nearby is the **Gallery of Art Books,** on the third floor of the Plaza Mercado at 116 W. San Francisco St. (tel. 988-2050), specializing in exactly what its name implies, and **Santa Fe Booksellers,** 203 W. San Francisco St. (tel. 983-5278), with its excellent offerings in art and southwestern materials. **The Ark,** 133 Romero St. (tel. 988-3709), focuses on New Age materials. **Trespassers William,** 327 Aztec St. (tel. 982-4100), is a children's book dealer. Santa Fe also has several shops dealing in rare and used books, including **Parker Books of the West,** 142 W. Palace Ave. (tel. 988-1076).

There are three relaxed newsstands-cum-coffeeshops in the downtown area: **Downtown Subscription,** 130 W. Palace Ave. (tel. 983-3085); the **Galisteo News & Ticket Center,** 201 Galisteo St. (tel. 984-1316); and **La Fonda Newsstand,** 100 E. San Francisco St. (tel. 988-1404).

BUSES: The **bus station** is at 858 St. Michaels Dr. (tel. 471-0008).

Greyhound/Trailways and **Texas, New Mexico & Oklahoma Coaches (TNM&O)** link Santa Fe with Albuquerque and Denver. There are six round trips daily between Albuquerque and Santa Fe; a one-way ticket costs $7.50 at this writing.

CHILI LINE: This local trolley service (tel. 989-8595) runs three tourist-oriented routes through the central city from the Sanbusco Market Center at the west end of Montezuma Street. Its principal routes are the **Historic Old Santa Fe,** which loops the city in two different itineraries from the Plaza to the hillside museums; and the **Cerrillos Road Express,** which runs south out the strip to the Villa Linda Mall and returns to Sanbusco. Both services run hourly from 9 a.m. to 6 p.m. daily except Sunday. Additional Thursday- through Saturday-evening service operates down Cerrillos Road and around the Plaza between 6 and 9:30 p.m. Courtesy stops can be arranged along any route by calling 989-8595.

An all-day ticket, good for 24 hours (ask for transfers), is $3 for adults, $1.50 for seniors and children.

CHINESE MEDICINE: Surprisingly, Santa Fe is one of the national leaders in this field, with three separate colleges here for students of acupuncture, herbology, and related arts. Nearest downtown is the **Southwest Acupuncture College and Chinese Medical Clinic,** 712 W. San Mateo Ave. (tel. 988-3538). There are also traditional Chinese elixir bars in the Villa Linda Mall and Las Tres Gentes Marketplace.

CHIROPRACTIC: There are 24 chiropractors listed in the telephone directory. I can recommend Guruchander Singh Khalsa, a Texas Sikh, at the **G.R.D. Health Clinic,** 301 E. Palace Ave., Suite 3 (tel. 984-0934).

CLIMATE: Santa Fe is consistently 10° cooler than the nearby desert but gets the same sunny skies, averaging more than 300 days of sunshine out of 365. Midsummer (July-August) days are dry and sunny (around 80°), with brief afternoon thunderstorms common; evenings are typically in the upper 50s. Winters are mild and fair, with occasional (and short-lived) snow (average annual snowfall is 32 inches). Average annual rainfall is 14 inches a year, most of it in summer; relative humidity is 45%. The prevailing winds average 15 miles per hour from the southwest.

For **current weather information,** call 988-3437.

Month	Avg. High	Avg. Low	Avg. Precip. (inches)	% Sun- shine
January	40	19	0.7	72
February	43	23		70
March	51	29		71
April	59	35	1.0	73
May	68	43		74
June	78	52		80
July	80	57	2.4	68
August	79	56		71
September	73	49		77
October	62	38	1.2	79
November	50	28		76
December	41	20		72

COLLEGES: **St. John's College** (tel. 982-3691) is affiliated with the main St. John's campus facility in Annapolis, Md. It is coeducational and nondenominational. The **College of Santa Fe** (tel. 473-6011), founded in 1947, is an independent private liberal arts college affiliated with the Christian Brothers. **Santa Fe**

Community College (tel. 471-8200), which opened in 1983, is a state-supported college with transfer programs to four-year universities.

DENTISTS: There are dozens listed in the phone directory. Most work in the medical office area near the intersection of St. Francis and St. Michael's Drives, several miles south of downtown. Among those near downtown, **Dr. Leslie E. La Kind,** 623 Don Gaspar Ave. (tel. 988-3500), offers 24-hour emergency service.

DOCTORS: Perhaps the most extensive clinic is the **Lovelace-DeVargas Medical Group,** 141 Paseo de Peralta (tel. 982-0881 for urgent care, 982-3246 for family care), in the DeVargas Center Professional Building at DeVargas Mall, between the Plaza and the Sheraton Hotel. It's open daily including evenings, by appointment, at 9 a.m. for family medical care; at 8 a.m. for urgent care (no appointment needed), every day of the year.

EMERGENCY: Dial 911 for police, sheriff, fire department, or ambulance.

FIRE DEPARTMENT: Dial 911 for emergencies, or 982-2029 for non-emergencies. The main fire station is at 2029 Murales St.

GASOLINE: You'll find Chevron, Exxon, Gulf, Phillips 66, and Texaco stations in Santa Fe, as well as a number of cut-rate independent operators.

GLASSES: If yours are broken or lost, you can get one-hour prescription service from the **Quintana Optical Dispensary,** 109 E. Marcy St. (tel. 988-4234), in downtown Santa Fe. The outlet is open Monday through Friday from 9 a.m. to 5 p.m., and on Saturday from 9 a.m. to noon.

HOSPITAL: The **St. Vincent Hospital,** 455 St. Michael's Dr. (tel. 983-3361), is a 268-bed regional health center. Patient services include urgent and emergency-room care, ambulatory surgery, diagnostic radiology, cancer diagnosis and treatment, behavioral sciences, and a family recovery center for adolescent substance abuse.

LAUNDRY AND DRY CLEANING: You'll find **Shockey's Coin-op Laundry** at 755 Cerrillos Rd. (tel. 983-9881), just outside the downtown perimeter, open every day from 6 a.m. to 10:30 p.m. **One Hour Martinizing,** in five locations including

200 E. Water St. downtown (tel. 982-8606), handles dry cleaning and drop-off laundry Monday through Saturday from 7 a.m. to 6 p.m.

LIBRARIES: The **Santa Fe Public Library** is half a block from the Plaza at 145 Washington Ave. (tel. 984-6780). There's a branch library at the south end of the city in Villa Linda Mall, and another, larger branch—the La Farge Branch—at 1713 Llano St. (tel. 473-7260), just off St. Michael's Drive.

LIMOUSINES: If you're inclined to indulge yourself, try **Limotion,** 1476 St. Francis Dr. (tel. 982-LIMO).

LIQUOR LAWS: Drinking age in New Mexico is 21. Bars are required to close at 2 a.m.; on Sunday they can only open between noon and midnight. Wine, beer, and spirits are sold at licensed supermarkets and liquor stores. A special allowance must be granted for liquor to be dispensed in proximity to any church.

LITERATURE: The classic Santa Fe novel is Willa Cather's *Death Comes for the Archbishop,* based on the life of 19th-century Bishop Jean-Baptiste Lamy. Also recommended are Rudolfo Anaya's autobiographical *Bless Me, Ultima,* about Hispanic village life, and any of Tony Hillerman's bestselling mystery novels, such as *The Dance Hall of the Dead.* If you're a history buff, seek out the work of Paul Horgan or Marc Simmons. Robert L. Casey's *Journey to the High Southwest: A Traveler's Guide* is perhaps the best complete guide to the Four Corners region. For a travel guide covering more of New Mexico, as well as Arizona and Colorado, try *Frommer's Dollarwise Southwest.*

LOST PROPERTY: Contact city police at 473-5000.

MAPS: Free city and state maps are easily obtained at tourist information offices.

Members of the **American Automobile Association** can get maps at no cost from the AAA office at 1511 5th St. (tel. 982-4633).

The latest **Mobil Road Atlas** contains the most accurate New Mexico maps including the revised 1988 state highway numbers.

NEWSPAPERS: *The New Mexican,* a Gannett Corporation property, is Santa Fe's daily newspaper. Offices are at 202 E. Marcy Ave. (tel. 983-3303). The weekly *Santa Fe Reporter,* published on Wednesday, is often more willing to stir dirt; its entertainment listings are excellent.

For more complete national and world news, you should read either of the two Albuquerque papers, the *Journal* or the *Tribune*. Both are readily available in Santa Fe.

PHARMACIES: Two are especially convenient to the Plaza: the **Santa Fe Pharmacy,** at 125 Lincoln Ave. (tel. 984-8202), open from 8 a.m. to 6 p.m. Monday through Friday and 9 a.m. to noon on Saturday; and the **Medicine Shoppe Pharmacy,** at 217 E. Palace Ave. (tel. 982-2541 or 983-6281), open from 9 a.m. to 5:30 p.m. Monday through Friday and 9 a.m. to noon on Saturday. Emergency and delivery service can be arranged with the **Medical Center Pharmacy,** adjacent to St. Vincent Hospital on St. Michael's Drive (tel. 983-4359).

PHOTOGRAPHY: Most picture-taking needs, from film purchases to camera repairs to 24-hour processing, can be handled by **The Camera Shop,** 109 E. San Francisco St. (tel. 983-6591), or **Camera & Darkroom,** 216 Galisteo St. (tel. 983-2948).

POLICE: In case of **emergency,** dial 911. All other inquiries should be directed to the main **Santa Fe Police Station** at 2515 Camino Entrada (tel. 473-5000, or 473-5080 after 5 p.m. and weekends). The **Santa Fe County Sheriff's Office** is in the county courthouse, Grant Avenue and Johnson Street (tel. 984-5060).

POPULATION: In 1986 the official figures were 54,860 for the city, and 81,400 for Santa Fe County.

POSTAL SERVICES: The **Main Post Office** fronts on South Federal Street two blocks north and a block west of the Plaza (tel. 988-6351). The branch **Coronado Station** is at 541 W. Cordova Rd. (tel. 983-7677). Most of the major hotels have stamp machines and mailboxes with twice-daily pickup. The ZIP Code for central Santa Fe is 87501.

RADIO AND TELEVISION: Santa Fe has ten radio stations—four of them AM, six FM—which offer listeners everything from country-western to Hispanic salsa music, '50s oldies to modern rock, news, and information. Many more Albuquerque stations are easily heard from Santa Fe. **KCHF-TV (Channel 11)** is the local television station; the three Albuquerque stations all have offices in the state capital.

RELIGIOUS SERVICES: Roman Catnolics are the most visible group in Santa Fe, with eight churches and the venerable **St. Fran-**

cis Cathedral. Visitors are welcome to attend services at the Franciscan cathedral, 131 Cathedral Pl., one block from the Plaza (tel. 982-5619). Masses are held five times on Sunday and holy days (including a Spanish-language mass) and three times on weekdays; hours are posted on the front door.

Other denominations active in Santa Fe include Anglican, Assembly of God, Baptist, Charismatic, Christian and Missionary Alliance, Christian Science, Church of Christ, Church of God, Disciples of Christ, Episcopal, Foursquare Gospel, Friends, Jehovah's Witnesses, Lutheran, Methodist, Nazarene, Seventh-day Adventist, and United Church of Christ. The Church of Jesus Christ of Latter-day Saints (Mormon) has two local wards, and there is also a Jewish synagogue.

Many New Age adherents meet in small discussion groups. A good source of information is the **Galisteo News & Ticket Center** at 201 Galisteo St. (tel. 984-1316). Organized groups include Baha'i, Buddhist (Mountain Cloud Zen Center), Eckankar, I AM Sanctuary, and Unitarian-Universalist.

ROAD CONDITIONS: Information on conditions in the Santa Fe area can be obtained from the State Police (tel. 827-9300) or by dialing 983-0120.

SENIOR DISCOUNTS: Many establishments offer discounts of 10% or more to card-carrying members of the American Association of Retired Persons (AARP).

SHOE REPAIRS: Most convenient to downtown Santa Fe is the **Jacobs Shoe Repair Shop,** 646 Old Santa Fe Trail (tel. 982-9774).

STORE HOURS: Most shops are open from 9 a.m. to 6 p.m. Monday through Friday, and from 9 a.m. to noon or 1 p.m. on Saturday. Some downtown and mall shops may remain open all day on Saturday and even on Sunday afternoons, particularly during the May-to-October tourist season.

TAXES: There's a 5.625% state sales tax on all merchandise and services. The city of Santa Fe charges an additional 4% bed tax on hotel rooms, for a total of 9.625% tax, according to the Santa Fe Convention and Visitors Bureau.

TAXIS: It's best to telephone for a taxi, for they are difficult to flag from the street and there are no cab ranks. There are no meters, but set fares exist for given distances. Expect to pay an average of about $2 per mile—unless you get coupons at the public library downtown for a 50% discount. The two companies—**Capital City Cab** (tel. 988-2090) and **Village Taxi** (tel. 988-9990)—have a common dispatch.

TELEPHONES: The **area code** for New Mexico is 505. For **directory assistance** within New Mexico, dial 411; outside of the state, dial 1, followed by the area code and 555-1212.

TIME: New Mexico is on Mountain Standard Time, one hour ahead of the West Coast and two hours behind the East Coast. Thus when it's 10 a.m. in Santa Fe, it's noon in New York, 11 a.m. in Chicago, and 9 a.m. in Los Angeles. Daylight Saving Time is in effect from April to October.

TIPPING: In normal circumstances, plan to leave 15% to 20% of your bill for waiters and waitresses in restaurants and lounges. A tip of 50¢ per bag is appropriate for hotel bellmen and airport porters. If you're staying longer than a night or two in a hotel, tip the chambermaid about $1 a night.

TOUR OPERATORS: These are subdivided into city, walking, and regional tours. There is some overlap in services.

City Tours

Gray Line Tours, 858 St. Michael's Dr. (tel. 471-9200 or 983-6565), offers the trolley-like "Roadrunner," leaving the Plaza (Lincoln Street and Palace Avenue) several times daily except Sunday, beginning at 9 a.m., for 75-minute tours of historic downtown Santa Fe. The cost is $6 for adults, $3 for children under 12. A half-day City Drive commences at 9 a.m. and 1 p.m., with a charge of $12. There is free pickup at hotels if reservations are made in advance.

RojoTours, 228 Old Santa Fe Trail, Suite A (tel. 983-8333), is a locally owned tour-booking service, also offering reservation and transportation service.

Santa Fe Detours, La Fonda Hotel Lobby, 100 E. San Francisco St. (tel. 983-6565, or toll free 800/DETOURS), is perhaps the city's most extensive booking service.

Walking Tours

Historical Walking Tours of Santa Fe, Las Tres Gentes Marketplace, 418 Cerrillos Rd. (tel. 984-8235). Lifelong Santa Feans Frank Montano and Kathy Montoya offer three tours: the deluxe, leaving at 9:30 a.m. for 2½ hours, at $8.50 per person; Orientation, leaving at 1, 2:30, 4, and 5:30 p.m. for 1¼ hours, at $5; and sunset, departing at 7:30 p.m., lasting 1¼ hours, for $5.

New Earth Treks, 964 Old Santa Fe Trail (tel. 982-6879), has walking tours and visits to Indian pueblos.

RojoTours (see above). Heather Fields leads walking tours twice daily, at 10 a.m. and 1 p.m., for $10 per person (children free). Fields is a native New Zealander who has lived in Santa Fe for 13 years.

Santa Fe Walks (tel. 983-6565, or toll free 800/DE-TOURS), offers tours conducted by Waite Thompson, author of "The Santa Fe Guide" (available locally). They leave the Santa Fe Detours desk at the La Fonda Hotel twice a day in summer, at 9:30 a.m. and 1:30 p.m., for 2½-hour tours of the historic and modern city. The cost is $10 per person, all inclusive; children under 14 are free with a parent.

Storyteller Joe Bussell (tel. 988-3377) leads tours emphasizing the city's arts and history twice daily, at 9:30 a.m. and 2 p.m., beginning in the Hotel St. Francis lobby. The cost is $10 per person.

Walk of the Town Tours, 611 Salazar St. (tel. 983-6499), offers recorded-cassette guided downtown walking tours.

Regional Tours

Chamisa Touring Service, Route 7, Box 125, Santa Fe, NM 87505 (tel. 988-1343), has custom-designed tours of the region, conducted by local educators or anthropologists who ride with you in your own car.

Discover Santa Fe, P.O. Box 2847, Santa Fe, NM 87504 (tel. 982-4979), is a group travel coordinator.

Gray Line Tours (see above). Tours include the following: Taos and Taos Indian Pueblo, full day, beginning at 9 a.m., for $35; Bandelier National Monument and Los Alamos, half day, leaving at 1 p.m., for $25. The combination Roadrunner and Bandelier–Los Alamos tour departs at 9 a.m., for $28. All tours operate daily except Sunday.

Rain Parrish, 535 Cordova Rd., Suite 250 (tel. 984-8236). Parrish is a Navajo anthropologist and former museum curator who takes small groups for visits to pueblos. Half-day rates are $70 for two, $90 for four; the full-day charge is $125 for two, $160 for four. A two-day advance reservation is required; a week's notice is needed if a meal is desired at the pueblo ($10 additional charge). Parrish does her best business on pueblo dance and feast days, April through November.

RedBird Tours, 2823 Camino Principe (tel. 471-4761), an Indian-owned and -operated business, offers overnight tours of pueblo homes, including dance and feast days, storytelling, and special healing rituals. Fishing and wildlife photography trips are also arranged, as well as visits to Taos and the Puye Cliff Dwellings. Guides will ride in your car or take you in theirs.

Rocky Mountain Tours, 102 W. San Francisco St., Suite 5 (tel. 984-1684), is a group tour specialist and offers private guide services. River-rafting trips and journeys on the Cumbres & Toltec Scenic Railway are arranged.

RojoTours (see above). Everything from pueblo tours to horseback riding, river rafting and bicycling can be arranged.

Santa Fe Detours (see above). Arrangements can be made for the Cumbres & Toltec Scenic Railway overnight special (from $27); river rafting on the Rio Grande ($35 for a five-hour family trip, $70 for a thrill in the "Taos box," $150 for an overnight journey in the Chama Canyon Wilderness); trail riding ($25 for a half day, $50 for a full day, $125 overnight); and cross-country skiing ($28 for a half day, $45 for a full day).

Southwest Safaris, P.O. Box 945, Santa Fe, NM 87504 (tel. 988-4246). This air service offers three separate trips to Arizona from the Santa Fe Airport: to Monument Valley ($299 per person), leaving at 7:30 a.m. and returning at 4 p.m., including a four-wheel-drive excursion; to the Grand Canyon ($299), 7 a.m. to 4 p.m.; and to Canyon de Chelly ($225), 8 a.m. to 1 p.m. Bookings can be made through Santa Fe Detours.

TOURIST INFORMATION: The **Santa Fe Convention and Visitors Bureau** is located in Sweeney Center at the corner of Marcy and Grant Streets downtown (P.O. Box 909), Santa Fe, NM 87504 (tel. 505/984-6760, or toll free 800/528-5369). The **New Mexico Economic Development and Tourism Department** is in the Joseph Montoya Building, 1100 St. Francis Dr. (tel. 505/827-0300, or toll free 800/545-2040). The **Santa Fe Chamber of Commerce** is at 333 Montezuma St. (tel. 505/983-7317).

USEFUL TELEPHONE NUMBERS: You'll find the following agencies or services at the numbers listed: **City of Santa Fe offices** (tel. 984-6500), **Crisis Intervention Center** (tel. 982-2771), **New Mexico Environmental Improvement Division** (tel. 827-9329), **poison control** (tel. toll free 800/432-6866), **Rape Crisis Center** (tel. 982-4667), **Sangre de Cristo Mental Health Services** (tel. 982-8516), and time and temperature (tel. 473-2211).

CHAPTER III

WHERE TO STAY IN SANTA FE

□ □ □

Santa Fe has become one of the "in" places to vacation in the United States. With its growth in tourism, so the hotel/motel industry has grown.

Although Santa Fe has some 45 hotels, motels, bed-and-breakfast establishments, and other accommodations, rooms can still be hard to come by at the peak of the tourist season. You can get year-round assistance from **Santa Fe Central Reservations,** 1210 Luisa St., Suite 10 (tel. 505/983-8200, or toll free 800/982-7669). The service will also book transportation and activities. Emergency lodging assistance is available free after 4 p.m. daily by calling 988-4252.

There may not be a "bad" place to stay in "The City Different." From downtown hotels to Cerrillos Road motels, from ranch-style resorts to quaint bed-and-breakfast establishments, the standard of accommodation is universally high.

In perusing the following listing, it helps to be aware of the highly seasonal nature of the tourist industry in Santa Fe. Accommodations are often booked solid through the summer months, and most establishments raise their prices accordingly. Rates are usually increased further for Indian Market, the third weekend of August. But there's little agreement on the dates marking the beginning and end of the tourist season; whereas one hotel may not raise its rates until July 1 and may drop them again in mid-September, another may have higher rates from May to November. Some hotels recognize a shoulder season or increase rates again over the Christmas holidays. It pays to shop around during these "in-between" seasons of May-June and September-October.

In any season, senior, group, corporate, and other special rates are often available. If you have any questions about your eligibility for these rates, be sure to ask.

In this listing, I have placed hotels and motels in four different price categories:

Deluxe hotels are those with high-season doubles starting at $100 or more.

Upper Bracket rooms run $80 to $100 double during the high season, $85 or less in the off-season.

Moderate lodgings are those with high-season doubles priced between $50 and $85, and low-season doubles for under $65.

Budget accommodations offer double rooms for less than $50 during the summer peak season, somewhat less in the off-season.

Accommodations are further categorized according to the geographical region of Santa Fe in which they are located: Downtown, Northside, Cerrillos Road, or Southside.

Following the hotel/motel listings, you'll find suggestions for bed-and-breakfast accommodations, a youth hostel, nearby resort accommodations, and campgrounds and RV parks. On-site restaurants, bars, and other facilities are listed following the description of the accommodation.

A tax of 9.625% is added to all hotel bills in Santa Fe.

HOTELS AND MOTELS

DOWNTOWN: Everything within the horseshoe-shaped Paseo de Peralta, and east a few blocks on either side of the Santa Fe River, is considered downtown Santa Fe. None of these accommodations is beyond walking distance from the Plaza.

Deluxe

In 16th- and 17th-century Spanish folklore, Eldorado was a fabled city of gold. The **Eldorado,** 309 W. San Francisco St., Santa Fe, NM 87501 (tel. 505/988-4455, or toll free 800/CLARION), a Clarion hotel, carries on the image of luxury as northern New Mexico's only "four-star" accommodation. Santa Fe natives may complain about the architecture of this pueblo-like fortress facing Sandoval Street, but guests rarely do. A C-shaped, five-story hotel built around an enormous courtyard two blocks west of the Plaza, the Eldorado opened in April 1986. Its southwestern-style interior features an art collection appraised at more than $250,000, including antique furniture, Indian pottery, carved animals, and other works mainly by Santa Fe artists.

The guest rooms continue the regional theme. Many of them have beehive fireplaces in the traditional *kiva* style and decks or terraces with handmade furniture. The upper rooms in particular afford outstanding views of the Sangre de Cristo range (to the east) or the Jemez Mountains (looking west). Each room—tastefully appointed in pastel shades of lilac and red—has one king-size bed or two double beds, a tiled table flanked by easy chairs, floor-length drapes, a double closet, limited-edition lithographs on the walls, a remote-control TV in an armoire (with cable and in-house movies), a clock-radio, a direct-dial phone (local calls are 50¢), and thermostat-controlled heating and air conditioning. Each room has a mini-refrigerator with an honor bar. Amenities include terry-cloth robes, large-size shampoo and conditioner, lotion, and a lint brush. An updated weather report is provided nightly with turn-down service.

The Eldorado has 200 rooms and 18 suites. Rates for two people run $110 to $130 in the low season (November to April), $130 to $145 in the shoulder season (May-June and September-October), and $145 to $160 in the high season (July-August). Prices are $20 less for singles. Suites range from $150 to $205 double in the low season, $190 to $230 in the high season.

If you're willing to lay out $600 a night, you can stay in "Los Cielos," the Presidential Suite, which has hosted the likes of George Bush, Robert Redford, and King Juan Carlos I of Spain and his queen. With 1,500 square feet of floor space, this suite is like an art museum. It features a huge, exclusive deck ideal for parties.

The Eldorado has a rooftop pool and hot tub, with adjacent saunas and massage room. Hotel guests also have free membership in the Santa Fe Spa. The hotel employs a full-service year-round concierge, valet laundry service, and safe-deposit boxes. Stores on the premises include three art galleries, a jeweler, leatherworker, boutique, and sundry shop. There are ten meeting and conference rooms, the largest holding 400 for banquets.

There are also three restaurants, including the innovative and elegant Old House Restaurant on the foundation of the house that was torn down to clear space for the new hotel. Open from 6 to 10 p.m. nightly for dinner only, the Old House has a polished-wood floor, *viga-latilla* ceiling, *kiva* fireplaces, and other regional touches. Pueblo pottery and Hopi *kachina* dolls rest in wall niches amid a blue-green and white color scheme. For your meal, you might start with corn soup with poached Pacific oysters ($3.75), followed by sweetbreads ($6.25). Entrees run the gamut from beef, veal, and lamb to chicken and seafood; you may want to consider roast saddle of venison and chestnut purée in grand veneur

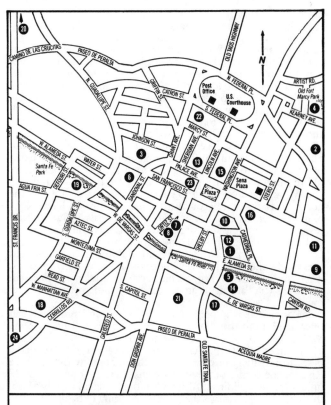

DOWNTOWN SANTA FE

KEY TO NUMBERED SIGHTS:

1. Best Western Inn at Loretto
2. Cross of the Martyrs
3. Eldorado Hotel
4. Fort Marcy Compound
5. Garrett's Friendship Inn
6. Hilton Hotel
7. Hotel St. Francis
8. Inn of the Governors
9. Inn on the Alameda
10. La Fonda Hotel
11. La Posada de Santa Fe
12. Loretto Chapel
13. Museum of Fine Arts
14. Oldest House
15. Palace of the Governors
16. St. Francis Cathedral
17. San Miguel Mission
18. Santa Fe Motel
19. Santuario de Guadalupe
20. Sheraton Hotel
21. State Capitol
22. Sweeney Center
23. Tourist Information
24. TraveLodge

sauce ($21.50) or broiled swordfish in homemade zucchini salsa ($16.50). The adjoining lounge features a weekly Friday-evening "Meet the Managers" one-hour cocktail party.

A more casual dining spot is the spacious Eldorado Court, open Monday through Saturday for breakfast and lunch from 7 a.m. to 2 p.m., and for Sunday brunch from 11 a.m. to 2 p.m. There are plans to redesign this red-carpeted lobby extension, but the tiled tables, wood-crafted chairs, and big fireplace will stay. Breakfast specials include eggs Norwegian on a brioche with smoked salmon ($7.75) and a Spanish hash of corned beef, eggs, and green chili ($6.50). Lunch offerings include Pasadena salad ($6.25), blue-corn chicken enchiladas ($7.50), sandwiches (from $6), and pizzas (from $6). The Eldorado Court Lounge, open daily from 4 p.m. to 2 a.m. (on Sunday to midnight), offers a variety of live entertainment from acoustic guitars to the baby grand.

More casual yet is Big Jo's Bar and Oyster Co., a deli at the north end of the central courtyard. Open daily from 11 a.m. to 11 p.m. or later, as business warrants, its specials include Cajun ceviche ($4.75), brie and pâté ($5.25), burgers (from $6), oysters and clams on the half shell, and various antipasto plates (from $8.75). It's also got a wide selection of domestic and imported beers and wines. Big Jo's really hops on hot summer afternoons, when the Green Chili Peppers big band (on Friday) and mariachi musicians (on Saturday) can be seen performing near the central fountain.

For visitors who prefer more intimacy than large hotels can offer, the **Inn on the Alameda,** 303 E. Alameda, Santa Fe, NM 87501 (tel. 505/984-2121, or toll free 800/552-0070, ext. 289), might be just the ticket. Four blocks from the Plaza and a block from gallery-intense Canyon Road, opposite the Santa Fe River at the corner of Paseo de Peralta, the inn contains just 37 units in three buildings. Although it only opened in July 1986, this small hotel preserves the spirit of old Santa Fe behind an exterior of adobe and adzed-wood pillars.

You'll catch the flavor as soon as you walk into the lobby, with its traditional *viga-latilla* ceiling construction. Just past the unobtrusive reception desk is a sitting room/library with handcrafted furnishings, soft pillows, and a rocking chair placed around a big fireplace. Piped light-jazz music adds to the *ambiente*. An elaborate continental breakfast (included in the room bill) is served here each morning, and refreshments are available at a full-service bar from 5 to 10 p.m. nightly.

The mood continues to the guest rooms, characterized by the pastel shades of contemporary southwestern décor. Each room features a king-size bed or two queen-size beds, a desk with three-drawer credenza, an additional table and chairs, cable TV with built-in AM/FM radio, and direct-dial phones (local calls are free, but there's a 50¢ surcharge on all long-distance calls). There are prints on the walls and wood-slat blinds on the windows, and heating and air conditioning is individually controlled. Some rooms have outdoor patios or private balconies.

Rooms are priced $80 to $125 single, from $90 double, November through May; $95 to $125 single, from $105 double, June through October. One suite (with a sundeck) goes for $150 in the off-season, $200 during the summer. The only charge for kids under 12 is an extra $5 for breakfast; a teenager or third adult in a room is charged $15.

Because the hotel serves only breakfast, room service is available from 7 to 11 a.m. only. Morning papers are delivered free to rooms, however, and there's a newsstand off the lobby. A tiled hot tub/spa is available by reservation. A concierge is on staff, and valet laundry service is offered. Small pets are accepted; child-care service can be arranged.

The Volper School of Culinary Art—instructed by Cindy Volper, former personal chef of New York Mayor Edward Koch—offers frequent Tuesday- and Thursday-evening classes at the Inn on the Alameda. The cost of $45 includes a full meal and drink. Call for advance registration (tel. 505/989-8998).

Upper Bracket

There's considerably more history behind the **Best Western Inn at Loretto,** 211 Old Santa Fe Trail (P.O. Box 1417), Santa Fe, NM 87501 (tel. 505/988-5531, or toll free 800/528-1234). This handsome, Pueblo Revival–style building was originally the Loretto Academy, a Catholic girls' school built in the late 19th century under the direction of Bishop Lamy. Although the building—which reopened as a hotel in 1975—has been fully renovated and expanded, bits and pieces of the original academy remain, including the famous Chapel of Our Lady of Light with its mysterious spiral staircase (see Chapter V, "What to See and Do in Santa Fe"). Another unique element of the Inn at Loretto is the use of hand-painted Mimbres designs. There are 7,200 of these colorful motifs, all different, on lobby, corridor, guest room, meeting room, and restaurant walls throughout the building. Staff artist Ross Martinez re-created work found on pottery of the 11th- and 12th-century Mimbres people of southwestern New Mexico.

The hotel, a little over one block from the southeast corner of the Plaza, is horseshoe-shaped, with room balconies or patios surrounding a landscaped outdoor courtyard with a fountain and pool. Inside, on the ground floor, is a veritable New Mexican shopping mall, with two art galleries, an additional folk-art dealer, two boutiques, a jeweler, a bookstore, a gift shop, a sundries shop, a liquor store, and a hair salon. Here also is where you'll find the Footsteps Across New Mexico audio-visual program (see Chapter V).

Of the 136 guest rooms, half feature a single king-size bed; the remainder, a pair of double beds. Southwest décor dominates, with etched-tin shades on intricate pottery-style lamps, Mexican tiles inset in writing and bedside tables, dried flower arrangements, and blue-toned regional motifs on bedspreads and drapes. All rooms have either a sofa or an easy chair with ottoman. About 75% have patios or balconies. Each has a refrigerator, cable TV with built-in radio, and direct-dial phone (no charge for local calls). Washer/dryer facilities are available to guests at no charge.

Prices for two are $96 to $108 May through October, $85 to $97 November through April; singles are $12 less.

Loretto's Los Rincones restaurant, notable for its intricate etched-tin chandeliers, is open daily from 6:30 a.m. to 9:30 p.m. On warm summer days, service is extended to the courtyard. Breakfast includes egg dishes, omelets, and local meals like chorizo burritos ($5.50). For lunch, consider an avocado and crab remoulade ($7), stuffed sopaipillas ($5), and sandwiches (from $4.25). Dinner entrees include bistec con chile ($14) and Los Rincones chicken, sautéed with red and green peppers, onions, tomatoes, pepperoni, green olives, and marsala wine ($11.25).

Hot spiced shrimp is cooked up during happy hour every Friday afternoon in the warm, mezzanine-ringed hotel lounge. It's open daily from 11 a.m. to 1 a.m. (to midnight on Sunday); there's live entertainment Tuesday through Saturday nights in summer, and a piano bar on Friday and Saturday nights in winter.

The Loretto can seat up to 200 for banquets. A large free parking area extends across the south side of the hotel.

Probably no hotel in Santa Fe is more famous than **La Fonda on the Plaza,** 100 E. San Francisco St. (P.O. Box 1209), Santa Fe, NM 87501 (tel. 505/982-5511, or toll free 800/523-5002). Often called "The Inn at the End of the Trail," it occupies a full block between the southeast corner of the Plaza, where a marker denotes the terminus of the Santa Fe Trail, and Bishop Lamy's St. Francis Cathedral.

When Capt. William Becknell and his trading expedition from Missouri pioneered the trail and arrived in Santa Fe in 1821, they found an inn—a *fonda*—on this site. With a boom in the number of trappers, traders, and merchants who began flocking to Santa Fe, a saloon and casino were added. Among its 19th-century patrons were President and Mrs. Rutherford B. Hayes, Gen. and Mrs. Ulysses S. Grant, and Gen. William Tecumseh Sherman. It is said that even William Bonney, alias Billy the Kid, worked at La Fonda for a time washing dishes.

The original inn was dying of old age in 1920 when it was razed and replaced on the same site by what is today La Fonda. The Atchison, Topeka & Santa Fe Railroad owned the hotel from 1925 to 1969 and leased it to the Harvey Houses chain. The most recent of a series of major additions was made in 1986, adding a three-story parking garage and rooftop restaurant.

Like the Loretto, La Fonda's architecture is of the Pueblo Revival style, imitation adobe with wooden balconies and beam ends protruding over the tops of windows. In its corridors, notable for their hand-painted designs, are two art galleries, an Indian artifacts outlet, a frame-and-print shop, a leather shop, a boutique, a beauty salon, a French pastry shop, and a newsstand with sundries.

Each of the 160 guest rooms and suites is a bit different from the next. That's particularly true of the bright color schemes: each piece of hand-carved Spanish-style furniture—from desk, chairs, and dresser to the headboard—is individually painted in a Hispanic folk motif, color-coordinated to other pieces in the room (but to nothing outside the room). All rooms have air conditioning, satellite TV, direct-dial phones (local calls are free), drapes, and a throw rug. Beds are king-size, doubles, or twins—the latter, high, old-fashioned beds.

All suites and deluxe rooms have mini-refrigerators, tiled baths, and more sophisticated artwork, including etched tin and stonework. Full suites—of which two have kitchen facilities—feature fireplaces, private balconies, antique furniture, Oriental carpets, and a large amount of closet and shelf space.

Standard room rates are $90 single, $100 double, July 1 through October 15 and the last two weeks of December; $75 single, $85 double, the remainder of the year. Deluxe units start at $115; mini-suites, $130 to $165; full suites, $170 to $295. There's no charge for children under 18 in the same room with their parents.

La Plazuela Restaurant, a tiled indoor-garden patio lit by a skylight, is open daily from 7 a.m. to 9:30 p.m. Its furniture is solid-wood Spanish colonial, and the waiters and waitresses are garbed accordingly. Fajitas and chicken enchiladas are luncheon delights. Dinner entrees, priced at $6.25 to $17, include regional specialties and other fine dishes such as lobster Delamar and veal marsala. The adjacent La Fiesta Lounge is open daily from 11 a.m. to 2 a.m. (on Sunday from noon to midnight), with nightly swing-era or mariachi entertainment appealing mainly to an older crowd.

The Carriage House Terrace, a spacious outdoor terrace on the third floor above the parking garage, serves lunches and light dinners daily except Wednesday until 8 p.m. in summer; there's bar service from 11 a.m. to closing. From the Bell Tower Lounge, at the southwest corner of the hotel, you can watch the sun set over the distant Jemez Mountains. This is the highest point in downtown Santa Fe, an impressive spot to end the day.

Hotel facilities include an outdoor pool, two indoor Jacuzzis, a cold plunge, and a massage room. There's also a tour desk and a guest-services desk open seven days a week. Pets may be allowed. Up to 180 people can be accommodated for banquets.

One of the city's loveliest hotels is **La Posada de Santa Fe,** 330 E. Palace Ave., Santa Fe, NM 87501 (tel. 505/986-0000, 505/983-6351, or toll free 800/727-5276). It is built around the Staab House, a historic mansion erected at the corner of the Paseo de Peralta four blocks east of the Plaza, between 1882 and 1886 by Abraham Staab, a German immigrant pioneer, for his bride, Julie. A three-story, mansard-roofed structure, the Staab House was the first brick building to be constructed in Santa Fe: materials were carried by wagon train from Missouri. It was equally well known for its richly carved walnut interior woodwork and the decorative scrolls and fluting on its doors and windows. Major social gatherings were frequently held in the house and its surrounding gardens and fruit orchards.

Today a specially commissioned oil painting of the Staab House hangs over the marble fireplace in the high-ceilinged Rose Room parlor, depicting the house as it was before the third floor burned down early in this century. The woodwork, copper-topped tables, and Victorian chairs separate the somber entry area, with its ponderous dark-wood ceiling beams, from the Staab House restaurant and bar and a half dozen haunted sleeping rooms.

Haunted? Yes, indeed. The mischievous but good-natured ghost of Mrs. Staab, who died the night of May 14, 1896, at the age of 52, is Santa Fe's best-known and most frequently witnessed spook. In particular, she is known to tease couples in her old bedroom, Room 252—the Honeymoon Suite.

The living and music rooms of the old Staab House have been fully restored in classical fashion as a lounge, with period furnishings, walnut woodwork, and museum-quality 19th-century art. The original dining room across the hall is now the Library, a red-carpeted overflow bar with a big piano and an inlaid oak floor as old as the building itself. Both rooms have hand-carved Italian marble fireplaces.

Entry to the Staab House Restaurant is through archways from the Rose Room. This dining area (open from 7 a.m. to 2:30 p.m. and 5 to 9:30 p.m. daily) has been fully restored with ceiling *vigas* and pueblo weavings and tinwork on the walls. From spring to early fall, food is also served outside on a big patio. House specialties are New Mexico cuisine and beef dishes. For breakfast, you can create your own deluxe house omelet, with up to three ingredients, for $5.50. Lunches include filet of catfish sandwich ($5), burgers (from $4.50), and a soup and salad bar (from $5). For dinner, you might start with a *tapas* plate for two ($9), then move either to a light meal like a wilted-spinach salad ($7) or an entree such as pork mezcal, sautéed with green chile, basil, red pepper, and mezcal ($15), or a mesquite-grilled trout piñon ($12.50). Mexican plates start at $5 for lunch, $7 for dinner.

With the exception of the six Victorian rooms contained in the Staab House itself, La Posada's 120 units are spread through 19 white adobe-style buildings on six acres of thoughtfully landscaped grounds. (The hotel employs a full-time crew to care for the gardens, including an apricot tree in the Margarita Courtyard that grew from cuttings offered by Bishop Lamy more than a century ago.) Each charming room is a little different from the next, with variations in size, shape, layout, and detail. Many objets d'art are one of a kind—a factor which often inspires repeat visitors to request "their" room year after year. But the *casitas,* the "little houses," share many common traits: outside entrances with wood-carved portals, handcrafted furniture and wrought-iron garden chairs, wood floors with throw rugs, painted tiles built into walls, cable TV/radio and telephones (local phone calls are 50¢). Two-thirds of the rooms have fireplaces or wood stoves; piñon firewood is provided daily. Some of the larger rooms have wet bars and/or refrigerators, walk-in closets, and big dressing tables. All bathrooms provide complimentary shampoo, conditioner, and body lotion, but a few have showers only (no tubs).

Finding your way around the hotel grounds, however, may be confusing. Get a map from the desk. The room numbers are in no particular order: No. 143, for instance, is between 195 and 196 and across from 116.

With the variation in room styles, there's a wide price range here: from $60 to $120 in the October-to-May low season, $75 and $140 in the high season. Suites cost up to $250. Children under 13 stay free with their parents. If you're visiting in the low season, you may want to look into some of the hotel's packages, providing breakfasts, one dinner, and museum admissions or shopping coupons for four days, three nights, costing between $150 and $190 per person, double occupancy.

La Posada—the name means "resting place"—has an outdoor swimming pool, and hotel guests can request passes to the nearby Fort Marcy pool and sports complex. Laundry facilities are available. On the premises are a gift shop, boutique, beauty salon, and realtor. Free valet parking is offered.

The Inn of the Governors, Alameda and Don Gaspar Ave., Santa Fe, NM 87501 (tel. 505/982-4333, or toll free 800/234-4534), is considered one of the best examples of Territorial architecture in downtown Santa Fe. Opened in 1965 three blocks south of the Plaza, it was fully renovated in early 1988 to the tune of $1 million.

There are 100 rooms: 54 standard motel units, 26 moderately priced rooms in the Senators Wing, and 20 deluxe accommodations in the Governors Wing. They have white stuccoed walls and color schemes of mauve and azure, with bedspreads of Indian-feather motif. Most of the creatively decorated larger units have Mexican handcrafted furniture and headboards, turned folk-art and wrought-iron lamps, mirrors of etched tin, washed-turquoise writing desks, and *kiva* fireplaces (wood provided daily). The spacious Governors rooms include wooden balconies, wall-size 19th-century pueblo photographs, and L-shaped seating to divide the sleeping and living areas. All rooms have in-room coffee makers, refrigerators with honor bars, and telephones (local calls are 30¢). All units also have TVs in Santa Fe–style armoires with built-in radio/alarm clocks.

The inn features an outdoor swimming pool and valet laundry service. If Fido's traveling with you, he's welcome to stay.

Rates from January 1 to May 15 and November 1 to December 15 are $65 standard, $85 in the Senators Wing, $105 in the Governors Wing, for two person, $10 for each additional person. From May 16 to October 31 and December 16 to 31 they increase to $90 (standard), $110 (Senators), and $135 to $150 (Governors).

The Old Forge restaurant (tel. 982-4141), which underwent a complete facelift in the 1988 renovation, looks out on Don Gaspar Avenue. Pastel adaptations of salmon and sea green highlight the décor. A luncheon grill and barbecue is served on an outdoor patio. Dinner entrees, featuring veal specials, fresh fish, and pasta daily, are priced from $9 to $14. The restaurant is open daily from 6:30 a.m. to 2 p.m. and 5 to 10 p.m. The casual and intimate adjoining lounge is open six days from 11 a.m. to 11 p.m. and on Sunday from noon to 10 p.m. There's a piano bar here nightly in summer, Tuesday through Saturday in winter.

The belltower of the **Hilton of Santa Fe,** 100 Sandoval St. (P.O. Box 2387), Santa Fe, NM 87504 (tel. 505/988-2811, or toll free 800/336-3676 or 800/HILTONS), is a city landmark. A square, three-story hotel two blocks west of the Plaza, the Hilton is built around a central pool and patio area, covering a full city block between Sandoval and Guadalupe Streets, San Francisco Street, and the Alameda. The lobby, with its *viga-latilla* ceiling, has a feeling of true hospitality. There's cozy seating around a *kiva* fireplace, flanked on one side by a cactus, on the other by the sculpture of a howling coyote.

The 155 units are clean and spacious, furnished with king-size, queen-size, or double beds. Each room—with forest-green carpets and drapes, pastel patterned bedspreads, and potted plants —has a deck or balcony, couch or two easy chairs and a table, four-drawer credenza, modern-art prints and a mirror on the white walls, cable TV/radio/alarm clock with in-house movies, and direct-dial phone (local calls cost 50¢). There are two sinks, one inside the bathroom, one outside at a dressing table. Amenities include shampoo, lotion, bath and facial soap, and shoe polish. Seasonal rates—based on size, availability, and room location (poolside or streetside)—are $80 to $135 from June 15 to October 15, $59 to $109 the rest of the year. There's no charge for children sharing a room with their parents.

The Hilton has two restaurants occupying the premises of the historic Casa de Ortiz, which has been incorporated into the hotel. In the Piñon Grill, with its intimate candlelight service around a *kiva* fireplace, you can't miss the ancient beams and pillars of the main house construction. The Chamisa Restaurant and Lounge, with casual garden-style tables amid lush greenery under a large skylight, is built on the home's enclosed patio.

Open continually from 6:30 a.m. to 11 p.m., the two restaurants share a menu. For breakfast, you might opt for a Santa Fe omelet with green chile, onions, and cilantro ($6.25). Popular lunches are the City Different fruit salad ($6.25), the Mexican combination platter ($8), or any of a variety of sandwiches ($6 to $8). Dinner offerings include broiled salmon steak with herb butter (market price), char-grilled San Francisco pork chops ($15), breaded gulf shrimp stuffed with crabmeat in sauce Rosine ($14), and fettuccine Alfredo ($9). Wines are available by the glass.

The Hilton has banquet seating for up to 500 guests. Courtesy car service is available. Other facilities include a Jacuzzi and a gift shop.

Moderate

The Santa Fe hostelry perhaps most evocative of a past era is the **Hotel St. Francis,** 210 Don Gaspar Ave., Santa Fe, NM 87501 (tel. 505/983-5700, or toll free 800/666-5700). Once the De Vargas Hotel, a 1924-vintage politicians' gathering place where more business may have been conducted in the 1930s and '40s than in the State Capitol, the inn closed its doors in 1984 and reopened as the St. Francis in January 1987 after a $6-million makeover. Listed on the National Register of Historic Places, it is less than two blocks south of the Plaza.

The spacious lobby is still a popular spot for political rallies. With its original tile floor, high-backed Edwardian chairs and sofas around glass tables, and its big fireplace (with Cupid designs), it's also an ideal setting for afternoon teas—which are, in fact, served daily at 3 p.m. Note the antique (and operable) "weight and fate" machine, telephone console, and phone boxes near the foot of the staircase.

The St. Francis has 81 distinctive units with high ceilings and casement windows. Thirty of them are tiny "baby rooms" with barely enough room for a double bed, two chairs, and a table atop a Chinese rug on a hardwood floor. But like all other rooms, these also have a refrigerator, a closet safe, and an individual thermostat. Most units have maroon carpeting, big brass or iron beds with calico bedspreads and drapes, brass lamps, cushioned rattan chairs, an antique cherrywood desk or table, telephone, and remote-control TV/radio (local reception only) in a Santa Fe–style armoire. There are brass fittings in the porcelain pedestal sinks and full baths of Mexican marble, with shampoo and lotion as amenities. From October 16 to June 15 singles are priced $50 to $85; doubles, $60 to $95. Prices increase by $10 between June 16 and October 15.

There's no pool here, but the concierge can arrange for guests to swim and use other facilities at the Fort Marcy complex. The hotel offers free parking, valet laundry service, and facilities for the handicapped.

Francisco's restaurant, open daily from 7 a.m. to 2 p.m. and 5:30 to 9:30 p.m., specializes in northern Italian cuisine. Guests can sup either in the large, elegant dining room, with pink marble-topped tables and hanging lamps, or al fresco in the patio area, with its vine-covered walls. Lunches feature zuppa di giorno ($2.50), fresh pastas including fettuccine Cappe (scallops in brandy cream sauce; $7.50), and a Tuscany steak-and-cheese sandwich ($6). Dinners are moderately priced, and can be completed with cups of cappuccino.

The De Vargas Bar, which incorporates the earlier hotel's copper-topped counter, offers sidewalk seating for people-watchers. Between 2 and 5:30 p.m., when the restaurant is closed, sandwiches and seafood snacks can be purchased here for $3 to $6.

Then there's the silver tea service from 3 to 5:30 p.m. daily in the lobby. Finger sandwiches, scones, and pastries—prepared by the hotel's own pastry chef—are served with six varieties of tea from India, Ceylon, China, and France (or coffee, if you prefer). Imported ports, sherries, and champagnes are also available. It's $7 for the full buffet, $1.50 for tea only, and walk-ins are welcome. In July and August, after-opera refreshments are served in the lobby in the early-morning hours.

A step down in elegance, but still clean and comfortable, is **Garrett's Friendship Desert Inn,** 311 Old Santa Fe Trail, Santa Fe, NM 87501 (tel. 505/982-1851, or toll free 800/552-0070, ext. 230). The nearest motel to the Plaza—just three blocks south, on the Santa Fe River across from the New Mexico state land office

—it offers 83 units and four suites on two floors. A heated swimming pool, offices of Avis Rent-a-Car, and a travel agency are on the premises.

The rooms have standard furnishings and unobtrusive southwestern décor: olive- or rust-colored carpets, rich wood headboards, patterned pastel bedspreads of blue or reddish-brown, a single watercolor on the white walls, a four-drawer credenza, dark drapes on the big windows, and a large tiled dressing table. The TV/radio has local reception only; local phone calls are 50¢. Pets are accepted here. Rates from September 15 to June 15 are $49 for rooms with queen-size beds, $59 for suites (by request) or rooms with king-size or two double beds. Prices increase by $10 between June 16 and September 14.

From the cozy lobby, you can walk directly into the Village Inn Pancake House, a franchised family restaurant open daily from 7 a.m. to 8 p.m.; or Geno's Lounge, open from 5 to 10 p.m. daily, with live entertainment on Thursday and Friday only, from 5 to 8 p.m.

Budget
One of the city's often-overlooked bargains is the **Santa Fe Motel,** 510 Cerrillos Rd., Santa Fe, NM 87501 (tel. 505/982-1039, or toll free 800/552-0070, ext. 299). There are three parts to this inn, located about half a mile south of the Plaza on the main thoroughfare leading into the city. The older two-story, 14-unit motel section behind the manager's home and office was built in the 1950s and fully remodeled in 1983. Two annex buildings, adobes dating from around the turn of the 20th century, contain five and three units respectively, and there's a separate two-bedroom house for rent across an adjacent street.

One big bonus here is that most rooms have kitchenettes, complete with two-burner stoves and mini-refrigerators, fully stocked with pans, dishes, and utensils. A typical room has maroon carpeting, pastel-colored bedspreads with southwestern motifs, two queen-size beds, a four-drawer dresser, a table and two chairs, nature prints on the walls, cable TV with HBO, and telephone (local calls are 50¢). Annex rooms have full kitchens, queen-size beds, and hide-a-bed couches. One unit in the Salazar House—renovated with its original *viga* ceilings intact—has a fireplace. The nearby Thomas House, on West Manhattan Drive, is a fully equipped home with living and dining rooms and off-street parking.

Fresh-brewed coffee is served each morning in the office, where a bulletin board posts listings of Santa Fe activities.

Off-season rates (October 15 to June 15) for singles are $35 standard, $40 with kitchenette, $45 in the annex; the charge for each additional person is $5. Rates increase by $10 across the board in summer. For the Thomas House, the charge is $85 to $125 for up to six guests. Weekly rates can be arranged in winter. Children 12 and under are free with adults; there's no extra charge for cribs.

Practically next door is the **Travelodge–Santa Fe,** 646 Cerrillos Rd., Santa Fe, NM 87501 (tel. 505/982-3551, or toll free 800/255-3050), with 49 motel-style units and a heated outdoor swimming pool.

Each room has a king-size bed or two queen-size beds with floral-patterned bedspreads and drapes, chocolate-brown or emerald-green carpets, a two-drawer credenza, table and chairs, cable TV, and telephone (local calls are 50¢). Some rooms also have a small desk. Rates from May 14 to October 21 begin at $47 single, $49 to $55 double; the rest of the year they run from $30 single, $32 to $36 double.

NORTHSIDE: This area, within easy reach of the Plaza, includes accommodations that lie beyond the loop of the Paseo de Peralta on the north.

Upper Bracket

If you're in town for the Santa Fe Opera, you'll have a hard time finding an accommodation closer than the **Sheraton de Santa Fe,** 750 N. St. Francis Dr., Santa Fe, NM 87501 (tel. 505/982-5591, or toll free 800/325-0759). No hotel in northern New Mexico makes it easier for you to get around without your own car. The amphitheater is only three miles north up U.S. 84/285; the Sheraton provides free drop-off and pickup. The Plaza is barely 1¼ miles southeast; the hotel has limousine service on call between 6 a.m. and 10 p.m. to take you there or anywhere else within the city limits at no charge. The Sheraton even has a winter shuttle to the Santa Fe Ski Basin ($10 round trip) and direct limo service to and from the Albuquerque airport ($55 for two with 24-hour advance notice).

Once you're at the Sheraton, though, you may find it hard to leave. You can watch an in-house artist convert a blank canvas into a stirring portrait or regional landscape. You can have free run of all facilities at the adjacent Santa Fe Spa, the city's top health club. If you're a summer visitor, you can delight to the Spanish quicksteps of Maria Benitez and the Estampa Flamenca Dance Company.

The Sheraton has 133 rooms and 28 suites. Each standard room, decorated in shades of browns, tans, and oranges, has a king-size bed or two double beds with light floral bedspreads, easy chairs, vanity, table, four-drawer dresser, lithographs on the walls,

TV/radio with local reception, direct-dial phone (local calls are 50¢), and alarm clock. A refrigerator can be installed on request.

Mini-suites are more spacious with older "Santa Fe–style" furnishings—including an armoire containing the TV—and private balconies. In addition to all the above, each parlor suite has a Murphy bed and *kiva* fireplace in the living room, a big dining area, and a hotplate kitchenette with a wet bar and refrigerator.

Rates from June 15 to September 15 are $85 single, $95 double, $115 for a mini-suite, and $135 for a parlor suite. The rest of the year you'll find singles at $65, doubles at $75, mini-suites at $90, and parlor suites at $115. Children under 18 are free in the same room as a parent.

The Mariposa Dining Room is a glass-enclosed patio with rich décor: high-backed mahogany chairs with burgundy upholstery, hanging wood chandeliers over mauve tablecloths, outstanding local art on the walls, and a baby grand in a corner. The restaurant is open daily from 6:30 a.m. to 10 p.m. Lunch offerings include the likes of a tostada compuesta ($5) and a Sheraton sandwich, with grilled corned beef, breast of turkey, ham, swiss and cheddar cheese, and a green chile strip ($5). At dinner you can start with the prosciutto melon ($4.50) or avocado surprise salad ($5); move on to shrimp Dijon ($13) or veal Oscar ($15); and finish with almond amaretto mousse ($4) or cherries jubilee ($5).

The adjacent Lookout Lounge, with its light-wood décor, offers live soft-rock music nightly. It's open from 11 a.m. to 2 a.m. six days a week, to midnight on Sunday.

Sheraton facilities include a gift and sundries shop, coin-op guest laundry, and banquet space for up to 200 people. All guests have a *USA Today* delivered free to their rooms each morning. The hotel will accept pets; child-care service is also available.

The Sheraton has its own outdoor pool, sauna, and Jacuzzi. Next door, the Santa Fe Spa (tel. 984-8727) has an indoor lap pool; racquetball courts; free weights and Universal machines; classes in aerobics, dance, yoga, and karate; massage therapy; and steamrooms. Sheraton guests get free membership. The spa is open Monday through Friday from 6 a.m. to 9 p.m., on Saturday from 8 a.m. to 8 p.m., and on Sunday from 9 a.m. to 5 p.m.

An alternative to hotel stays, for those who like a "home away from home," is the **Fort Marcy Compound,** 320 Artist Rd., Santa Fe, NM 87501 (tel. 505/982-6636, or toll free 800/666-2729). Only four to five blocks northeast of the Plaza, these privately owned condominiums, nestled in a tastefully landscaped desert garden, are leased by the day or by the month.

Some archeologists believe the land now occupied by the Fort Marcy Compound was the site of an Indian pueblo existing around the year 1000. More certainly, it's adjacent to Old Fort

Marcy Park, former location of the Fort Marcy Military Reservation, a 16-acre, 19th-century outpost on a hilltop above Santa Fe. There are few memories of the fort today; the park is notable for its overlook of downtown.

Some 65 condo units are available. Each is a full upstairs/downstairs apartment with a living and dining room, a full kitchen, one to three bedrooms, and 2 or 2½ baths. Each unit is individually furnished by its owner, who nevertheless must meet compound standards for rentals. A typical apartment has handcrafted wood and leather furnishings, and is decorated with regional arts and crafts. In the living room are a sofa bed, an easy chair with an ottoman, coffee table, fireplace, satellite TV with video-cassette recorder, and stereo tape deck. In the dining room are a full-size table and six chairs. The kitchen, in addition to a four-burner stove and refrigerator, has a microwave oven, coffee maker, toaster, and dishwasher; the cupboards are stocked with staples. Bedrooms generally have queen-size beds, private balconies, and plenty of shelf space, and normally portable TVs and radio/alarm clocks. Each unit has a private phone line, so guests are encouraged to make any long-distance calls collect or on credit card.

Rates for two people, from January through May and September 1 to December 14, are $60 for a one-bedroom unit, $85 for a two-bedroom, and $110 for a three-bedroom. In June and July, prices rise to $80 for a one-bedroom, $105 for two, and $130 for three. During the month of August and from December 14 to 31, units cost $100 for one bedroom, $125 for two, and $150 for three. Additional guests (beyond two) are charged $10 apiece. Monthly rates start at $725 for one bedroom in the low season, $1,500 in high season.

The Fort Marcy Compound has a large guest laundry with 12 washers and six dryers, an indoor, year-round swimming pool, and a hot tub. Other athletic facilities are two blocks downhill in the city-run Fort Marcy sports complex on Washington Avenue. Child-care service can be arranged for those who require it.

CERRILLOS ROAD: Santa Fe's major commercial strip is U.S. 85, the main route to and from Albuquerque before the construction of the Interstate 25 freeway. It's about 5¼ miles from the Plaza to the Villa Linda Mall, which marks the southern extent of the city limits.

Moderate

A stone's throw toward downtown from the mall is the **Howard Johnson Plaza-Hotel,** 4048 Cerrillos Rd., Santa Fe, NM 87501 (tel. 505/473-4646, or toll free 800/654-2000). As you enter, you may be startled by the four-story atrium lobby. High on the ceiling-length fireplace is a ceremonial Plains Indian shield decorated with buffalo claws, horns, and lightning bolts; it's considered a symbol of strength, unity, and power. Lush plants and overstuffed couches and chairs stand against stuccoed white walls. Colorful serapes and vines hang from the balconies of upper floors, reached via glass-enclosed elevators rising through the atrium.

The 131 units are tastefully appointed with brown carpets, multicolored drapes, and navy-blue or carmine bedspreads on one queen-size bed or two double beds. Regional prints hang on white walls. Furnishings include a dresser/credenza, table with two chairs, remote-control cable TV with built-in radio/alarm clock, and direct-dial phones (local calls are 50¢). There's a hairdryer at the dressing table in every room, and amenities include shampoo, conditioner, and body lotion. The 14 spacious suites have king-size beds and wet bars. No-smoking rooms and facilities for the handicapped are also available.

Standard rates, Memorial Day weekend through mid-October, are $65 single, $70 double, $5 per additional person (they increase by $20 on Indian Market weekend only). The remainder of year, rates are $48 single, $52 double. Suites are priced to $145.

The Howard Johnson has a small outdoor/indoor pool, a sauna and whirlpool, and a small weight room on the second floor. Adjacent to the lobby is a gift shop. There's valet laundry and courtesy-car service, as well as ample parking. The hotel accepts pets and makes child-care arrangements. Three meeting rooms can seat up to 180.

Earl's restaurant is open daily from 6:30 a.m. to 2 p.m. and 5 to 10 p.m. An elegant coffeeshop, it features rich wood décor, Santa Fe–style furniture, and potted trees. Try "corney yokes" (eggs with corned-beef hash; $3.75) for breakfast, or Texas-style chili ($2.75), winner of the 1987 Santa Fe Chili Cookoff, for lunch. Reasonably priced dinners range from fettuccine Alfredo ($6.50) to an eight-ounce butcher-block filet ($11.50).

La Cantina Lounge, open from 11 a.m. to 1 a.m., has festive Mexican décor beneath a skylight, with patio seating available. There's live entertainment Wednesday through Sunday evenings.

Often considered the other "better" hotel along Cerrillos Road is the **Best Western High Mesa Inn,** 3347 Cerrillos Rd., Santa Fe, NM 87501 (tel. 505/473-2800, or toll free 800/528-1234), about four miles south of the Plaza. The High Mesa has 152 standard rooms with Southwest regional décor. Each room has plush carpeting, one king-size bed or two queen-size beds, a wet bar and refrigerator, a combination desk/three-drawer dresser, satellite TV with built-in radio and in-room movies, and direct-dial phone (free local calls). An additional 55 suites have a separate sitting room with a couch and TV. Five luxury suites have full kitchens with dishwashers, huge desks, and remote-control TVs. No-smoking rooms and facilities for the handicapped are available.

Fringe benefits include a year-round heated indoor pool with a skylight, a pair of 24-hour Jacuzzis, a new exercise room with a Universal gym and free weights, a coin-operated guest laundry, a message board in the lobby with information on local events, a gift counter, child care, and courtesy-car service. There's also free bus service to San Juan Indian Bingo games Wednesday through Saturday nights. Up to 400 people can be accommodated for meetings and banquets.

There are four rate schedules. From January through June, singles are $45 to $49 and doubles cost $49 to $59. July 1 to August 21, singles go for $61 to $71; doubles, $66 to $76. From August 22 to October 15, singles are priced at $44 to $54; doubles, $49 to $59. The low season is October 16 to December 31, when singles cost $36 to $46; doubles, $46 to $56. Suites, single or double, are $55 to $80 most of the year. There's always a 10% discount for guests 55 years of age and older. Kids under 16 stay free in the same room as their parents.

Alfredo's restaurant is open daily from 6 a.m. to 9:30 p.m. for breakfast, lunch, and dinner. You can expect gourmet coffeeshop fare here, with breakfasts priced from $3; dinner entrees, $7 to $11. Kids' menus are also available.

Right at the Villa Linda Mall, **La Quinta Motor Inn,** 4298 Cerrillos Rd., Santa Fe, NM 87501 (tel. 505/471-1142, or toll free 800/531-5900), is the local entry in the 200-strong Texas-based La Quinta chain. A *quinta* (pronounced "*keen-*ta") is a villa in the Spanish language, and like a vacation home, this three-story motel is friendly and gracious toward visitors.

There are 130 units, appointed with light-wood décor, adobe-colored carpets, regional-design bedspreads and drapes in lime-green patterns, and specially commissioned prints on beige walls. Each room has one king-size bed or two extra-long double beds, a credenza, a table and chairs, a satellite TV/radio with pay in-house movies, a direct-dial phone (free local calls), a bathroom heat lamp, and individually controlled heating and air conditioning. Every room is stocked with the current edition of *Newsweek* magazine. La Quinta also has eight rooms for the handicapped, and nearly 50% of its rooms are designated for nonsmokers.

The airy-looking lobby, replete with tile floor and handmade furnishings, has a 24-hour desk, complimentary coffee, and bell service. The hotel has a kidney-shaped outdoor swimming pool and ample parking. Rover needn't spend the night in the car; he's welcome in your room.

Rates from June 1 to October 15 are $52 to $57 single, $57 to $62 double, $5 extra for each additional person. From mid-October until the following June, rates are $10 less across the board. AAA members pay only $30 on weekends, $35 on weekdays, with an association coupon.

The Kettle, a pleasant 24-hour coffeeshop, is across the parking lot from La Quinta. Here, you can dine on a stack of buttermilk pancakes for just $2, half-pound burgers from $3.50, a salad bar for $3.25, or dig into a wide selection of dinner entrees for only $4.75 and up.

At the north end of Cerrillos Road, just south of the Paseo de Peralta and only three-quarters of a mile from the Plaza, is the **Budget Inn of Santa Fe,** 725 Cerrillos Rd., Santa Fe, NM 87501 (tel. 505/982-5952, or toll free 800/552-0070, ext. 241). The Budget Inn offers 160 modest look-alike units, each with one queen-size bed or two double beds, brown- and blue-striped bedspreads, and reading lamps. A desk with a built-in four-drawer dresser stands on the tan carpet, while Santa Fe Opera and Santa Fe Fiesta posters add color to the walls. Each room has cable TV (with three movie channels) and a direct-dial phone (local calls are 25¢). Units for the handicapped are available. There's an outdoor swimming pool and plenty of parking. Guests are entitled to 10% discounts at the adjacent Mr. Steak restaurant.

Rates, from June 1 to September 15 and December 25 to January 2, are $52 single, $60 double, $68 with two double beds, and $9 per extra guest. Rates increase $10 to $20 for Indian Market weekend. Off-season prices officially run $38 to $50, but a frequently available Sunday-to-Thursday "super-saver" rate makes singles and doubles available for $28 to $30. Be sure to inquire.

The **Quality Inn,** 3011 Cerrillos Rd., Santa Fe, NM 87501 (tel. 505/471-1211, or toll free 800/228-5151), was until recently known as the Santa Fe Inn. Most of its 100 spacious units have beige carpeting, one queen-size bed or two double beds with tan-and-blue bedspreads, reading lamps, a dresser with two deep drawers, a table and chairs, Santa Fe Opera prints on the walls, 12-channel cable TV, direct-dial phone, and individually controlled thermostat heating. A patio deck or balcony faces inward toward the impressive outdoor pool. Some kitchenettes are available. Deluxe king-size units have a wet bar, a refrigerator, and a long dressing table.

No-smoking rooms are well marked from the well-lit, carpeted corridors. A courtesy van is available on request, and there's a hot tub and shuffleboard on the pool deck. Pets are accepted and child-care can be arranged.

Rates from June 1 to September 15 are $50 to $55 single, $55 to $60 double. The rest of the year, singles are $38 to $42; doubles, $40 to $44.

The Quality Inn coffeeshop, open from 7 a.m. to 1 p.m. and 5 to 9 p.m. daily, has nice wood décor and upholstery with a regional motif. Big breakfasts are priced from $4, New Mexican fare starts at $4 for lunch, and full dinners start at $9.

Another entry in a nationally known chain is the **Ramada Inn,** 2907 Cerrillos Rd., Santa Fe, NM 87501 (tel. 505/471-3000, or toll free 800/2-RAMADA). Guests enter a moderately small but neat, high-ceilinged lobby with seating around tables atop Oriental rugs, a garden nestled beneath the staircase landing, and hanging chile ristoles and hanging ferns.

From the lobby, you're directed to one of 106 spacious units. Each has king-size or double beds on rust-colored carpets, matching pastel bedspreads and drapes, five-drawer credenza, writing table and chairs, dressing table, cable TV with built-in radio, and direct-dial phone (local calls are 25¢). There's an outdoor swimming pool and a hair salon on the premises. The Ramada accepts pets and will schedule child care.

From May 16 to August 31, singles are priced at $50 to $52; doubles, $57 to $59 (higher rates are applicable during the Indian Market). The rest of the year, singles go for $34 to $45; doubles, $41 to $52. Special rates are offered to AAA and AARP members. Children under 18 stay free in their parents' room.

The Back Stage Bar & Grill is open daily from 6 to 10 a.m. and 5 to 9 p.m. for breakfast and dinner only. In the basement, Mad Dog's Lounge has live rock 'n roll on Thursday, Friday, and Saturday nights.

Budget

One of Santa Fe's premier values is **El Rey Inn,** 1862 Cerrillos Rd. (P.O. Box 130), Santa Fe, NM 87504 (tel. 505/982-1931). El Rey means "The King," so it's no coincidence that all guests are treated royally by the friendly, easy-going staff of this motel, notable for its carefully tended grounds and 56 thoughtfully maintained units two miles from the Plaza.

The white stucco buildings, shaded by large elms and spruce trees, are adorned with bright trim around the doors and hand-painted Mexican tiles inset in the walls. No two rooms are alike, but most have traditional *viga* ceilings, cornflower blue or rust carpets, rose-colored Southwest-motif bedspreads on brass beds, opera prints on the walls, and Santa Fe–style wood furnishings including a desk, easy chair, love seat, nightstand, and three-drawer dresser. Each room has cable TV (with a built-in radio/alarm clock), a walk-in closet, and a handsome blue-and-white tiled bathroom. Nine units have kitchenettes, and another five have wet bars with refrigerators. Nine other units, including two of the kitchenettes, have fireplaces; piñon firewood is supplied. Eight stylish poolside terrace units feature private outdoor patio areas, and the motel also features five passive solar units.

One of El Rey's most elegant rooms is the large sitting room adjoining the office. Appointed with antique Territorial-style furniture (including an early organ), this is a place where guests are welcome at all hours to sip complimentary coffee while reading or playing cards and board games. Through a small chamber stocked with snack machines is the breakfast room, where complimentary continental breakfasts are served at six tables beneath a skylight, beside a *kiva* fireplace.

Full-time gardeners maintain the 3½-acre grounds, which include a picnic area, an outdoor play area for kids, and a swimming pool and hot tub beside cabañas at the rear of the complex, as far as possible from busy Cerrillos Road. The motel also has a coin-op guest laundry and ample parking.

Rates from May 1 through September 30 are $41 to $68, depending on the size and type of room required. The remainder of the year prices range from $34 to $55. Suites are priced to $93.

Like the El Rey, one of the big selling points of the **Best Western Lamplighter Motel,** 2405 Cerrillos Rd., Santa Fe, NM 87501 (tel. 505/471-8000, or toll free 800/528-1234), is its spacious and attractive grounds. Trees and shrubbery surround a grassy inner courtyard adjacent to a large heated indoor pool and hot tub. La Conquistadore coffeeshop is open daily, and snacks can be purchased in the lobby.

There are 64 units in a well-kept older building and a newer annex. Each older room has rust-colored carpeting, matching bedspreads and drapes in red-and-blue Southwest motifs, a two-drawer credenza, a writing table with two chairs, hanging lamps, satellite TV with built-in radio (high above the beds on a wall rack), and direct-dial phone (free local calls). Some rooms have small refrigerators; all have complimentary coffee makers. Somehow, the framed print of a sports car doesn't fit.

The annex rooms feature stronger regional décor: sand paintings and Cerro Gordo watercolors on the walls, matching bedspreads and drapes in adobe-colored pottery designs. The TV sits on a long credenza of rich wood, and there are reading lamps above the beds.

Rates from January 1 to May 8 and November 4 to December 31 are $30 to $40 single, $32 to $45 double. Between May 9 and November 3 singles are priced at $38 to $44; doubles, $43 to $50 (marginally higher on Fiesta and Indian Market weekends). Suites range from $60 to $70, according to season.

The **Warren Inn,** 3357 Cerrillos Rd., Santa Fe, NM 87501 (tel. 505/471-2033, or toll free 800/331-7700, 800/351-5500 in California), has 168 units—all a real bargain because they have kitchenettes, complete with sink, two-burner hotplate, and refrigerator. You just provide the food, the pots and pans, and other utensils. Even if you choose not to cook, a continental breakfast, included in your room price, is served each morning in the Club Room.

The green-carpeted units have queen-size, double, or twin beds, nine-drawer dressers, tables and chairs, large closets, cable TVs, and direct-dial phones (local calls are 25¢). Guest facilities include a swimming pool, coin-op laundry, and barbecue grills in the garden.

Some 88 studio rooms are open year round; the other 80 are rented on a long-term basis, except in summer when they, too, are available daily. Rates June through September are $23 single, $28 double; during the off-season rates drop to $21 single, $26 double.

Vaguely Spanish looking, with its red-tile roof and white stucco exterior, the two-story **Allstar Inn,** 3695B Cerrillos Rd., Santa Fe, NM 87501 (tel. 505/471-4140), is one of Santa Fe's best values. Its 121 rooms are appointed in masculine tones of brown and green, with beige bedspreads and drapes, and silk-screen prints on the walls. Furnishings include a desk, dresser, satellite TV, and direct-dial phone (free local calls). The motel has an outdoor swimming pool and an elaborate snack-vending room.

Between April and September, rates run $23 single, $27 double. The rest of year they're $20 single and $28 double. Each additional person is charged $5.

An anomaly in this tourist town is the **Super 8 Motel,** 3358 Cerrillos Rd., Santa Fe, NM 87501 (tel. 505/471-8811, or toll free 800/843-1991): its rates ($27 single, $29 double) stay the same year round.

There are 60 units, each with the same simple décor found in Super 8s across America: red carpets, beds with orange bedspreads, Lazy Boy recliners, white walls with no adornment except a lone mirror. There's cable TV and free local calls from the direct-dial phone.

The **Rodeway Inn,** 2900 Cerrillos Rd., Santa Fe, NM 87501 (tel. 505/473-4281), is one of Santa Fe's older lodgings, dating to the 1950s. It offers room guests a complimentary continental breakfast in its spacious lobby.

There are 80 units, each with "Halloween" appointments: chocolate-brown carpets and orange bedspreads on the beds. Furnishings include a desk, four-drawer dresser, couch, table, and chairs. Each room has satellite TV with built-in radio and direct-dial phones (local calls are 25¢). There's also a swimming pool and a guest laundromat.

Rates start at $38 single, $43 double, May to September; and $27 single, $32 double, October to April.

Typical of many small privately owned motels on the Cerrillos Road strip is the **Cactus Lodge**, 2864 Cerrillos Rd., Santa Fe, NM 87501 (tel. 505/471-7699). This ma-and-pa operation has 25 units, including four two-bedroom suites which can sleep up to nine people. Each room is furnished with queen-size or double beds, a desk or three-drawer dresser, table, and chairs. Each has satellite TV and telephones (local calls are 25¢). Pets are welcomed.

Rates from Memorial Day to Labor Day are $36 single, $38 double, $55 for suites. During the rest of year prices drop $10 across the board.

SOUTHSIDE: These properties are two to three miles south of downtown Santa Fe but roughly an equal distance east of Cerrillos Road, on or near the other two main north-south arteries: St. Francis Drive (U.S. 84/285 Bypass) and Old Pecos Trail (U.S. 84/285).

Deluxe

The **Residence Inn**, 1698 Galisteo St., Santa Fe, NM 87501 (tel. 505/988-7300, or toll free 800/331-3131), opened in July 1987 as Santa Fe's only all-suite hotel. It's a member of a Marriott-affiliated chain, a connection which should leave little question as to its quality.

The inn has 96 attractive suites in 12 buildings, three-quarters of them one-bedroom studios with one king-size bed or two double beds. The remaining two dozen are deluxe penthouse suites. All units are fully self-contained, even to the point of having their own hot-water heaters and air compressors.

Studios are appointed with sea-green carpets and pastel striped bedspreads and upholstery. Furnishings include a sofa sleeper or love seat and chair beside the fireplace, two spacious closets with full-mirror sliding doors, remote-control satellite TV with built-in radio, a bedside alarm clock, and a direct-dial phone with free local calls. The kitchenette has a full refrigerator and range, a microwave oven, coffee maker, and popcorn popper. There's seating for four at the counter. A dressing table with its own sink is outside the bathroom, and a complimentary copy of *USA Today* is delivered to the room each morning.

In addition to all of the above, penthouse suites have an

additional bedroom in an open loft, a queen-size Murphy bed in the living room, a full dining room table, and two baths.

Complimentary continental breakfasts are served to all guests from 6:30 to 9:30 a.m. weekdays, to 10 a.m. on weekends. A courtesy car is available to drop guests off at the Plaza, 2¼ miles distant, and pick them up later in the day. Those who remain at the inn can enjoy an outdoor pool, three hot tubs, jogging trail, and sport court with facilities for paddle tennis, basketball, badminton, volleyball, and racquetball. There's a coin-op laundry on the premises, barbecue grills on the patio, and deli refrigerators and snack racks adjacent to the office. Child care is easily arranged.

There's always something going on weekday evenings in the friendly lobby seating area. On Monday, Wednesday, and Thursday from 5 to 6:30 p.m., complimentary drinks and hors d'oeuvres are served according to a variety of themes, like Wine and Cheese Night, Pizza Night, and Fiesta Night. Classic films are shown on Tuesday and Friday.

Room rates from January 3 to May 26 are $65 for studios, $89 for penthouses, for one or two guests. From May 27 to June 30, and September 1 to 15, they increase to $89 and $115. In July and August studios are priced at $105; penthouses, at $140. From September 16 to December 15 they drop again to $69 and $94. Finally, rates between December 16 and January 2 are $95 and $125. Weekly and monthly rates are available on request.

Moderate

The **Town House Motel,** 2239 Old Pecos Trail, Santa Fe, NM 87501 (tel. 505/982-1943), is the only motel on the approach to Santa Fe via I-25 from Las Vegas, Lamy, Galisteo, and other towns to the east and southeast.

There are 20 spacious, if somewhat spartan, rooms. Each unit has a rust-colored carpet and white walls, a double bed, small desk and chair, coffee table, cable TV with built-in radio, and direct-dial phone (local calls are 25¢). But the heating system is outdated, the closets lack doors, and the bathrooms need a handyman's attention.

Rates from May 20 to September 30 seem a bit high: $48 single, $52 double. The rest of year they drop to $25 single, $30 double. Two kitchenette apartments are available for $85 a night in summer, $450 a month the rest of the year.

The Town House has an outdoor pool with a big deck. Pets are welcomed.

Scampone's Italian Restaurant, adjacent to the motel, offers filling dinners for as little as $8. The restaurant is open daily from 6:30 a.m. to 2 p.m. and 5 to 10 p.m.; the bar stays open later.

BED-AND-BREAKFASTS

Of a growing number of bed-and-breakfast establishments catering to visitors to Santa Fe, four in particular stand out. All of them are within easy walking distance of the Plaza.

The **Grant Corner Inn**, 122 Grant Ave., Santa Fe, NM 87501 (tel. 505/983-6678), occupies an early-20th-century manor at Johnson and Grant Streets, a mere three blocks west of the Plaza.

Each of its 11 guest rooms is furnished with antiques, from brass or four-poster beds to armoires and quilts. Each has a portable cable TV, private phone (free local calls) and clock radio, watercolors and limited-edition lithographs on the walls, and monogrammed terrycloth robes, herbal shampoo and soap in the private bathroom. Most rooms also have ceiling fans and small refrigerators. All incoming guests find a fruit basket awaiting them.

But each room also has its own character. No. 3, for instance, has a hand-painted German wardrobe closet dating from 1772 and a wash basin with brass fittings in the shape of fish. No. 8 has an exclusive outdoor deck which catches the morning sun. No. 9 is a student's dormer, with a sunlit writing desk and art and architecture books on the shelves. No. 11 has an antique collection of dolls and stuffed animals arranged around the top of the room on a shelf. The inn's office, on your right as you enter, doubles as a library and gift shop, and has hot coffee and tea at all hours. Opposite are the living and dining rooms. Breakfast is served here each morning in front of the fireplace, or on the front veranda during the warm months of summer.

Those morning meals are so good that an enthusiastic public pays $8.75 a head ($5.75 for young children) to brunch here on Saturday from 7:30 a.m. to noon and on Sunday from 8 a.m. to 1 p.m. (It's included in the room price for Grant Corner Inn guests, of course.) The menu changes daily but always includes fruit frappe, a fresh fruit plate, a choice of two entrees (such as banana waffles and eggs Florentine), homemade pastries, and coffee and tea (with free refills). Guests with lighter appetites can opt for a cereal buffet of Nutrigrain, homemade granola, and fresh fruit ($3.50 for the public).

Rates at the Grant Corner Inn haven't changed since June 1986. Singles are priced at $45 to $50; average-sized doubles, $65 to $80; deluxe doubles, $90 to $110. Five rooms can accommodate a third person for $15 extra. Children over 5 are welcome; pets are not. The inn is closed the last three weeks of January each year.

Innkeeper Louise Stewart—a graduate of the Cornell Hotel School and daughter of Jack Stewart, founder of the famous Camelback Inn in Scottsdale, Arizona—also rents out the Grant Corner Inn Hacienda, at 604-F Griffin St., about six blocks north of the inn. This two-bedroom condo is majestic with its cathedral ceilings, combining the traditional (exposed *vigas*) and the modern (skylights). The rate of $190 a night for four people, $15 per additional up to seven, includes breakfast at the inn and daily maid service.

More truly traditional is **El Paradero** ("The Stopping Place"), 220 W. Manhattan Ave., Santa Fe, NM 87501 (tel. 505/988-1177). This building began as a circa-1810 Spanish adobe farmhouse; doubled in size in 1878, when Territorial-style details were added; and incorporated Victorian touches, clear in the styling of its doors and windows, in 1912. It opened in 1982 as a bed-and-breakfast, the second in Santa Fe and third in the state of New Mexico.

There are 12 rooms here, each one different. Nine ground-level rooms surround a central courtyard. These skylit chambers have clean white décor, simple hardwood floors, folk art and hand-woven textiles on the walls, and carved headboards. Three newer, more luxurious upstairs rooms, added in the past ten years, have tile floors and baths, and private balconies. Three rooms have fireplaces. Eight rooms have private baths; four others share. All rooms have sinks, individually controlled heating, and private phones (local calls are 50¢). There are no televisions.

The entire downstairs, with its impressive *viga-latilla* ceilings, is common space. That includes a parlor, a living room with a piano and fireplace, and the dining room, where a full gourmet breakfast is served daily from 8 to 9:30 a.m. The meal includes homemade muffins or bread, fresh fruit, fresh-squeezed orange juice, coffee, and a different entree each day (it's always pancakes on Sunday).

Here's the rate schedule: March 31 to October 31, downstairs and patio rooms are $55 single, $65 double, with private bath; $15 less with shared bath. Upstairs and fireplace rooms go for $65 single, $75 double, with private bath; $20 less with shared bath. November 1 to March 30, downstairs and patio rooms are $48 single, $56 double, with private bath; $10 less with shared bath. Upstairs and fireplace rooms are $60 single, $70 double, with private bath; $15 less with shared bath.

A block from El Paradero and half a mile from the Plaza, **Pueblo Bonito,** 138 W. Manhattan Ave. (at Galisteo Street), Santa Fe, NM 87501 (tel. 505/984-8001), occupies a former circuit judge's century-old adobe hacienda and stables. Private court-yards and narrow flagstone paths give it a look of 19th-century elegance, while adobe archways lead to hybrid rose gardens shaded by prolific apricot and pear trees. Guests are invited to help themselves to the fruit.

The 14 *casitas* are each named for a Pueblo tribe of the surrounding countryside. Every one—decorated with fresh flowers daily and Indian rugs on wood or brick floors—has a queen-size bed, fireplace, portable cable TV, and radio/alarm clock. Bathrooms are small but attractively tiled.

There are three classes of rooms. Three are "preferred stable suites," each with an elaborate and fully stocked kitchen, living/dining room with cozy seating beside the *kiva* fireplace, and bedroom with five-drawer dresser. A couple of ordinary suites have *viga* ceilings, big closets, refrigerators, and wet bars. The remainder are standard units with locally made willow headboards and couches, love seats, dining alcove, old Spanish-style lace curtains, and copper-etched mirror.

Continental breakfasts are served from 8 to 10 a.m. daily on the sundeck, or if you prefer, room service. They include fresh juice, fruit in season, croissants and pastries, and coffee or tea.

There are no phones in the rooms, but a pay phone is available for use, and the office accepts messages for guests. There's also a coin-op laundry on the premises. Guests may also choose to watch TV and sit around the fireplace with Amy and Herb Behm and their four cats.

Rates from June through October and during holiday periods are $65 to $80 single, $75 to $90 double, $115 for stable suites. Fall-winter rates are $15 less across the board. Kids are welcome; pets are not.

The **Preston House,** 106 Faithway St., Santa Fe, NM 87501 (tel. 505/982-3465), is a different sort of building for the City Different—it's a 102-year-old Queen Anne home. That style of architecture is rarely seen in New Mexico, especially painted sky-blue with white trim. The house's owner, noted silkscreen artist and muralist Signe Bergman, adores its original stained glass.

Located five blocks east of the Plaza, off Palace Avenue near La Posada hotel, the Preston House has nine rooms with period antiques and exquisitely feminine décor. Each has floral wallpaper and lace drapes. Many rooms have brass beds covered with quilts. Most also have a desk and dresser; some have decks or ceiling fans, and several have fireplaces. What once were closets have been converted to private bathrooms (only two rooms must share a bath). Sherry is complimentary in all rooms.

There's a telephone and large television in the living room; six portable TVs are available for those who need Johnny Carson and David Letterman to help them sleep at night.

A continental buffet breakfast is served daily from 8 to 10 a.m. in dining room. On nice days many guests choose to take their meal to the rear patio, where there are five tables for dining. An afternoon tea and snack is also served.

The Preston House also has two cottages in the rear of the main building and an adobe home across the street, all with private phones and refrigerators. The cottages have skylights and large fireplaces; the adobe contains a kitchenette, separate bedroom and sitting room, and a private patio.

Rates for two, including breakfast, are $45 and $58 for a shared bath, $75 and $90 for a private bath, $90 and $98 for a room with a fireplace in the main house. Cottage units are $110, and the adobe home rents for $115 nightly.

HOSTELS

Backpack travelers, vagabonds, and other severe budget watchers will find the **Santa Fe International Hostel,** 1412 Cerrillos Rd., Santa Fe, NM 87501 (tel. 505/988-1153 or 983-9896, or 247-4204 in Albuquerque), to be a godsend. It's only 1½ miles south of the plaza, and a mere half mile from the bus depot.

There are 14 mens' dorm bunks here, 12 womens' dorm bunks, and 14 more beds in an overflow dorm priced at $8 a night for American Youth Hostels members, $10 for nonmembers. Couples and families can nestle into double beds in two spartan private rooms for $20 a night (additional kids are half price). If you don't have your own linen, that will cost you $2.

Regular hostelers will find the Santa Fe hostel to be relatively liberal. There's no curfew or wakeup time, no deadline for check-in or check-out; and the office is open continually from 7 a.m. to 11 p.m. But no smoking is allowed in the building, and all guests must do a daily chore to help keep maintenance costs down.

Use of the common kitchen costs $1 a day, a charge that entitles guests to free snacks and the use of all staples in the pantry. A laundry fee of $1 includes soap. In the main common room, through which guests enter, are a piano, bulletin board (packed with budget travel information), pay phones, and a book rack (perhaps including this book).

Hostel warden Preston Ellsworth also runs the Rio Bravo River Tours service from an office at the rear of the hostel. If you're considering river rafting, this may be the place to start.

GUEST RANCHES AND RESORTS

More than a century ago, when Bishop Jean-Baptiste Lamy was the spiritual leader of northern New Mexico's Roman Catholic population, he often escaped clerical politics by hiking 3½ miles north over a ridge into the Little Tesuque Valley. There he built a humble chapel and retreat he named Villa Pintoresca ("Picturesque Villa") for its lovely vistas.

Today Lamy's 1,000-acre getaway has become **The Bishop's**

Lodge, P.O. Box 2367, Santa Fe, NM 87504 (tel. 505/983-6377), 3 miles north of the Plaza on Bishop's Lodge Road. Purchased in 1918 from the Pulitzer family (of publishing fame) by Denver mining executive James R. Thorpe, it has remained in one family's hands for seven decades. That gives it continuity in theme and direction not often found in the visitor industry.

The bishop himself planted the orchard and garden, and dug the irrigation ditches that are today maintained by a full-time gardening staff. And his tiny chapel, recommended for inclusion in the National Register of Historic Places, is a prime tourist attraction with its high-vaulted ceilings, painted-glass windows, hand-built altar, and menorah-like candelabra.

Most guests today come with their families to take part in the wide range of activities offered. Most popular is horseback riding —the lodge has 60 horses in its corral. Daily guided rides of 1½ to 2 hours, covering a variety of desert and mountain terrain for $18 per person, leave daily except Sunday at 9:30 a.m. and 2 p.m. There are breakfast rides and picnic rides in July and August, and private rides by appointment. For kids, there's a pony ring and introductory riding programs.

Other sports include tennis on the four tournament-grade courts, and there's a full-time pro, a well-equipped tennis shop, and classes for kids from 6 years old; skeet and trap shooting on the lodge's own fully automatic ranges, where gun rentals and instruction are available; swimming, with a lifeguard on duty in the solar-heated pool from 10 a.m. to 6 p.m. daily (saunas and a whirlpool are adjacent to the pool cabaña); aerobics classes, shuffleboard, croquet, and Ping-Pong; and children's fishing in a stocked trout pond. Kids 4 through 12 get special attention in summer, when counselors lead them in a daytime program of hiking, swimming, arts and crafts, pony rides, Indian culture, and outdoor games.

Three large adjoining rooms with wrought-iron chandeliers and wall-size Indian-theme oil paintings comprise the Bishop's Lodge dining room, a popular spot for Santa Feans. They keep coming back for its buffets (breakfast at $9, lunch at $10, and Sunday brunch at $16) and dinners. Appetizers like wild mushrooms gratiné and escargots sauce enshallot are priced between $6 and $7. Entrees include pollo verde with pesto and goat cheese ($15.50), carne de puerco asada al Obispo ($16), and piccata of veal with fettuccine Alfredo ($17). Attire is casual at breakfast and lunch but more formal at dinner, when men are asked to wear a sport coat and women a dress or pants suit. Daily hours are 7:30 to 9:30 a.m. for breakfast, noon to 1:30 p.m. for lunch, 6:30 to 8:30 p.m. for dinner, and noon to 2 p.m. for Sunday brunch. El Charro Bar offers a full vintage-wine list for the restaurant.

There are 68 guest rooms in seven buildings. All are appointed in earth tones and feature handcrafted cottonwood furniture, regional artwork, and etched-tin trim. They've got TV (with local five-channel reception) and direct-dial phones (local calls are 50¢, with a $1 surcharge for long distance). Guests receive a complimentary fruit basket on arrival. Bathrooms have a full range of amenities, from shampoo and body lotion to bath gel and suntan lotion.

Standard suites have a bedroom nook apart from the living area. Deluxe units have a *kiva* fireplace, brass beds, a private deck or patio, walk-in closets, and a refrigerator, as required. Older-style deluxe rooms have flagstone floors and *viga* ceilings. Deluxe suites have a fireplace in the bedroom as well as the living room and artwork of near museum quality throughout.

Rates at the Bishop's Lodge—open only from mid-April through New Year's Day—are European Plan (meals not included) or Modified American Plan (includes breakfast and dinner daily, and services of the children's program). The European Plan applies anytime except in July and August. During June, daily rates for two are $110 in a standard room, $145 in a standard suite, $165 in a deluxe room, and $210 in a deluxe suite. At other times, rates are $95 in a standard room, $115 in a standard suite, $140 in a deluxe room, and $185 in a deluxe suite. Additional persons are charged $12. The Modified American Plan is in effect from June through Labor Day. Rates in June are $150 for a standard room, $185 for a standard suite, $205 for a deluxe room, and $250 for a deluxe suite. Rates July 1 through Labor Day are $185 for a standard room, $210 for a standard suite, $230 for a deluxe room, and $280 for a deluxe suite.

A 15% service fee is added to all charges, including room, restaurant, bar, transportation, and activities, in lieu of tipping. Credit cards are not accepted, but personal or company checks (with proper identification) are.

If you watched television in the 1960s, you might remember a short-lived series called "Guestward Ho!" It was filmed at **Rancho Encantado,** Route 4, Box 57C, Santa Fe, NM 87501 (tel. 505/982-3537). Located eight miles north of the city off N.M. 592 in quiet chaparral country near Tesuque Pueblo, this elegant adobe guest ranch purposely keeps itself small. Built in 1932, it had only 12 rooms when it was purchased by the Egan family in 1968, and they've added only 10 more on the ranch site since. The intimacy is a major part of its homey charm.

As you enter the handsome main lodge, you'll discover a traditional southwestern décor of hand-painted tiles, ceiling *vigas,* brick floors, antique furniture, Pueblo carpets, and Hispanic art objects hanging on stuccoed walls. A large fireplace, in the corner of the living room/lounge, is lit whenever the air is chilly.

There are seven bedrooms in the lodge. Also on the ranch site are five "cottage rooms" with fireplaces; eight "casitas" with living rooms, fireplaces, and refrigerators; and two luxury suites (with all of the above and more) in Casa Piñon.

Across the highway, spread through a 91-acre tract of ranch property, is Pueblo Encantado. These 72 split-level adobe condominium units are privately owned but are administered by the Rancho. Each has a living room, dining room, fully stocked kitchen, one or two bedrooms, 1¾ baths, and a private patio. There are fireplaces in the living room and master bedroom. Condo guests are entitled to full use of all services and facilities at the Rancho Encantado.

The most popular activities are horseback riding, swimming, and tennis. Each day, wranglers lead morning and afternoon rides on the ranch's 160-acre spread and into the Sangre de Cristo Mountains (there's a kiddie ring for the little ones). The swimming pool and hot tub, beside the Cantina Bar, are covered in winter for year-round relaxation. (Pueblo Encantado has its own pool for condo guests.) Tennis lessons are given on the resort's three all-weather courts. Guests can also take part outdoors in hiking, shuffleboard, and horseshoes, or engage in pool, chess, backgammon, and cards in the library.

Anyone planning dinner in Rancho Encantado's fine gourmet restaurant is advised to book a table well in advance. New Mexican, American, and continental specialties are served here in white stuccoed décor beneath the glance of wild-game heads and serene *santeros* in wall niches. Locals love to dine at sunset, when there's a spectacular view of the Jemez Mountains on the western horizon.

Breakfasts (served from 7:30 to 10 a.m.) feature the likes of Belgian waffles ($4) and Egans' holey toast ($5.25); lunches (11:30 a.m. to 1:30 p.m.) include taco salad and crêpes du jour (both $7). If you're here for dinner (6 to 8:30 p.m.), consider starting with angels on horseback ($6) or splitting a classic Caesar salad ($9.50 for two). Entrees—including soft-shell crabs ($15), pescado Encantado (fresh swordfish in puff pastry; $16), crispy roast duck Polynesian ($15.50), and a marvelous chateaubriand ($43 for two)—are served with salad, potato or rice, vegetable, rolls, and beverage. There's also a "light and lean" à la carte menu, and a special quick-service opera-goers' menu for those July and August nights.

Three rate schedules are employed. From May 27 to September 5 and December 16 to January 2, guests at the main lodge pay

$145 to $155; in cottages, $155 to $175; in casitas, $200; in Casa Piñon, $215 to $225; in one-bedroom condos, $230 to $250; and in two-bedroom condos, $260 to $300. From March 25 to May 26 and September 6 to December 15, rates for the main lodge are $120 to $130; cottages, $130 to $150; casitas, $175; Casa Piñon, $180 to $190; one-bedroom condos, $195 to $215; and two-bedroom condos, $215 to $255. Between January 5 and March 24, you pay $85 to $100 in the main lodge, $115 to $125 in the cottages, $150 in the casitas, $155 to $165 in Casa Piñon, $165 to $185 in the one-bedroom condos, and $185 to $220 in the two-bedroom condos. (All rates are European Plan, with no meals included.)

At the other end of the resort spectrum is the **SunRise Springs Resort,** Route 14, Box 203, La Cienega, Santa Fe, NM 87505 (tel. 505/471-3600, or toll free 800/772-0500), a former counterculture retreat that has evolved into an elaborate meditation and wellness center for enthusiasts of New Age metaphysics. The 69-acre resort is built around a series of spring-fed ponds in the Rio Grande Valley, a 15-minute drive south of Santa Fe. Its program aims at providing a total body experience—physical, mental, emotional, and spiritual.

At a glance, here's what you get: (1) a staff that includes a full-time holistic M.D., a chiropractor-nutritionist, and specialists in such therapies as acupuncture, shiatsu, yoga, Trager bodywork, colonic irrigation, and deep-tissue and other forms of massage; (2) sports facilities, including a large swimming pool and childrens' pool, tennis and volleyball courts, bicycling and roller skating, and an aerobics room with exercise equipment; (3) a dry sauna and sweat lodge beside the springs, a Jacuzzi by the pool, and two large hot tubs, one of them for guests who prefer not to wear clothes when soaking; (4) several shops, including Merlin's Closet and the Crystal Room, a New Age bookstore; the Inner Game pro shop, with sports equipment and clothing; and Devas garden shop, with a variety of materials for organic growers; and (5) Indian storytelling for kids in an authentic teepee.

The Excellerated Learning Forum contains "alpha chambers," egg-shaped lounge chairs that employ high-frequency tones to stimulate brain-wave activity, enhance relaxation and meditation, and accelerate learning. Participants may watch videos or listen to music or success tapes in guided visualization sessions.

Nearby, the Vision Resource Center caters to New Agers' goal of real as well as spiritual wealth. It offers computer services and tutorials, a large selection of business and personal-development software, a reading room and library—and an astrologer for chart preparation and consultation.

Central to the resort is a botanical garden, created with emphasis on organic and permaculture growth techniques. Its vegetable garden is planted in a wheel shape, according to the 12 astrological signs, and its herb garden resembles a mandala pattern used in meditation.

The Blue Heron gourmet restaurant specializes in wild game and vegetarian meals. Diners appreciate the Japanese motif: dried *ikebana* flower arrangements on the tables, blue porcelain table settings featuring *koi* (carp) designs, and *haiku* poetry on the menus: "The flash of a wing / the colors of pond and sky / Ah! the Blue Heron!"

Breakfasts (like eastern omelets with apple-chutney sauce) and lunches (such as chile rellenos stuffed with tofu and wild rice and breaded in blue corn) are priced in the $5 to $8 range. Dinners are the most popular meal here; you might start with roasted vegetables in bamboo leaves or smoked pheasant salad (both $4.25) and follow with an entree like mesquite-roasted blue marlin ($14), roast rack of lamb ($18), or almond tempeh and pan-fried noodles ($13.75). On Friday night a special seven-course Japanese dinner is offered for $20 per person or $37.50 per couple.

The Blue Heron also has a daily low-sodium, low-cholesterol menu and full bar service. It's open daily for breakfast from 8 to 10 a.m., for lunch from 11 a.m. to 2:30 p.m., and for dinner from 5:30 to 9 p.m. Sunday brunch ($14 per person) is served from 11:15 a.m. to 2:30 p.m. Reservations are suggested.

The 32 guest apartments, notable for their eclectic décor and unusual color combinations, are in two buildings which overlook the central gardens on the north and south. The typical room (if there is one) is brightly painted in all colors of the rainbow, with floral bedspreads and a generous use of Mexican tiles. Furnishings include a dresser, a desk with a chiropractically approved chair, two other chairs, antique night tables with marble tops, a big-screen satellite TV with VCR attachment, lots of closet and shelf space, and potted shrubbery. In the art deco tile bathroom are two robes, a hairdryer, and herbal shampoo, conditioner, and lotion. Each guest building has its own breakfast lounge with a big mosaic fireplace, tape deck, refrigerator, and coffee pot.

Nightly rates of $100 single, $120 double, with breakfast, are in effect from June 1 through October 15. From April 16 to May 31 and October 16 to January 14 they drop to $75 single, $90 double. Rates of $63 single, $80 double, apply from January 15 to April 15, but do not include breakfast. Four small garret rooms (with shared baths) are rented year round at $50, single or double. Weekly rates, including use of all resort facilities and three meals a day, start at $950 per person, double occupancy. Winter ski packages are available for $74.50 per person per day, double occupancy.

Coming from Santa Fe, you can reach SunRise Springs by turning west at the Santa Fe Downs racetrack and proceeding 2½ miles on County Rte. 54. From Albuquerque, leave I-25 at exit 271 and continue 3.3 miles on N.M. 22. The resort is just north of Las Golondrinas outdoor museum.

CAMPGROUNDS / RV PARKS

At least six private camping areas, mainly for recreational vehicles, are located within a few minutes' drive of downtown Santa Fe. Typical rates are $12 for full RV hookups, $7 for tents; be sure to book ahead at busy times. The sites are:

Apache Canyon KOA, Route 3, Box 95A, Santa Fe, NM 87505 (tel. 505/982-1419), located 11 miles southeast of Santa Fe at exit 294 of I-25, offers full hookups, pull-through sites, tent sites, picnic tables, showers, rest rooms, laundry, store, playground, recreation room, propane, and dumping station.

Los Campos RV Resort, 3574 Cerrillos Rd., Santa Fe, NM 87501 (tel. 505/473-1949), located just five miles south of the Plaza, has 95 spaces with full hookups, picnic tables, showers, rest rooms, laundry, and grocery store.

Piñon RV Park, I-25 Frontage Road, Santa Fe, NM 87501 (tel. 505/471-9288), is opposite the Santa Fe Downs racetrack ten miles south of the Plaza. This facility has full hookups, tent sites, showers, rest rooms, laundry, and public telephones. AARP members get a 10% discount.

Rancheros de Santa Fe Camping Park, Route 3, Box 94, Santa Fe, NM 87505 (tel. 505/983-3482), eight miles southeast of Santa Fe, is reached from exit 290 off I-25 and welcomes tents, motor homes, and trailers with full hookups. More than 80 sites are set in 22 acres of piñon and juniper forest. Facilities include tables, grills and fireplaces, hot showers, rest rooms, laundry, grocery store, swimming pool, playground, games room, TV lounge with nightly movies, public telephones, and propane.

Tesuque Pueblo RV Campground, Route 5, Box 360-H, Santa Fe, NM 87501 (tel. 505/455-2661, or 455-2407 after 8:30 p.m.), ten miles north of Santa Fe along U.S. 84/285, has full hookups, pull-through sites, tent sites, showers, rest rooms, laundry, hot tub, swimming pool, and a store selling jewelry and fishing gear.

The Trailer Ranch, 3471 Cerrillos Rd., Santa Fe, NM 87501 (tel. 505/471-9970), has 46 RV sites with full hookups, a swimming pool, clubhouse, and summer shuffleboard.

In addition, there are three forest sites along N.M. 475 toward the Santa Fe Ski Basin. All are open May to October. Overnight rates start at about $5, depending on site choice.

Hyde Memorial State Park, P.O. Box 1147, Santa Fe, NM

87503 (tel. 505/827-7465), is eight miles from the city. This facility has shelters, water, tables, fireplaces, firewood, and pit toilets.

In the **Santa Fe National Forest,** P.O. Box 1689, Santa Fe, NM 87504 (tel. 505/988-6940), are Black Canyon, with 44 sites, and Big Tesuque, with 10 units. Black Canyon, just past the state park, has clean water and sites for trailers up to 32 feet in length. Big Tesuque, 12 miles from town, has fishing but no drinking water. Both have pit toilets.

CHAPTER IV

THE RESTAURANTS OF SANTA FE

□ □ □

Santa Feans take their eating seriously. In fact, they've coined a name for their unique blend of Hispanic and Pueblo Indian recipes: northern New Mexico cuisine.

This isn't the same as Mexican cooking, or even those American distortions sometimes called "Tex-Mex" or "Cal-Mex." It's a consequence of southwestern history. As the native Indians taught the Spanish conquerors about their corn—how to roast it, how to make corn pudding, stewed corn, corn bread, cornmeal, and posole (hominy)—the Spanish introduced their beloved chiles, adding spice to the cuisine and ultimately developing such famous strains of chile as Chimayo, Pojoaque, and Española Improved.

Lovers of tacos, burritos, and enchiladas will find them here, although they may not be quite as you've had them before. Tacos, for instance, are more often served in soft rolled tortillas than in crispy shells. Tamales are made from cornmeal mush, wrapped in husks and steamed. Chile rellenos are stuffed with cheese, deep-fried, then covered with green chile.

Here's a sampling of some of the more regional dishes that might be hard to find outside the Southwest:

Blue corn: This Pueblo vegetable produces a crumbly flour widely used in tortilla shells, especially for enchiladas.

Carne adovada: Tender pork marinated in red chile, herbs, and spices, then baked.

Chorizo burrito (also called a breakfast burrito): Mexican sausage, scrambled eggs, potatoes, and scallions wrapped in a flour tortilla with red or green chile and melted jack cheese.

Empanada: A fried pie with nuts and currants.

Huevos rancheros: Fried eggs on corn tortillas, topped with cheese and red or green chile, served with pinto beans.

Fajitas: Strips of beef or chicken sautéed with vegetables and served on a sizzling platter.

Green chile stew: Locally grown chiles cooked in a stew with chunks of pork, beans, and potatoes.

Sopaipillas: A lightly fried puff pastry served with honey as a dessert or side dish.

Vegetables and nuts: Unusual local ingredients as piñon nuts, jicama, and prickly pear cactus will often be a part of your meals.

Of course, in a city as sophisticated as Santa Fe, there are many other cuisines available as well. Some chefs create new recipes incorporating regional foods with non-indigenous ingredients; their restaurants are referred to in this listing as "nouvelle cuisine." Others stick with steak and seafood. Many offer continental or European menus. And there are some unusual cuisines also available in Santa Fe, including Afghani and Vietnamese.

There are literally hundreds of restaurants in Santa Fe, from luxury establishments with strict dress codes right down to corner hamburger stands. The following sampling classifies my recommendations by the area of the city and the type of food offered. Price ranges are included within each listing, but generally I've put the higher-priced restaurants immediately beneath each heading and the budget establishments toward the end.

DOWNTOWN

REGIONAL CUISINE: At historic **La Casa Sena,** 125 E. Palace Ave., across from St. Francis Cathedral (tel. 988-9232), two restaurants look into a spacious garden patio. The elegant main dining room occupies the Territorial-style adobe house built in 1867 by Civil War hero Maj. José Sena for his wife and 23 children. In the adjacent La Cantina, waiters and waitresses sing arias and Broadway show tunes as they carry platters from kitchen to table.

The cuisine in the multicolored dining room—a veritable art gallery with museum-quality landscapes on the walls and Taos-style handcrafted furniture—might be described as northern New Mexican with a continental flair.

Lunches, priced $6 to $8, include butifarra con migas (fresh conejo sausage with garlic and herbs; $8) and chicken enchiladas (on blue-corn tortillas with green chile and cheese, Spanish rice, and beans; $6.75). Evening diners may start with tamal de salmon (salmon mousse steamed in a cornhusk; $4.50) or calde de frijole negro (purée of black-bean soup with Amontillado sherry; $2.50), then move to the entrees. House specials include trucha en terracotta (fresh trout wrapped in vine leaves and baked in clay; $15.75) or filete bistec (filet mignon with cilantro béarnaise; $17.75). Meals are served with vegetables, blue-corn muffins, and salad. Desserts include chocolate mousse torte, piñon tarts, and avocado lime pie (all $2.75). There are 150 wines on the vintner's list, a dozen of which are available by the glass.

Lunches are served Monday through Saturday from 11:30 a.m. to 3 p.m.; dinners, daily from 5:30 to 10 p.m. The main dining room is also open for Sunday brunch from 10 a.m. to 3 p.m.

La Cantina's singers concertize Thursday through Sunday from 6 to 11 p.m. with a repertoire that (in 1988) included *Oklahoma!*, *Fiddler on the Roof*, *West Side Story*, and *The Fantasticks*. To go along with the light entertainment, La Cantina presents a light and reasonably priced menu Monday through Saturday from 11 a.m. to 3 p.m. and daily starting at 5 p.m.

Lunches ($5.75 to $7.75) include a vegetarian burrito ($6) and red chile pasta salad with prickly pear cactus ($7.25). Salads are popular for dinner—consider the O'Keeffe salad (Belgian endive, radish, nasturtium, avocado, and yellow pepper with poppyseed dressing; $5.75) and the Sena salad (guacamole, feta cheese, artichoke hearts, red onions, jicama, lettuce, and blue-corn chips; $7.25). Entrees, including green chile stew and enchiladas, are priced $6.50 to $12.75. A children's menu offers burritos and burgers for $2.50.

La Tertulia, 416 Agua Fria St. (tel. 988-2769), is at least as historic as La Casa Sena: it's housed in a former convent that once belonged to the 18th-century Santuario de Guadalupe across the street. Thick adobe walls separate six dining rooms, among them the old chapel and a restored "Sala" (living room) containing a valuable Spanish colonial art collection. There's also an outside garden patio for summer dining.

Dim lighting and *viga*-beamed ceilings, shuttered windows and wrought-iron chandeliers, lace tablecloths and hand-carved *santos* in wall niches lend a feeling of historic authenticity to this elegant restaurant.

A highlight of the menu is Spanish paella, an olio of seafood, chicken, chorizo sausage, vegetables, and rice, served with black-bean/jalapeño soup and sopaipillas, priced at $13.75 per person for two or more. Gourmet regional dishes include filet y rellenos (chiles rellenos with a filet mignon; $14), carne adovada ($8), pollo adovo ($9.75), and camarones con pimientos y tomates (shrimp with peppers and tomatoes; $10). If you feel like dessert, try capirotada (bread pudding; $1.75) or natillas (custard; $1.75). Many diners request the bar to bring them a pitcher of the home-made sangría ($11.75).

La Tertulia—its name means "The Gathering Place"—is open from 11:30 a.m. to 2:30 p.m. and 5 to 9:30 p.m. daily except Monday. Reservations are advised.

Tomasita's Santa Fe Station, 500 S. Guadalupe St. (tel. 988-5721), may be the restaurant most consistently recommended by local Santa Feans. Why? Some point to the atmosphere; others cite the food and prices. Hanging plants and wood décor accent this spacious brick building, adjacent to the old Santa Fe railroad station. Traditional northern New Mexican entrees, including vegetarian dishes and daily specials, are priced from $4 to $6. It's open daily except Sunday, with full bar service, from 11 a.m. to 10 p.m.

Don't be surprised if you have to wait for a table at the **Guadalupe Café,** 313 Guadalupe St. (tel. 982-9762). Santa Feans line up at all hours to dine in this casually elegant café with tall potted plants and cushioned seats. Breakfasts include huevos rancheros ($4.25) and chorizo burritos ($4.50); on the lunch menu are Mexican chicken salad ($5) and crabmeat enchiladas ($7). Dinner includes everything from breast of chicken relleno to chile cheese chimichangas for a top price of $9. Daily specials include fresh fish, crêpes, and pastas; don't miss the famous chocolate-amaretto adobe pie for dessert. Meal times are 7 a.m. to 2:30 p.m. Tuesday through Friday, 8 a.m. to 2 p.m. on Saturday and Sunday for brunch, and 5:30 to 10 p.m. Tuesday through Saturday for dinner. Beer and wine are served.

Queues also form outside **The Shed,** half a block east of the Palace of the Governors at 113½ E. Palace Ave. (tel. 982-9030). A luncheon institution since 1954, it occupies several rooms and the patio of a rambling hacienda built in 1692 and inhabited from 1879 to 1940 by Gov. Bradford Prince and his family. Festive folk art adorns the doorways and walls, while Indian corn and chile rissoles dangle in the windows. The food is basic but delicious, a compliment to traditional Hispanic Pueblo cooking. Enchiladas, tacos, and burritos, all served on blue-corn tortillas with pinto beans and posole, are priced between $4.50 and $5.25. Dessert specials are priced at $1.75 and $2—try the mocha cake. The Shed is open from 11 a.m. to 2:30 p.m. Monday through Saturday. Beer and wine are available; credit cards are not accepted.

The Shed's sister restaurant, under the same ownership, is **La Choza,** at 905 Alarid St. (tel. 982-0909), near Cerrillos Road's intersection with St. Francis Drive. A casual eatery with cowhide chairs and round tables beneath *vigas,* it's especially popular on cold days when diners gather around the wood-burning stove and fireplace. The menu is similar to the Shed's, with dishes like green chile stew, chili con carne, and carne adovada also on the menu. Vegetarians and children have their own menus. Beer and wine are served. Lunch prices run $4.50 to $5.50; dinner entrees range from $5.50 to $6.50. La Choza is open daily except Sunday from 11 a.m. to 9 p.m., though it closes an hour earlier on winter weeknights.

The rustic establishment kitty-corner from the Hotel St. Francis is **Café Pasqual's,** 121 Don Gaspar Ave. (tel. 983-9340), a big favorite of budget-watching travelers. Not only does it have a common table where solo journeyers can get acquainted with others; but it has an innovative menu with reasonable prices. The lengthy breakfast menu, served all day, features omelets, pancakes, cereals, and huevos motulenos—like rancheros but with fried bananas ($5.75). Soups, salads, sandwiches, and Mexican dishes run $4.75 to $6.25 at lunch, and there's a delectable grilled trout in cornmeal with green chile and toasted piñon for $7. There are also daily pasta specials, homemade desserts, imported beers, and wine by the bottle or glass. The frequently changing dinner menu offers grilled meats and seafoods, plus vegetarian specials, for $9 to $11. Pasqual's is open daily from 7 a.m. to 3 p.m., for Sunday brunch from 8 a.m. to 2 p.m., and for dinner from 5:30 to 10 p.m. Friday through Monday.

At **Tia Sophia's,** 210 W. San Francisco St. (tel. 983-9880), diners enjoy breakfast and lunch while seated at big wooden booths. Breakfasts include chorizo omelets and eggs with blue-corn enchiladas for $3.50; a popular lunch is the Atrisco plate green chile stew, a cheese enchilada, beans, posole, and a sopaipilla for $4.75. Hours are 7 a.m. to 2:30 p.m. Monday through Saturday.

Josie's Casa de Comida, 225 E. Marcy St., opposite Cienega Street (tel. 983-5311), is an unpretentious little white house with casual Mexican décor open for lunch only, from 11 a.m. to 4 p.m. Monday through Friday. Everything is home-cooked and made to order, which means there's a 20-minute minimum wait for diners. But it's worth it: a complete Mexican dinner, with a taco, rolled enchilada, chile relleno, tortilla, lettuce, and beans, costs just $5. Josie's is unlicensed, and caters to vegetarians.

The Burrito Co., 111 Washington Ave. (tel. 982-4453), is probably downtown Santa Fe's best fast-food establishment. You can people-watch as you dine on the outdoor patio or enjoy the garden-style poster gallery indoors. Order and pick up at the counter. Breakfast burritos are just $3; after 11 a.m. you can get traditional Mexican meals with lots of chiles for a top price of $5. The eatery is open from 7:30 a.m. to 9 p.m. Monday through Saturday and 11 a.m. to 5 p.m. on Sunday. There's a branch at 3297 Cerrillos Rd. (tel. 471-5700) with drive-through service.

NOUVELLE CUISINE: For my money, the best food in Santa Fe is served at **e.k. mas fine food,** 319 Guadalupe St. (tel.

989-7121). The name of this unimposing restaurant is a play on the Spanish words *y que mas,* and after dining here, you, too, will probably be asking (despite a full stomach): "And what else?"

Sharing an open brick courtyard with Moe's Ribs, an ice-cream parlor, and a home-furnishings shop, e.k. mas occupies several rooms of an old house. The décor is quaint, to say the least: the walls are painted pink and adorned with regional watercolors, red "chile" lights are strung around the windows as if it were always Christmas, a potted palm is cooled by ceiling fans, and beehive fireplaces are aglow in winter.

Chef Robert Goodfriend is a master of the culinary arts, but he doesn't lord it over his guests with exorbitant prices. It's rare for any entree to be priced higher than $16, and full dinners start at just $7 with the vegetarian pasta of the day.

The cuisine is appropriately described as "international." Italian and Greek dishes are always on the menu, along with innovatively prepared continental specialties. Daily blackboard specials always include seafood: when it's available, the grilled yellowfin tuna with a ginger-pesto cream sauce ($16) is outstanding. Other entrees include braised lamb shank with mushrooms, tomatoes, carrots, potatoes, onions, and garlic ($11), and stuffed chicken breast with brie, herbs, mushrooms, and leeks, wrapped in phyllo ($9). All meals include French bread with herbal butter, house salad, potatoes, and vegetables. Desserts are terrific, especially the sweet potato/pecan pie ($3.50). The lunch menu is similar, but features lighter meals. Prices range from $4.75 for Greek horiatiki to $8.25 for a veal stew.

Service is extremely friendly and efficient, though you may have to wait 25 minutes in the open courtyard for dinner—even with reservations. With a mainly local clientele, waiters are discouraged from rushing anyone out.

e.k. mas has no lounge, but the restaurant offers an oenologist's delight of 55 wines from lesser-known California vintners. As many as 10 are available by the glass. And 16 beers from mini-breweries are also featured.

The restaurant is open from 11:30 a.m. to 2 p.m. Wednesday through Saturday for lunch, 5:30 to 9:30 p.m. Wednesday through Sunday for dinner. Sunday brunch is also served; call for hours.

Young Santa Fe professionals love the **Santacafe,** 231 Washington Ave. (tel. 984-1788). A casually formal restaurant in the 18th-century Padre Gallegos House, 2½ blocks north of the Plaza, its service and presentation are impeccable. Low lighting, soft jazz, and simple white décor dominate all four dining rooms. Crayons are provided for doodlers who can't resist the temptation presented by the shelf paper covering the linen tablecloths. Each of the rooms has a fireplace for winter heat, and there's an outside courtyard for summer diners.

T-shirted waiters present a menu which varies seasonally. A year-round favorite is the $7 "sampler" of three salad specials—for example, egg noodle salad in sesame-seed sauce, shrimp and shredded-crab salad, and an artichoke heart/calamari salad. Lunch and dinner appetizers include Chinese dumplings filled with shrimp, spinach, and mushrooms ($6), and roasted peppers with fresh buffalo mozzarella ($5). Luncheon diners may select from an omelet, pasta, and pizza of the day, or perhaps a grilled Coho salmon or filet mignon (each $9). Dinner grills, priced between $13 and $16, include salmon, veal, lamb, and a chicken breast with Chimayo chile miso lime butter. Soba noodles with tofu and fresh vegetables ($11) keep non-meat-eaters happy. All breads and desserts are homemade, including the rum pecan pie ($5) and the ginger ice cream ($3).

The Santacafe has a popular wine bar with a full liquor license. Drinks and appetizers are served until late at night.

Hours are 11:30 a.m. to 2:30 p.m. Monday through Friday for lunch, 5:30 to 10:30 p.m. nightly for dinner. The restaurant is closed Sunday in winter.

The city's No. 1 "trendy" restaurant at this writing is the **Coyote Café,** 338 E. DeVargas St. (tel. 983-1615). Owner-chef Mark Miller, formerly of San Francisco's Fourth Street Grill, has talked extensively about his kitchen on national television, with the result that tourists throng here, but locals shy away from the pricey menu. In summer, in fact, reservations are recommended two to three days in advance.

The Coyote Café overlooks DeVargas Street from tall windows on the second floor of a downtown building. Beneath the skylight, set in a cathedral ceiling, is a veritable zoo of avant-garde animal sculptures. Rattan seats with animal-skin upholstery are posed around painted plasterboard tabletops.

The cuisine, prepared on a pecan-wood grill in an open kitchen, is traditional southwestern with a modern twist. Dinner guests, for example, might start with cured duck and tequila–black-bean quesadillas ($7) or a marisco platter of scallops ceviche, Chipotle shrimp, and smoked fish ($9). Entrees range from rellenos with smoked corn, mushrooms, tomato, and cheese ($10.75) and paillard of pork loin with Chipotle-peanut sauce ($15.50) to striped bass Veracruzana ($17.50). Drinks are available from a full bar.

Lunch is served from 11:30 a.m. to 2 p.m. Monday through Friday; dinner, from 5:30 to 10 p.m. Monday through Thursday, to 11 p.m. on Friday and Saturday. Sunday brunch is also popular. The Coyote Café is closed annually during March and April.

A large patio on the Alameda, facing the huge cottonwood trees beside the Santa Fe River, is the distinguishing mark of the **Café del Rio,** 235 Don Gaspar Ave. in Springer Plaza (tel. 989-9106). The spacious interior is reminiscent of the rustic dinner theater that once occupied these premises.

Lunches, priced from $4 to $6.25, include a variety of New Mexico specialties, homemade soups, and fresh salads. Deep-fried cornmeal oysters ($7) are a big favorite. Midday is also a good time to indulge in the imaginative dessert menu ($3 to $4.25), which includes a strawberry pecan cake and a chocolate Kahlúa truffle cake in coconut cream.

Dinners begin with an *antojito* ("fancies") menu ($2.50 to $6), featuring the likes of goat-cheese-and-mushroom quesadillas and a steamed artichoke with lemon-mustard aeoili. That's followed by a selection of four daily specials ($9 to $14), usually pasta, seafood, and poultry. If it's available, try the linguine in mascarpone cream sauce with roasted tomatoes, oysters, mushrooms, chives, basil, and garlic. All meals are served with a fresh green vegetable and two thick blue-corn pancakes.

A wine list emphasizes California and New Mexico vintages; beer is also served. Classical and light-jazz music are piped in, and some evenings there may be live performances.

The Café del Rio is open from 11:30 a.m. to 10 p.m. Tuesday through Sunday. Sunday brunch is served until 2:30 p.m.

El Farol, 808 Canyon Rd. (tel. 983-9912), is the place to head for local ambience and oldtime flavor. The Canyon Road artists' quarter's original neighborhood bar (its name means "The Lantern"), its low ceilings and dark-brown walls have now also become the home of one of Santa Fe's largest and most unusual selections of *tapas* (bar snacks and appetizers). There are 35 varieties of *tapas,* including such delicacies as pulpo a la Gallega (octopus with Spanish paprika sauce; $4.75), grilled cactus with ramesco sauce ($4.25), conejo y vino (rabbit with tomatoes, olives, and wine; $4.75), and Moroccan eggplant ($2.75). Guests who proceed to the entrees ($14 and $15) often opt for the Cornish game hen—butterflied, cooked with rosemary, and served with ginger sauce.

Jazz, folk, and ethnic musicians play most nights. Dinner is served from 6 to 10 p.m. Tuesday through Saturday; the bar is open nightly from 4:30 p.m. In summer there's an outdoor patio seating 50. Reservations are suggested.

Just down the road is **Celebrations,** 613 Canyon Rd. (tel. 989-8904), housed in a former art gallery. Beautiful stained-glass windows and a *kiva* fireplace shed light on the wood décor; in summer, guests can also dine on a brick patio.

Three meals are served daily. Breakfast (8 a.m. to 2:30 p.m.)

might be a Canyon omelet ($4.75), orange French toast ($3.75), or berries in cream with bananas ($3). Lunch (from 11 a.m.) includes soup, pasta and pizza specials, sandwiches like the oyster poorboy ($7), and salads (the Cobb salad is $4.50). Northern New Mexico specialties run $3.75 to $4.75.

The dinner menu—served from 5:30 to 9 p.m. Tuesday through Saturday in summer, Thursday through Saturday in winter—changes weekly. Diners might start with fried bocconcini with fresh tomato and basil sauce ($5), then progress to an entree like red snapper with avocados and lemon sauce ($12), shrimp brochettes with Chimayo chile and pineapple salsa ($14), or grilled ribeye with rosemary potatoes ($15).

Homemade desserts ($1.50) include cheesecake and fruit tarts. California wines are available by the bottle or glass. There's also a choice of beers, herbal teas, and mineral water.

Located right off Guadalupe Street, the **Garfield Grill,** 322 Garfield St. (tel. 988-9562), does its thing in casual art deco décor: polished white inside and outside with Day-Glo green trim. The menu, featuring home-grown herbs and vegetables, changes weekly. Appetizers might include a creamy beet soup ($2.75) or cheese-and-chive ravioli with fresh herb tomato sauce ($3.75). Entrees are priced $10 to $12, and always include at least one seafood and at least one beef dish. A house favorite is fresh cod or sea bass with spinach-cream sauce ($12). Heading the dessert list is a strawberry sorbet bombe filled with pistachio mousse ($3.50).

Beer and wine are available. Dinner only is served, from 5:30 to 10 p.m. Wednesday through Sunday, to 9 p.m. in winter. Reservations are recommended.

Also art deco, albeit in a self-described "southwestern desert diner chic," is **The Zia,** 326 S. Guadalupe St. (tel. 988-7008). Its eclectic furnishings—in a renovated 1880 adobe coal warehouse —include a stainless-steel soda fountain, a wood-burning pizza oven, an outdoor patio, and Pueblo Indian motifs throughout.

Like the décor, the menu tries to be all things to all people, catering to vegetarians and meat lovers, mild-palated Americans and adventurous ethnic diners. Homemade soups, salads, sandwiches, and pastas are served anytime, along with black-bean flautas ($3.75), green chile stew ($4), and Greek spinach salad ($6). Among the daily lunch specials, priced from $5.75 to $7, are East Indian curry (Wednesday) and spanakopita (Thursday). Dinners, starting at $7.25, include shrimp and fettuccine ($10.25) and lamb chops with jalapeño mint jelly ($13.75). Pizzas are served from 5:30 p.m.; try the shrimp and artichoke-heart special, at $8.50.

The full-service bar offers wines by the glass and 14 beers, including Guinness on tap. There's live entertainment on weekends. Hours are Monday through Thursday from 11 a.m. to 10 p.m., on Friday and Saturday to 11 p.m., and on Sunday from 10 a.m. to 2 p.m. for brunch and 5 to 10 p.m. for dinner.

STEAKS AND SEAFOOD: It's hard to miss the **Ore House on the Plaza,** 50 Lincoln Ave. (tel. 983-8687), the most popular restaurant on Santa Fe's central park block. Its second-story balcony, at the southwest corner of the Plaza, is an ideal spot from which to watch the passing parade while enjoying lunch or cocktails; when the weather's too cold for a Plaza perspective, there's a big fireplace indoors.

The décor is southwestern, with plants and lanterns hanging amid white walls and booths. The menu is heavy on fresh seafood and steaks. Daily fresh fish specials include salmon and swordfish (poached, blackened, teriyaki, or lemon, for $15 and up), rainbow trout ($10), lobster, shrimp, and oysters (market prices). Steak Ore House, an eight-ounce cut of beef wrapped in bacon and topped with crabmeat and béarnaise sauce ($15.25), and chicken Ore House, a grilled boneless breast finished with sweet ham and cheese, asparagus spears, and béarnaise ($12), are local favorites. The Ore House caters to vegetarians with its fresh pasta primavera ($10). Luncheon diners often opt for the spinach salad with honey-lemon dressing ($3.50) or the freshly ground sirloin burger ($6). Children's dishes are also available.

The bar, with music nightly, is proud of its 64 "custom" margaritas. It also has a selection of domestic and imported beers and an excellent wine list.

The Ore House is open daily from noon to 3 p.m. for lunch and 5:30 to 10 p.m. for dinner. Reservations are suggested.

Legislators and lobbyists from the adjacent State Capitol make a habit of dining and drinking at **The Bull Ring,** 414 Old Santa Fe Trail (tel. 983-3328). Impressive impressionistic paintings adorn the walls of this old adobe hacienda, now a series of small dining rooms.

Steaks, starting at $10, are the dinner specialty. Much ballyhooed is the Bull Ring steak, a 13-ounce charcoal-broiled New York cut with sautéed mushrooms or onions, red or green chile, or au poivre sauce ($14.50). Seafood dishes include Spanish red or Panama white shrimp ($17.50) and 12-ounce Alaskan king crab legs ($19). Caesar salads are prepared tableside for $4 per person. New Mexican blue-corn specialties run $5.25 to $9 for lunch or dinner; fajitas are $7. Midday diners can also select half-pound hamburgers or other sandwiches, from $4.50 to $8.

Lunch is served from 11:30 a.m. to 2:30 p.m. Monday through Friday; dinner, 5:30 to 9:30 p.m. Monday through Saturday. Reservations are recommended.

The Bull Ring's lounge is one of Santa Fe's most active, with live rock music and dancing. It opens with the restaurant and doesn't close until 2:30 a.m. nightly except Sunday. You can order off the bar menu and enjoy the oil paintings of regular customers hanging on the walls.

There's nightly live music of a different sort at **Vanessie of Santa Fe,** 434 W. San Francisco St. (tel. 982-9966). The talented Doug Montgomery holds forth at the large piano bar, caressing the ivories with a repertoire that ranges from Bach to Gershwin to Barry Manilow.

A five-item menu, served at large round wooden tables beneath hanging plants, never varies: roast chicken ($8), fresh fish ($10), New York sirloin ($12.50), filet mignon ($12.50), and rack of lamb ($12.50). Portions are large, and are served with baked potatoes or onion loaf, fresh vegetables or salad for $1.50 extra per item. The cheesecake served for dessert ($4) is large enough to feed three. The wine list is limited to a choice of two: Domaine St. George cabernet sauvignon or chardonnay, at $10 per bottle.

Dinner is served from 5:30 to 10:30 p.m. seven days a week. Vanessie opens an hour earlier for cocktails.

Ogelvie's Bar & Grille, 150 Washington Ave. (tel. 988-3855), caters to local businessmen and women from the rear of the First Interstate Bank Building, behind the Palace of the Governors a block from the Plaza. A casual restaurant with wicker chairs, an outdoor patio, and an unusual "greenhouse room," it serves lunch, dinner, and a late-night bar menu.

Luncheon offerings include homemade soups (from $2.25) and salads (from $3), burgers and other sandwiches (from $4), pastas (from $6), and huevos de casa Ogelvies, the house version of huevos rancheros ($4.75). Heading the dinner menu is steak Ogelvie (a filet wrapped in bacon with king crab meat, covered with sauce béarnaise; $14.50) and pollo verde (boneless chicken sautéed with piñons, shredded zucchini, and green chile in a light cream sauce; $9.50). American Heart Association light meals are priced $4.50 to $8.50. A children's menu is available.

Ogelvie's is open daily June through mid-September from 10 a.m. to 4 p.m. for lunch and 5 to 10:30 p.m. for dinner. Winter hours are 11 a.m. to 4 p.m. and 5 to 10 p.m. Reservations are suggested. There are other Ogelvie's restaurants in Taos and Albuquerque.

Nothing on the menu at the **San Francisco Bar & Grill,** 114 W. San Francisco St. in Plaza Mercado (tel. 982-2044), is priced over $8.50. Open every day of the week from 11 a.m. to 11 p.m., this easy-going eatery offers casual dining amid simple décor in three seating areas: the main restaurant, an indoor courtyard beneath a three-story atrium, and an outdoor patio with its own summer luncheon grill.

The most popular menu items may be the sausages—beef, pork, and chicken, all homemade. Diners can opt for a hot Italian sausage sandwich (with feta and provolone cheese, sautéed onions, and bell peppers; $5.50) anytime, a quarter-pound grilled bratwurst ($4.50) for lunch, or the Santa Fe sausage plate (served over black beans; $6.50) at dinner. A half-pound hamburger ($4.25), fresh broiled fish sandwich ($5.50), and Copenhagen pasta salad ($5) are served at all hours. The dinner menu includes fresh Boston bluefish ($7), grilled pork chops ($7.25), and New York strip steak ($8.50). There's full bar service with draft beers and daily wine specials.

Some say the **Fresco Mesquite Grill & Tapas Bar,** 142 Lincoln Ave. (tel. 982-4583), is the best grill restaurant in the city. Angus beef, veal, lamb, pork chops, and fresh fish ($10 to $14) are prepared in front of diners' eyes over an open mesquite-wood grill. There's an adobe oven for pizzas, fresh pasta (from $5), and a large *tapas* bar offering cold and warm appetizers for lunch or after-hours supper. Lunch is served inside or on the patio from 11 a.m. to 2 p.m. Monday through Friday; dinner is available daily from 5:30 to 10 p.m. The full bar remains open for cocktails and *tapas* until nearly midnight.

CONTINENTAL: Many consider **The Compound,** 653 Canyon Rd. (tel. 982-4353), to be at the head of its class in Santa Fe dining. A past winner of several national awards, this restaurant is set on beautifully landscaped grounds amid tall firs and pines on the south bank of the Santa Fe River. It's reached by a long driveway off Canyon Road, at the rear of an exclusive housing compound.

The interior décor yields to the natural setting. There is little adornment except for a large rainbow mural and a wall of *santos* in niches. Entrees start at $15 and climb much higher. Specialties are Dover sole, pepper steak, and lamb and veal dishes. Seafood and vegetables are delivered fresh daily; bread and pastries are baked on the premises. There is, of course, an extensive wine list.

Dinner only is served, from 6:30 to 11:30 p.m. Tuesday through Saturday. Service is extremely formal and elegant: gentlemen must wear a coat and tie, and young children are not admitted. It almost goes without saying that reservations are essential.

San Pasqual, patron saint of the kitchen, keeps a close eye on **The Pink Adobe,** 406 Old Santa Fe Trail (tel. 983-7712). This popular restaurant is in the center of the 17th-century Barrio de Analco, across the street from the San Miguel mission and a mere half block from what is billed as "the oldest house" in the United States. A Santa Fe institution since 1946, it occupies an adobe home believed to be at least 350 years old.

Guests enter through a narrow side door to a series of quaint, informal dining rooms with tile or hardwood floors. Stuccoed walls display original modern art or Priscilla Hoback pottery on built-in shelves.

At the dinner hour the Pink Adobe is at its continental best, with the likes of escargots ($5.25) and shrimp remoulade ($5.50) as appetizers. Entrees, priced at $12.50 to $16.75, include shrimp Créole, poulet marengo, tournedos bordelaise, lamb curry, and porc Napoleone. Lobster salad runs $15.75. Lunch has more New Mexican and Cajun dishes, including a house enchilada with egg ($6), turkey-seafood gumbo ($7.25), gypsy stew (chicken, green chile, tomatoes, and onions in sherry broth with cheese and corn bread; $6.75), and a fruit-and-cheese board ($7.50). Salads and sandwiches run $5.75 to $7.50, and a fine soup du jour is $4.50 a bowl.

Lunch is served from 11:30 a.m. to 2:30 p.m. Monday through Friday; dinner is offered from 5:30 to 10 p.m. daily. Reservations are suggested.

One last note: There's no smoking in the Pink Adobe. That privilege is reserved for patrons of the Dragon Room, the lounge across the alleyway from the Pink Adobe. Under the same ownership, the Dragon Room has a separate menu from its parent establishment, with traditional Mexican foods in the $8 to $10 range. The full bar is open from 11:30 a.m. to 2 a.m. daily.

Another friendly lounge, this one with a casual piano bar, is the **Carriage Trade Restaurant y Cantina,** 724 Canyon Rd. (tel. 982-3541). Open daily, its lunch offerings of Brazilian salad with heart of palm ($5), omelet niçoise with vegetable ratatouille ($5), and seafood crêpes ($6.25) are particularly popular. Evening diners can start with shrimp à la Borghese ($5), progress to roast duckling aux framboises ($11.50) or tournedo of beef Aztec ($12.50), and conclude with tarte Tatin ($3.50). The intimate dining room, with brass-topped tables, is divided by a walkway from the cantina.

FRENCH: Santa Fe's premier French restaurant, **Comme Chez Vous,** 116 W. San Francisco St. (tel. 984-0004), is high on the third floor of the Plaza Mercado. You might not find it exactly "like your place," as the translation of the establishment's name might imply, but you will find fine cuisine in a light, airy décor. Entrees, including fresh seafood, veal, quail, duck, and prime rib, run the gamut from a vegetarian pasta ($13) to carré d'agneau aux framboises ($22). All meals are served with vegetables and rice or potatoes. Luncheon diners often opt for a bowl of delicious soup à l'oignon ($2.50).

The restaurant has an extensive French wine list and a summer balcony popular with midday diners. Lunch is served from 11:30 a.m. to 2 p.m. Monday through Saturday; dinner, daily from 6 to 9:30 p.m. (from 5:30 p.m. during the opera season). There's also a continuous menu (from 11:30 a.m. to 11 p.m.) in the elegant lounge, where solo musicians often perform.

ITALIAN: When construction crews in 1959 were excavating the Burro Alley site of Dona Tules's notorious 19th-century gambling hall, they came across an unusual artifact: a brass door-knocker, half in the shape of a horseshoe, the other half resembling a saloon girl's leg, complete with stocking and high-heel boot. That knocker today is the logo of **The Palace,** 142 W. Palace Ave. (tel. 982-9891), which maintains the Victorian flavor but none of the ill-repute of its predecessor.

Red velvet wallpaper, dimly lit chandeliers, marble-topped tables, and high-backed chairs provide a classy yet casual décor for the restaurant—which, by the way, is huge. It seats 325, plus another 125 in summer on the garden patio.

Brothers Lino, Piedro, and Bruno Pertusini have carried on a long family tradition in the restaurant business: their father was chef at the famous Villa d'Esta on Lake Como, Italy. The Pertusinis' menu is predominantly northern Italian but contains a few French and continental dishes as well. Lunches, priced from $5 to $8, include coquille of fresh seafood ($7), ravioli Ortolana ($6.50), and salade niçoise ($6.75). Full dinners, all in the $9 to $16.50 range, include agnolotti campagnola (veal and chicken pasta; $10.50), steak au poivre verte ($16.25), trout al Balsimico ($13.50), and scallopine Villa Borghese (with julienne of artichoke bottoms; $15). The wine list is long and well considered.

Lunch is served from 11:30 a.m. to 3 p.m., and dinner is from 6 to 10 p.m. or later, Monday through Saturday. Reservations are suggested.

You can see the famous door-knocker above the bar of the spiffy saloon, open daily except Sunday from 11:30 a.m. to 2 a.m. There's dancing to a live combo here on Friday and Saturday nights, and a piano bar every night.

Babe's, 731 Canyon Rd. (tel. 983-3512), has one of Santa Fe's most romantic settings for dinner: a lush greenhouse. Brilliant bougainvillea and other flowers surround the brick courtyard, in the center of which is a moss-cloaked fountain. An art gallery, with works by European and regional artists, adjoins the dining area.

Babe's is famous for its homemade pastas—like fettuccine

Babe's ($11), a mixture of peas, prosciutto, mushrooms, and onions in a butter-cream and parmesan cheese sauce. Canneloni, manicotti, puttanesca, and other pastas are served with salad and garlic toast.

Those who come for lunch (served from 11 a.m. to 3 p.m. daily) can choose spaghetti al pesto ($6), three-topping pizza ($6.50), chef's salad ($6.25), turkey blue-corn enchilada ($6.25), or many other items. Dinner entrees, with salad, pasta, and vegetable, include steaks, chicken, scampi, and fresh fish, all priced from $11.50 to $15.50. Artichoke hearts Domenica ($5) are a good way to start dinner, and cassata siciliana ($3) is a fine way to conclude. Australian and French vintages share the wine menu with Italian favorites. Dinner is served from 6 to 10 p.m. daily, and reservations are recommended.

Billie Holliday, Bessie Smith, and other early-20th-century jazz and blues singers hold forth on tape and record in the casual bar. There's live Dixieland jazz here on Friday, a wandering minstrel on Saturday, and a dart tournament every Tuesday. Pasta, pizza, and enormous hamburgers ($5.50) highlight the bar menu, served until midnight.

The Rafters Spaghetti Warehouse & Bar, 550 Montezuma St. in Sanbusco Market Center (tel. 988-1080), may offer the best value of any restaurant in Santa Fe: full pasta dinners, with appetizers, salad, sourdough bread, coffee or tea, and spumoni ice cream, for a top price of $10. Spaghetti runs $5 to $7; the menu also includes cheese manicotti ($7), lasagne ($7.25), cannelloni Florentine ($7.25), fettuccine in clam sauce ($7.50), chicken cacciatore ($8.25), and veal parmigiana ($9). Kids can choose between spaghetti marinara ($3) and ravioli ($3.50). They get a fruit cup, soft drink or milk, and chocolate ice cream with their meal—and if they're good, a helium-filled balloon.

Lunch features sandwiches, soups, salads, and pastas in the $4 to $5 range, served beneath a skylight and hanging ferns in a rustic atmosphere with a heavy dark-wood touch.

The Rafters' bar is the longest in Santa Fe. It's popular among sports fans, who appreciate its big-screen television and two additional TVs hanging over the bar. "Attitude adjustment hour" comes from 4:30 to 6 p.m. weekdays, when drinks are discounted and snacks are free. Well brands are all major label; there's a good choice of domestic and imported beers, Italian and California wines.

The Rafters is open Monday through Friday from 11 a.m. to 3 p.m. and 5 to 11 p.m., on Saturday and Sunday from noon to 11 p.m. Reservations are not taken.

Victor's Ristorante Italiano & Bar, 423 W. San Francisco St.

(tel. 982-1552), with its whitewashed Mediterranean-style décor, is within shouting distance of the Eldorado and Hilton hotels. Northern Italian cuisine is the specialty, including veal (try the saltimbocca), seafood (scallops, poached salmon, fresh trout), and homemade pasta (the tortellini is locally famous). Lunches run $5 to $9; dinners, $8 to $16. Victor's antipasto, a mouthwatering tray of meatballs, sausages, and imported cheeses, is the most popular late-night bar snack.

Lunch hours are 11:30 a.m. to 2:30 p.m. Monday through Friday; dinner is served from 6 to 10:30 p.m. Sunday through Thursday, until 11 p.m. on Friday and Saturday. The bar stays open later. Reservations are required for parties of five or more.

Como's Ristorante Italiano & Pizzeria, 125 W. Water St. (tel. 989-9549), is an informal bistro a couple of blocks from the Plaza best known for its pizzas and calzone, filled with provolone, ricotta, and mozarella cheeses. Scampi, linguine with clams, lasagne, and other pastas are on the dinner menu. Beer and wine are served. Lunches run $3 to $8; dinners, $4 to $11. Como's is open for lunch Monday through Saturday from 11 a.m. to 2:30 p.m. and on Sunday from 1 to 3 p.m.; for dinner, daily from 5:30 to 11 p.m.

Upper Crust Pizza, 329 Old Santa Fe Trail (tel. 983-4140), in an adobe house with its front patio adjacent to the old San Miguel mission, may have Santa Fe's best pizzas. Meals-in-a-dish like the Grecian gourmet (feta and olives) and the whole-wheat vegetarian (topped with sesame seeds) are priced from $7 small to $12.50 large. You can choose between indoor seating or 30-minute free delivery. Beer and wine are served, as well as salads, calzones, and stromboli. No reservations or credit cards are accepted. Hours are 11 a.m. to 10 p.m. Monday through Thursday, to 11 p.m. on Friday and Saturday, and noon to 10 p.m. on Sunday.

JAPANESE: The **Shohko-Cafe and Hiro Sushi,** 321 Johnson St. (tel. 983-7288 or 983-7364), which opened a decade ago, was Santa Fe's first Japanese restaurant. Located at the corner of Guadalupe Street next to the Eldorado Hotel, it has a sushi bar, seating 17 people, with 30 fresh varieties of raw seafood. Here is where to indulge in teriyaki dishes, sukiyaki, yakitori (skewered chicken), and yakisoba (noodles), and a uniquely southwestern Japanese treat: green chile tempura. There are also some Chinese plates on the menu. Wine, imported beers, and hot sake are available.

Lunch, served from 11:30 a.m. to 2 p.m. Monday through Friday, ranges from $4 to $8. Dinner, offered Sunday through Thursday from 5:30 to 9 p.m. and on Friday and Saturday to 10 p.m., is priced from $7 to $15. Reservations for dinner are recommended.

Just a block away is **Sakura,** 321 W. San Francisco St. (tel. 983-5353). Once known as Taro's, this Japanese restaurant is notable for its tatami rooms—small private dining rooms with cushions for sitting cross-legged on mats. There's a sushi bar here too, and other specialties like sashimi, tempura, teriyaki, and sukiyaki. Entrees are priced $3.50 to $12.50. Japanese beer, sake, and wine are available. Sakura is open daily except Monday for lunch and dinner until 9 p.m.

AFGHANI / INDIAN: The honor of being Santa Fe's most unusual restaurant might fall to **Hassina's Afghani Cuisine,** 227 Don Gaspar Ave. in the Santa Fe Village (tel. 989-8268). Diners enter through a side door opposite a parking lot, sit on the floor at low tables in a long, narrow room draped with Middle Eastern carpets, and perhaps (if entertainment is scheduled) listen to a sitar player as they eat.

The cuisine of Afghanistan has been influenced both by India and the eastern Mediterranean. This is a good place to get acquainted. Start with an appetizer like bolani (eggrolls filled with spiced leeks and lentils, served with a yogurt dip; $4.50), then move on to the main course—perhaps khorma (a lamb-and-vegetable stew with texmati rice; $10.50) or vegetarian sabsi (spinach stew seasoned with nuts and served with brown rice and yogurt; $7.50). There are also chicken and seafood courses. Wash it down with a big cup of chai (black tea with cardamon; $1.25).

Hassina's is open for dinner from 6 to 9 p.m. Tuesday through Saturday. Call for possible lunch hours in summer.

Albuquerque has several East Indian restaurants, but Santa Fe has only one: **Rama's Cuisine,** 418 Cerrillos Rd. in Las Tres Gentes marketplace (tel. 983-1747). Combination plates (to eat in or take out) include an entree, vegetables, yogurt, chutney, and papadum chips. Dishes include chicken Madras ($6.50), coconut fish curry ($7), lamb Mysore ($7.50), shrimp sambal ($8), scallops in oyster sauce ($9), and trout tikka ($9). Rama's is open Monday through Saturday from noon to 2:30 p.m. and 5:30 to 9 p.m.

BUDGET DINING: Perhaps the most charming deli in town is **Becker's Delicatessen,** 403 Guadalupe St. (tel. 988-2423). Fresh flowers and clean paper doilies are placed on the wood tables daily, and wrought-iron windows lend an old-world touch to the no-smoking atmosphere. Sandwiches combine a fine selection of imported and domestic cheeses, smoked fish and meats, and/or homemade sausage. Pasta, salads, breads, desserts, and espresso are also available. The take-out counter is open all day, of course. Breakfast and lunch are served weekdays from 7 a.m. to 5:30 p.m. and Saturday from 8 a.m. to 5:30 p.m. Closed Sunday. Prices range from $3 to $5 for breakfast and $5 to $7 for lunch.

A block away is a favorite of the sweet-tooth set: **the Swiss Bakery & Restaurant,** 320 Guadalupe St. (tel. 988-3737). You'll hear raves about the stuffed croissants and cappuccino served at breakfast ($3 to $4), and the quiches and individual pizzas available at lunchtime ($4 to $6). Also on the menu are croissant sandwiches, homemade soups, salads, and vol-au-vent. Pastries and cakes are baked fresh daily and served in the Tea Room, open all day. Beer and wine are also available. The Swiss Bakery serves breakfast from 7 to 10:50 a.m. and lunch from 11:30 a.m. to 3 p.m. Monday through Saturday. Tea Room service is continual from 7 a.m. to 6 p.m. weekdays, to 5 p.m. on Saturday.

Another popular breakfast-and-lunch spot on the west side of downtown is **O.J. Sarah's,** 106 N. Guadalupe St. (tel. 984-1675), so called because of the owner's attachment to orange juice and other wholesome foods. Breakfasts, priced between $3 and $4.50, include such unusual items as cottage cheese pancakes topped with hot raspberry sauce and three-egg omelets filled with spinach, avocado, mushrooms, and cheese. Granola is homemade. For lunch ($3.25 to $5.50), consider a spinach-artichoke salad, a guacamole burrito, or a sour-cream chicken enchilada—or play it safe with sandwiches on home-baked bread and a fruit smoothie. O.J.'s is open from 7 a.m. to 1:30 p.m. Monday through Friday. Credit cards are not accepted.

O.J. Sarah has opened a second restaurant in a shiny silver Santa Fe Rail car. Called the **Super Chief Diner,** it's parked on a platform at 531 Guadalupe St. (tel. 983-3080). Everything here is '50s, from the music to the soda jerk behind the counter. Remarkably, the prices seem almost like the '50s too. Eggs and pancakes, served all day, are priced $3 to $5. Burgers are $3.50; polish sausage, $3; chili, $4 a bowl. Shakes, malts, and ice-cream sodas all run $2. Super Chief is open from 8 a.m. to midnight Sunday through Thursday (except Wednesday, when it's closed); until 2 a.m. on Friday and Saturday.

Croissant-lovers appreciate **Patis CorBae,** a bakery and café behind the State Capitol at 422 Old Santa Fe Trail (tel. 983-2422). There are 15 varieties of the French sandwich rolls, from chocolate almond to egg, ham, and swiss cheese, priced no higher than $2. Other sandwiches run $3.25 to $5; quiche is $3.25, soup is $2.35 a bowl, and there are weekday luncheon specials. Early risers can enjoy fruit granola ($3.25) for breakfast with a cup of espresso or cappuccino. The café, with indoor and outdoor seating, is open daily from 7 a.m. to 3:30 p.m.

Santa Fe Gourmet, 72 W. Marcy St. (tel. 982-8738), offers delectable home-style sandwiches just a couple of blocks north of the Plaza. Homemade soup and salad are included with all sandwich entrees, including the Italian veggie hero ($4.50). Picnic lunches can be made to order. It's open for breakfast and lunch Monday through Friday from 7 a.m. to 3:30 p.m. and on Saturday from 10 a.m. to 3 p.m.

You may sing the praises of the "Say Amen" desserts at **Carlos' Gospel Café,** 150 Washington Ave. (tel. 983-1841), in the inner courtyard of the First Interstate Bank Building. First, though, try the tortilla or hangover (potato-corn) soups (at $3.25 a bowl), or the deli sandwiches (from $4). Desserts are $2.25. Carlos' has outdoor tables, but many diners prefer to sit indoors, reading newspapers or sharing conversation at the large common table. Gospel and soul music play continually; posters and oil paintings of many of the performers cover the walls.

By contrast, easy-listening New Age music fills the air and modern religious art dominates the simple décor at **the Nighthawk Café,** 225 E. DeVargas St. (tel. 982-4799). Sharing an old adobe home with a lowercase bookstore, "burnt horses," it's the frequent venue of prose and poetry readings, one-act plays, and lectures. A menu of "chemical-free" foods is served from 7:30 a.m. to 10:30 p.m. Monday through Friday, 10 a.m. to 10:30 p.m. on Saturday and Sunday. Top price is $3.50 for a tuna melt on a toasted English muffin, liver pâté with French bread, or baked brie with toasted almonds and apple slices. There's a selection of quiches, soups, and salads, and a list of ten black and herbal teas.

Moe's Ribs, 319 N. Guadalupe St. (tel. 983-9729), carefully guards its reputation as Santa Fe's No. 1 purveyor of woodsmoked and barbecued meats—especially pork ribs and brisket chicken, but also including beef, ham, and sausage links. All cooking is done naturally over a hardwood pit and served with Moe's own sauce. All platters are priced under $10. There are all-you-can-eat nights for ribs ($8) on Tuesday and chicken ($7) on Wednesday. Beer and wine are available. Moe's is open daily from 11 a.m. to 9:30 p.m., with abbreviated winter hours.

Downtown Santa Fe's preferred hamburger stand is **RealBurger,** 227 Don Gaspar Ave. (tel. 988-3717), across from the St. Francis Hotel. Burgers with "the works" are priced no higher than $2.50; chili dogs ($1.75), fajitas ($4), and an enchilada plate ($3) are also on the menu. Earlier in the day you can get steak and eggs for $4.25 or a breakfast burrito for $3.25. It's open daily except Sunday from 7 a.m. to 5 p.m.

Late-night dessert-and-cappuccino people have a place to go too. It's the **Jean Cocteau Cinema and Coffee House,** 418 Montezuma St. (tel. 988-2711), in an alternative movie theater between Guadalupe Street and Sanbusco Center.

NORTHSIDE

REGIONAL CUISINE: About 7½ miles north of the Plaza and about 5 miles from the Santa Fe Opera, **Las Brazas,** on U.S. 285 in Tesuque (tel. 455-2111), has a wide reputation for its carnitas (sirloin bites) and carne adovada broiled over mesquite wood, both $9.75. Also on the dinner menu are almejas (clam strips with tostadas and salsa), crab-stuffed shrimp, and a combination seafood platter ($18.50). There's a good salad bar. Margaritas are sold by the glass or the pitcher ($7). Las Brazas is open daily from 11:30 a.m. to 9:30 p.m.

STEAK AND SEAFOOD: Life has never been dull at **El Nido,** "The Nest," five miles north of the Plaza on N.M. 22 in Tesuque (tel. 988-4340). This 1920s adobe home was a dance hall and later Ma Nelsen's brothel, before the restaurant opened in 1939. It's been drawing throngs of Santa Feans ever since for its food and atmosphere, lively bar, and occasional flamenco dance performances.

Scandinavian wood tables and chairs sit beneath *viga* ceilings, surrounded by *kiva* fireplaces and stuccoed walls covered with local artwork. On one of those walls is a mural painted in 1964 by Will Shuster, the artist who dreamed up the custom of burning Old Man Gloom during Santa Fe Fiesta.

Dinner only is served, nightly except Monday. The appetizer list ($4 to $6) features ceviche, steamed mussels, and half-shell or deep-fried oysters when available. Entrees ($9 to $19) include a variety of steaks, aged prime rib, stuffed chicken breast, king crab, shrimp, scallops, and broiled fresh fish specials such as salmon, swordfish, yellowfin tuna, and red snapper. Desserts ($2.75) are highlighted by the profiteroles, a puff pastry filled with vanilla ice cream and covered with chocolate sauce.

Hours are 5:30 to 10 p.m. Tuesday through Thursday and Sunday, to 10:30 p.m. on Friday and Saturday. The bar remains open until early morning. Reservations are suggested.

JAPANESE: The flashing knifework of hibachi chefs makes meals an entertaining experience at **the Japanese Kitchen,** 510 N. Guadalupe St. in DeVargas Center North (tel. 988-8893). Diners enter the restaurant on a wooden bridge across a small pond, then sit back and watch as *teppan* grill dinners of chopped steak, seafood, and chicken ($9 to $25) are prepared with Oriental finesse before their eyes. The menu also features tempura plates, vegetarian dishes, and daily specials. A sushi bar is open throughout the day; an all-you-can-eat luncheon buffet is priced at $5. The full bar offers numerous exotic cocktails, including mai tais.

The Japanese Kitchen is open from 11:30 a.m. to 2 p.m. Monday through Friday for lunch; 5 to 9:30 p.m. daily for dinner (to 10 p.m. on Friday and Saturday). Reservations are recommended.

CERRILLOS ROAD

REGIONAL CUISINE: A Santa Fe tradition for four decades, **Maria's New Mexican Kitchen** is at 555 W. Cordova Rd. just east of St. Francis Drive (tel. 983-7929). Established on this site in 1949 by Maria Lopez and her politician husband, Gilbert, the restaurant is a prime example of what charm can come from scavenging: bricks used in its construction came from the old New Mexico State Penitentiary, and most of its pre–World War II furniture was once used in the La Fonda Hotel. The five priceless wall frescoes in the cantina were painted by master muralist Alfred Morang (1901–1958) in barter exchange for food and drinks, and were painstakingly restored after former corporate broadcasting executive Al Lucero and his wife, Laurie, bought the restaurant in 1985.

But it's not the rustic décor that keeps people coming back. It's the high quality and generous portions of food. Award-winning beef, chicken, shrimp, and vegetarian fajitas are priced $8 to $10 for one, $14 to $19 for two. Lunches are priced under $6; dinners ($5.75 to $9.75) include blue-corn enchiladas, homemade pork or vegetarian tamales, chile rellenos, and Mexican-style ribs. Also on the menu are a 20-ounce Trailmaster sirloin steak with beans ($12), tasty green chile and posole stews ($3), and the unique tortilla burger ($6.75). There's also a child's plate for $3.75. From September through April, Tuesday is "Twos-day," when diners pay only $2 additional for a second meal.

One of Maria's special touches is an open tortilla grill, where cooks can be seen behind a glass partition making flour and corn tortillas by hand. In the cantina, bartenders still hand-shake margaritas, concoct homemade sangría daily, and offer a list of more than 60 premium wines and the full gamut of Mexican beers. Strolling mariachi troubadours perform on weekends.

Maria's is open Monday through Thursday from 11 a.m. to 4 p.m. and 5 to 10 p.m., on Friday from 11 a.m. to 4 p.m. and 5 to

10:30 p.m., on Saturday from noon to 4 p.m. and 5 to 10:30 p.m., and on Sunday from noon to 10 p.m. The restaurant closes somewhat earlier in winter.

Another longtime favorite of Santa Feans is **Tiny's Restaurant & Lounge,** at St. Francis Drive and Cerrillos Road in the Pen Road Shopping Center (tel. 983-9817 or 983-1100). First opened in 1948, it has added an elegant new indoor/outdoor patio and garden room with full food and cocktail service. Steaks and shrimp complement a menu that features fajitas and northern New Mexico entrees, such as chicken and guacamole tacos, at prices that average $8 for dinner. Daily lunch specials are in the $5 range. A very popular lounge has live entertainment weekends from 9 p.m. to 1:30 a.m. Meal hours are 11:30 a.m. to 2 p.m. Monday through Friday for lunch, 6 to 10 p.m. Monday through Saturday for dinner. Reservations are advised.

The **Old Mexico Grill,** 2434 Cerrillos Rd. in College Plaza South (tel. 473-0338), is unique among Santa Fe restaurants: it specializes not in northern New Mexican food, but in authentic Mexico City and regional Mexican cuisine. The restaurant's centerpiece is an exhibition cooking area with an open mesquite grill and French rôtisserie. Here, behind bright-blue tiles and beneath a raft of hanging copperware, chef Paul Salazar (formerly of San Francisco's Compton Place Hotel) prepares a tempting array of fajitas, tacos al carbon, and other specialties. Among the more popular dishes are pollo mole poblano ($8.75), chiles en nogada (in a walnut and cream-cheese sauce; $9), paella Mexicana ($10), and chuletas de puerco en adobo (grilled pork chops; $9.50).

Lunch entrees are priced $4.25 to $7; dinners, $6.25 to $12. There's a good choice of antojitos (appetizers), soups, and salads, and a choice of homemade desserts (including hazelnut-apricot torte) from $2.50 to $3.25. A full bar serves Mexican beers and margaritas. The atmosphere is casual with attentive service from blue-jeaned waitpersons who take personal interest in the clientele.

Hours are 11:30 a.m. to 3 p.m. Monday through Saturday for lunch, 5 to 9 p.m. Sunday through Thursday, to 9:30 p.m. on Friday and Saturday, for dinner. Reservations are not accepted.

Maria Ysabel, 2821 Cerrillos Rd. (tel. 473-2782), is a family affair. Former New Mexico Lt.-Gov. Roberto Mondragon, accompanied by his grandson, Chaco, often sings and plays the guitar on weekend nights while his wife, Bell, does the cooking. This casual, friendly restaurant serves eight-course family-style dinners ($8 to $12.50) and ample lunches ($4 to $7.25) that include huevos rancheros, as featured on "Good Morning, America." House specials include carne adovada, carnitas asadas, chicharron burritos, and blue-corn crabmeat enchiladas. There's a children's menu with dishes priced at $4, and several vegetarian offerings. Beer and wine are served. The restaurant is open Monday through Friday from 10 a.m. to 3 p.m. for lunch and 5 to 9 p.m. for dinner; on Saturday and Sunday, from 11 a.m. to 10 p.m.

A breakfast lovers' favorite is the **Tecolote Café,** 1203 Cerrillos Rd. (tel. 988-1362). The décor is simple, but the food is elaborate: eggs any style, omelets, huevos rancheros, served with fresh-baked muffins or biscuits and maple syrup. Luncheon specials include carne adovada burritos and green-chile stew, served with beer or wine. Entrees are priced $3.25 to $8. The Tecolote is open from 7 a.m. to 2 p.m. Tuesday through Sunday; closed Monday.

Cordelia's, 1601 Berry Ave. (tel. 988-1303), one block off Cerrillos Road at 2nd Street, has a second location on Rodeo Road West (tel. 471-6774). A favorite choice here is the Mexican combination plate ($9), with other entrees of tacos, enchiladas, and the like priced in the $5 to $6 range. Steaks and fish also are on the menu at this friendly family restaurant, and beer and wine are served. It's open Monday through Saturday from 11 a.m. to 8 p.m. for lunch and dinner.

Tortilla Flats, 3139 Cerrillos Rd. (tel. 471-8685), prides itself on its all-natural ingredients and vegetarian menu selections. A casual restaurant open daily from 7 a.m. to 9 p.m. for breakfast ($1.75 to $6.25), lunch ($1.25 to $6.50), and dinner ($1.75 to $7), it offers the likes of homemade blueberry pancakes, fajitas and eggs with a side of black beans, and blue-corn enchiladas, quesadillas, and chimichangas. Beer and wine are served, but no reservations or credit cards are accepted. There's a children's menu and take-out service.

STEAKS AND SEAFOOD: At 4220 Airport Rd., one block from the Villa Linda Mall, **Toushie's** (tel. 473-4159) is an oft-overlooked surprise on the south side of town. Its spacious, semi-circular seating area is an ideal place to listen to the mellow dance music of the Clark Pontsler Trio on Saturday nights, and an intimate area in which to enjoy a relaxing meal at other times.

Appetizers include escargots and sautéed mushrooms ($3.75 to $5.75); a wide choice of entrees might include a 16-ounce T-bone steak ($15), prime rib and baked shrimp ($16), and coquille of sea scallops and shrimp ($10). Regional dishes highlight the lunch menu, with a bowl of menudo at $4.50 and a combination plate of taco, tamale, and rolled enchilada at $7. Children's plates run $2.50 and up. A favored dessert is Toushie's Delight, a flaming sopaipilla, at $3.75.

Toushie's is open from 11:30 a.m. to 10 p.m. Monday

through Saturday and noon to 2 p.m. on Sunday. There's full bar service daily except Sunday to 1 a.m.

CHINESE: A pair of stone lions guard the ostentatious dragon-gate entrance to the **Hunan Chinese Restaurant,** 2428 Cerrillos Rd., in College Plaza South (tel. 471-6688). The pink-and-white décor, with a large aquarium and antique Oriental furniture, is reminiscent of a Chinese palace.

The hot, spicy Hunan- and Peking-style recipes prepared by chef-owner Min Lee are equally fascinating. Family dinners of Hunan shredded pork, sha-cha beef, and spiced chicken and shrimp are priced at just $9 per person, including eggroll, wonton soup, fried rice, tea, and fortune cookies. Or you can order à la carte: whole fish with hot bean sauce is $14, and Peking duck is $23 (advance order, please).

The ten-dish all-you-can-eat luncheon buffet is priced at $5.25, or $3.50 for diners under 8 years of age. There's also a full bar, and take-outs are welcomed.

Lunch is served weekdays from 11:15 a.m. to 2 p.m., weekends from 11:45 a.m. to 2 p.m.; dinner is available Sunday through Thursday from 5 to 9 p.m., on Friday and Saturday from 5 to 10 p.m.

There's more spicy food, pleasing the southwestern palate, at **Szechwan Chinese Cuisine,** 1965 Cerrillos Rd. (tel. 983-1558). Lunches, priced between $3.50 and $5, include fried rice, an eggroll, fried wonton, and homemade soup. Dinner starts at $4.50 and goes up to $20—the cost of Peking duck, made to order in 30 minutes, served with traditional pancakes and plum sauce. Some opt for the "sea treasures" seafood platter of shrimp, scallops, crab, fish, and vegetables stir-fried in a wine sauce. Other specialties include Lake Tung Ting shrimp, sesame beef, and General Chung's chicken. Wine is served, along with Tsingtao beer from China.

The restaurant is open Monday through Saturday from 11:30 a.m. to 2:30 p.m. and 5 to 9:30 p.m.; closed Sunday. Reservations are suggested.

The **Peking Palace,** 1710 Cerrillos Rd. (tel. 984-1212), specializes in the spicy Szechwan and much milder Cantonese cuisines. Twice-cooked pork and seafood go bah are among the house favorites, most priced in the $7 to $15 range. Lunch specials cost about $5. It's open from 11 a.m. to 9:30 p.m. Monday through Thursday, to 10 p.m. on Friday and Saturday, and to 11:30 p.m. on Sunday. Reservations are advised.

More typical Chinese-American food is the fare within the adobe walls of the **On Lok Yuen Restaurant,** 3242 Cerrillos Rd. (tel. 473-4133). Here's where you'll find longtime favorites like beef and chicken chow mein, chop suey, egg foo yung, sweet-and-sour pork, and shrimp fried rice. Luncheon specials, including soup, wonton, rice, and fortune cookie, run $4.25; dinner combinations for one to six are priced at $6.25 to $8 per person. On Lok Yuen is open Monday through Thursday from 11 a.m. to 2:30 p.m. and 4:30 to 9 p.m., on Friday and Saturday from 11 a.m. to 9 p.m.; closed Sunday.

Vietnamese and Chinese food are on the menu at **the Saigon Café,** 501 W. Cordova Rd., at the rear of the Osco Drug Center (tel. 988-4951). There are weekday breakfast and daily lunch buffets, and many dinner entrees under $6, such as cashew chicken and eggrolls. The Saigon prepares orders to go, and has beer and wine for those who prefer to dine in. It's open from 7 a.m. to 9 p.m. Monday through Friday, 11 a.m. to 9 p.m. on Saturday and Sunday.

VEGETARIAN: The **Natural Café,** 1494 Cerrillos Rd. (tel. 983-1411), may be unpretentious in appearance, but don't let that fool you. Its international menu of tasty vegetarian and seafood dishes is served in artsy garden surroundings by a competent cosmopolitan staff.

No fewer than seven national cuisines—Mexico (black-bean enchiladas), China (Szechuan vegetables), Indonesia (tempeh in gingered coconut sauce), Japan (seitan Parmesan), Lebanon (hummus with pita bread), Italy (pasta Verano), and the United States—are represented on the everyday menu. In addition, there are daily specials such as walnut fettuccine and mushroom Stroganoff, and homemade desserts sweetened with maple syrup or honey. Lunches start at $4.75 and range to $6.25, the price of a panfried trout sandwich with fresh basil and walnut sauce. Dinners, at $7 to $10, include soup or salad and homemade bread. Children's meals are priced at $5.25.

There are 21 wines and nine beers (including Warteck non-alcoholic beer), plus herbal teas, grain coffee, and other beverages on the beverage list.

The Natural Café is open for lunch Tuesday through Friday from 11:30 a.m. to 2:30 p.m., for dinner Tuesday through Sunday from 5 to 9:30 p.m. It does not accept reservations.

BUDGET DINING: Murphy's Law states: "Anything that can go wrong, will go wrong." That makes **Murphy's Law,** a restaurant at 1107 Cordova Rd. (tel. 983-8833), a contradiction in terms. Here, everything seems to go right.

Meals are served in a single large room with booths and darkwood furnishings. The breakfast menu, available all day, includes green-chile omelet ($4), breakfast burrito ($4.25), steak and eggs

($6.25), pancakes, Belgian waffles, and a Santa Fe special (two scrambled eggs with chorizo sausage, potatoes, biscuits, and gravy; $3.50). Lunch, priced $4.25 to $6.25, is served from 11 a.m.; regular offerings are meatloaf, chicken-fried steak, and hot turkey and roast-beef sandwiches with potatoes and vegetables. There's a choice of burgers, burritos, and enchiladas, and a frito pie for $3.50. There are daily luncheon specials, and in winter, an Early Bird Skiers Special.

Murphy's Law is open from 6:30 a.m. to 2 p.m. weekdays, to 1 p.m. weekends. I don't understand how it got its name, but that's fitting. As the law states: "If you can keep your head when all about you are losing theirs, you don't understand the problem."

Salad enthusiasts will love **Souper Salad,** 2428 Cerrillos Rd. in College Plaza South (tel. 473-1211). The all-you-can-eat salad bar is Santa Fe's largest, with more than 60 items. There's also a soup stove with four homemade soups daily, such as vegetable beef, cream of zucchini, broccoli cheese, and red beans, rice, and sausage; and a baked-potato bar with eight different toppings. Gingerbread and honey-buttered cornbread are served with all meals.

Fitting right in with the Depression-era antiques and 1930s atmosphere is the deli sandwich counter, whose offerings include the New Deal—sliced avocado, mushrooms, and swiss cheese on whole-wheat bread with house dressing ($3). The prices seem to be from another era as well: salad bar is $3.75; soup and salad, $4.25; soup and sandwich, $4.25; salad and sandwich, $4.50; baked potato, $3; avocado stuffed with tuna salad, $4. Younger diners (under 10) get a half sandwich plus soup or salad for $2; soup and salad are free to those 3 and younger. Prohibition being over, beer and wine are available.

Hours are 11 a.m. to 9 p.m. Monday through Saturday, and on Sunday from noon. Neither reservations nor credit cards are taken.

The **Chelsea Street Pub,** near the east end of the Villa Linda Mall (tel. 473-5105), is a casual shoppers' oasis with unfinished-log décor. Open daily from 11 a.m. to midnight (on Sunday from noon), its menu features half-pound gourmet hamburgers from $3.75 to $4.25 and New York–style deli sandwiches from $5 to $6. Barbecued ribs, chicken, fajitas, and salads are also on the menu. There's live entertainment (usually rock bands) nightly except Sunday, with exotic drinks and table snacks available at the bar.

Elsewhere in **Villa Linda Mall,** between six and eight fast-food outlets of different types surround a modernistic central pergola in a skylit sidewalk-café setting. This is a good place to settle family arguments about who wants to eat what—you can order separately and eat together.

Otherwise, the following **fast-food restaurants** can be found on Cerrillos Road between downtown and I-25: McDonald's (two), Kentucky Fried Chicken (two), Blake's LotaBurger (two), Burger King, Wendy's, Arby's, Long John Silver's, Taco Bell, Sonic, El Pollo Asado, and Baja Tacos. There's also a Pizza Hut.

There are also these **family restaurants** on Cerrillos Road: Little Anita's (New Mexican), Denny's, Mr. Steak, Sirloin Stockade, Western Sizzlin' Steakhouse, Village Inn, JB's Big Boy, and K-Bob's.

SOUTHSIDE

REGIONAL CUISINE: For more than 20 years **Dona Elena's Mexican Kitchen,** at 5th and Saint Michael's Drive (tel. 983-9941 or 982-3049), has been an institution. Noted for its carnitas and carne adovada in a unique chile caribe sauce, this family restaurant has a menu which ranges from huevos rancheros and stuffed sopaipillas to menudo (tripe stew) and hamburgers. There are daily breakfast specials for $2; lunches and dinners are priced under $9, and children's platters are much less. Beer and wine are served. It's open Sunday through Thursday from 7 a.m. to 10 p.m., on Friday and Saturday to midnight. Tuesday is a day off. No credit cards, please.

The **Green Onion,** 1851 St. Michael's Dr. (tel. 983-5198), has some of the hottest chiles and one of the rowdiest bars in Santa Fe. Roast-beef burritos and chicken enchiladas highlight a dinner menu on which there's nothing priced over $10. It's open daily except Sunday for lunch and dinner until 10 p.m.

STEAKS AND SEAFOOD: Santa Fe's most highly regarded steakhouse is the **Steaksmith at El Gancho,** a 15-minute drive up the Old Pecos Trail toward Las Vegas (tel. 988-3333). In a pioneer atmosphere of brick walls and *viga* ceilings, New York sirloin, filet mignon, and other complete steak dinners are priced from $9 to $15. There are fresh seafood specials nightly, such as oysters, trout, and salmon; a creative appetizer menu, ranging from ceviche Acapulco to grilled pasilla peppers and beef chupadero; a good salad bar; homemade desserts and bread; and a full bar and lounge that even caters to cappuccino lovers.

The Steaksmith is open for dinner on Sunday, Monday, Wednesday, and Thursday from 5:30 to 10 p.m., on Friday and Saturday until 11 p.m.; closed Tuesday. Reservations are recommended.

BUDGET DINING: Meat eaters love the **Bobcat Bite,** an unimposing place five miles southeast of Santa Fe on the Old Las Vegas

Hwy. (tel. 983-5319). High-quality steak dinners begin at just $8, and huge hamburgers are comparably priced. It's open Tuesday through Saturday from 11 a.m. to 7:45 p.m.

OUT OF TOWN

CONTINENTAL: Nestled in a grove of spruce and pine, eight miles east of Santa Fe at the entrance to Hyde Memorial State Park, is **The Evergreen,** on Hyde Park Road (tel. 984-8190). If the views en route to the Santa Fe Ski Basin don't take your breath away, the elevation might—you're 8,400 feet up in the Sangre de Cristo range.

Diners can enjoy an intimate candlelit atmosphere beside the fireplace or, in summer, bask in twilight on a flagstone patio. The menu, designed by the Evergreen's Swiss chef, highlights veal dishes, rack of lamb, beef Wellington, roast duck, live Maine lobster, and fresh fish specialties. Full dinners, including soup, salad, entree, vegetables, and sorbet, are priced from $12 to $25. Flambé desserts are extra. Tempting lunches run $5 to $9; Sunday brunch is $11.

Skiers are an important part of the Evergreen's clientele. The roadside bakery opens at 7 a.m. between Thanksgiving and Easter for early breakfasts; and when the skiers are returning from the slopes between 3 and 6:30 p.m., there's complimentary fondue in the lounge.

The Evergreen is open daily for lunch from 11:30 a.m. to 3 p.m. and for dinner from 6 to 10 p.m.; Sunday brunch is served from 10:30 a.m. to 2:30 p.m. The full bar is open from 11 a.m. to 11 p.m. daily, and features live music on Friday, Saturday, and Sunday. Reservations are suggested for dinner.

STEAKS AND SEAFOOD: Seventeen miles from the Plaza, but just across the road from the old Atchison, Topeka & Santa Fe Railroad station in Lamy, **The Legal Tender** (tel. 982-8425) is spectacularly faithful to the Wild West theme of the late 19th century. Built by John Pflueger as a general store in 1881, when the railroad first came to New Mexico, it has gone through a lot of changes. But the Victorian décor remains. The handcarved cherrywood bar is the same one Pflueger imported from Germany. A valuable collection of period paintings and prints covers the saloon walls. Two murals on the balcony, depicting the coming of the iron horse to the West, were commissioned for the 1916 Pan Pacific Exposition in San Francisco. After the Legal Tender took over in 1969 from the Pink Garter Saloon, the Americana Room was added; its tinned ceiling was from the original Hilton Hotel in San Francisco, and its drapes and chandeliers came from the presidential suite of Chicago's

Sherman Hotel. The building is listed on the National Register of Historic Places.

The food is equally worthy of recognition. Beef, chops, and seafood highlight the menu. For lunch, diners can consider a Tender's beef sandwich ($5.25), Hawaiian chicken sandwich ($5.75), red snapper Veracruz ($7), or Bombay chicken salad with curry dressing ($5.75). Dinner entrees include ribeye steak ($12), teriyaki beef kebab ($11), quail ($10.25), mountain rainbow trout ($11), shrimp Fiji ($15), and top sirloin and shrimp ($16). Hours are noon to 4 p.m. Monday through Saturday for lunch, 5 to 10 p.m. daily for dinner, and 11 a.m. to 3 p.m. on Sunday for brunch. Reservations are advised.

The bar features imported wines and beers and specialty cocktails. Say hello to bartender Mark Lee, a Lamy resident and modern-day Renaissance man: he's also a sculptor and jeweler, and conducts French- and English-language tours.

To reach the Legal Tender, take I-25 north toward Las Vegas, get off at exit 290, and follow it toward Galisteo until you see the signs for Lamy.

CHAPTER V

WHAT TO SEE AND DO IN SANTA FE

□ □ □

Santa Fe is one of the oldest cities in the United States and has long been a center for both the creative and the performing arts, so it is not surprising that the major sights in Santa Fe have to do with history and the arts. It would be easy to spend all your time sightseeing in the city without ever heading out to the pueblos, national parks, and the many other attractions in the surrounding area.

Leave at least two half days for visiting museums, two half days for walking tours of churches and historic sites, and at least one full day for browsing the art galleries of downtown and Canyon Road (see Chapter VI).

MUSEUMS

THE MUSEUM OF NEW MEXICO: The Museum of New Mexico system, 113 Lincoln Ave. (tel. 982-6366), comprises four museums and five state monuments. All four museums are in Santa Fe: the Palace of the Governors, the Museum of Fine Arts, the Museum of International Folk Art, and the Museum of Indian Arts and Culture.

The museums are open daily from 10 a.m. to 5 p.m., March through December. (They are closed on Mondays in January and February, and on the Thanksgiving, Christmas, and New Year's holidays.) Admission to each museum is $3 for adults, $1.25 for children 6 to 16; children under 6 are free. Two-day passes are good at all four museums and cost $5 for adults and $2.50 for children.

The flagship of the system is the **Palace of the Governors,** on Palace Avenue facing the Plaza (tel. 827-6483). Built in 1610 as the original Santa Fe capitol, it has been in continual public use longer than any other structure in the United States. It has been a seat of government for the Spanish (1610–1680 and 1692–1821), for the Pueblo Indians (1680–1692), for Mexico (1821–1846), and for the United States (1846–present). The Confederacy held it briefly in 1862. It was designated the Museum of New Mexico in 1909, two years before New Mexico's statehood, and has become (appropriately) the state history museum, with an adjoining library and photo archives.

A series of exhibits chronicle four centuries of New Mexico's Hispanic and American history, from the 16th-century Spanish explorations through the frontier era to modern times. Among the displays are early Jesuit maps and rare Franciscan hide paintings, restored governor's offices of the Mexican and 19th-century U.S. eras, a century-old chapel, and a model showing how the adobe palace itself has evolved through the centuries, alternately shrinking and expanding. Some cutaways of doors and windows show off early architecture.

Reminders of the early Indian heritage are scant in this museum, most having been moved to the new Museum of Indian Arts and Culture. Among those remaining are some ancient pottery from the Puye Plateau culture and a series of artifacts and photographs depicting a museum-sponsored study of Mayan sites in Mexico's Yucatán.

There are two shops here that visitors should not miss. One is the bookstore, with one of the finest selections of art, history, and anthropology books in the Southwest. The other is the print shop and bindery, in which limited-edition works are produced on hand-operated presses.

One of the most lasting impressions Santa Fe visitors bring home is not of the museum itself, but of the Indian artisans squatting shoulder-to-shoulder beneath the long covered portal facing the Plaza. Here on the shaded sidewalk, several dozen colorfully dressed members of local Pueblo tribes (plus an occasional Navajo or Hopi) spread their handcrafts—mainly jewelry and pottery, but also woven carpets, beadwork, and paintings. They sell directly to throngs of tourists who gather around hoping for a wholesale "deal," but who are often surprised to find that the natives have a keenly honed business sense. The museum reserves the portal space specifically for the Indians, who have been mainstays of Santa Fe art sales for many decades.

The **Museum of Fine Arts,** kitty-corner from the Plaza and immediately opposite the Palace of the Governors at the corner of Lincoln Avenue (tel. 827-4455), was the first Pueblo Revival-style building constructed in Santa Fe, in 1917. As such, it was a major stimulus in Santa Fe's development as an art colony earlier this century.

The museum's permanent collection of more than 8,000 works emphasizes regional art, including numerous Georgia O'Keeffe paintings, landscapes and portraits by all the Taos masters, and more recent works by such contemporary greats as R. C. Gorman and Amado Maurilio Pena. Northern New Mexico's Indians are well represented by small, colorful, stylized tempera paintings of costumed ceremonial dances and by a number of remarkable sculptures in three courtyards. There's also a collection of Ansel Adams photography. Modern artists, many of them far from the mainstream of traditional southwestern art, are featured in temporary exhibits throughout the year.

Beautiful St. Francis Auditorium, patterned after the interiors of traditional Hispanic mission churches, adjoins the Museum of Fine Arts; it hosts a wide variety of scheduled musical events including the Santa Fe Chamber Music Festival in July and August. A museum shop sells books on southwestern art, plus prints and postcards of the collection.

The rest of the state museum group is a short drive southeast of the Plaza, in the Sangre de Cristo foothills on Camino Lejo off Old Santa Fe Trail.

The **Museum of International Folk Art,** 706 Camino Lejo (tel. 827-8350), may not seem quite as typically southwestern as the others, but it's the largest museum of its kind in the world. It has a collection of more than 120,000 objects from over 100 countries, and is my personal favorite of the Santa Fe museums.

It was founded in 1953 by Chicago collector Florence Dibell Bartlett, who said: "If peoples of different countries could have the opportunity to study each others' cultures, it would be one avenue for a closer understanding between men." That's the basis on which the museum operates today.

The special collections include Spanish colonial silver, traditional and contemporary New Mexican religious art, Mexican Indian costumes, Mexican majolica ceramics, Brazilian folk art, European glass, African sculptures, East Indian textiles, and the marvelous Morris Miniature Circus. Particularly delightful are numerous dioramas—all done with colorful miniatures—of people around the world at work and play in typical town, village, and home settings. Recent acquisitions include American weathervanes and quilts, Palestinian costume jewelry and amulets, and Bhutanese and Indonesian textiles. Children love to look at the hundreds of toys on display.

Special exhibitions and related performances, lectures, and demonstrations are scheduled year round. The museum's 80,000-square-foot premises also include a research library and a shop where a variety of folk art is available for purchase.

Across the parking lot is the **Museum of Indian Arts and Culture,** 710 Camino Lejo (tel. 827-8941), which opened in July 1987 as the showcase for the adjoining Laboratory of Anthropology. Interpretive displays detail tribal history and contemporary lifestyles of New Mexico's Pueblo, Navajo, and Apache cultures, and more than 50,000 pieces of basketry, pottery, clothing, carpets, and jewelry—much of it quite ancient—is on continual rotating exhibit. Indian artisans are almost always present to demonstrate traditional skills, and native educators run a year-round participatory workshop.

The laboratory is a point of interest in itself, an exquisite example of Pueblo Revival architecture by well-known Santa Fe architect John Gaw Meem. Since the museum opened, the lab has expanded its research and library facilities into its former display wing. It was founded in 1931 by John D. Rockefeller, Jr.

OTHER MUSEUMS: The **Wheelwright Museum of the American Indian,** 704 Camino Lejo (tel. 982-4636), is not a member of the state museum system, but it's often visited on the same trip as the Folk Art and Indian museums by virtue of its proximity: next door. Once known as the Museum of Navajo Ceremonial Art, it was founded in 1937 by Boston scholar Mary Cabot Wheelwright in collaboration with a Navajo medicine man, Hastiin Klah, to preserve and document Navajo ritual beliefs and practices. In 1976 the museum changed its focus to include the living arts of all American Indian cultures.

Built of adobe in the shape of a Navajo hogan, the museum offers rotating single-subject shows of silverwork, jewelry, tapestry, pottery, baskets, and paintings. There's a permanent collection, of course, plus an outdoor sculpture garden with works by Allan Houser and other noted artisans. Demonstrations are planned occasionally, and the museum sponsors continuing scholarly research. In the basement is the Case Trading Post, an arts-and-crafts shop built in the image of a turn-of-the-century trading post such as was found on Navajo reservations.

The Wheelwright Museum is open daily, May through October, from 10 a.m. to 4:45 p.m. (on Sunday from 1 to 4:45 p.m.). The rest of the year it's closed Monday. Admission is by suggested donation: $2 for adults and $1 for children.

A couple of smaller Santa Fe museums also showcase the art of the region's Indians. The **Institute of American Indian Arts Museum,** 1501 Cerrillos Rd. (tel. 988-6281), displays the work of the institute's students and faculty in four to five major exhibits a year. Indians from 70 tribes attend this school, which is sponsored by the federal Bureau of Indian Affairs. Many of the outstanding works displayed at art galleries throughout the region were done by institute graduates.

The permanent collection is on display from early June to late August. An annual Christmas Student Exhibit Sale is held the first Sunday of December. The museum is open Monday through Friday from 8 a.m. to 5 p.m. and weekends from 10 a.m. to 5 p.m. Admission is free.

The **Indian Art Research Center,** 660 Garcia St. off Canyon Road (tel. 982-3584), a division of the School of American Research, houses one of the world's finest collections of Southwest Indian art. Admission is generally restricted to Native Americans, who may view the collection anytime at no charge. Others must make a group appointment (minimum of 10 people) at least two weeks in advance, and must pay $10 per person.

The School of American Research was created in 1907 as a center for advanced research in anthropology and related fields. It sponsors scholarships and educational programs.

Opened in early 1989 at the Armory for the Arts Complex, 1050 Old Pecos Trail, the **Santa Fe Children's Museum** (tel. 989-8359), offers series of free exhibits and hands-on displays for the whole family. Special theater performances for the younger set are regularly scheduled. Open Tuesday through Saturday from 10 a.m. to 5 p.m. and Sunday from noon to 5 p.m. Admission is $1.

One more very different sort of museum is **El Rancho de las Golondrinas,** otherwise known as the Old Cienega Village Museum, 15 miles south of the Plaza in La Cienega (tel. 471-2261). Once the last stopping place on the 1,000-mile El Camino Real from Mexico City to Santa Fe, this living 17th- and 18th-century Spanish village comprises a hacienda, village store, schoolhouse, and several chapels and kitchens. There's also a working molasses mill, wheelwright and blacksmith shops, shearing and weaving rooms, a threshing mill, and four water mills, as well as dozens of farm animals. The ranch is 400 acres in size, and a walk around the entire property is 1¾ miles in length.

Highlights of the year for Las Golondrinas ("The Swallows") are the Spring Festival (the first weekend of June) and the Harvest Festival (the first weekend of October). Authentically costumed volunteers demonstrate shearing, spinning, weaving, embroidery, woodcarving, grain milling, blacksmithing, tinsmithing, soapmaking, and other activities. There's an exciting atmosphere of Spanish folk dancing, music, and theater, and traditional oven-cooked food. Each festival Sunday the museum is open with a procession and mass dedicated to San Ysidro, patron saint of farmers.

This open-air museum has a limited season. On Wednesday and Saturday in June, July, and August, 2½-hour guided tours are offered at 10 a.m.; advance reservations are requested. On the first Sunday of July, August, and September there are open houses with self-guided tours from 10 a.m. to 4 p.m., at which costumed volunteers are active. The entry fee is $2.

CHURCHES

St. Francis Cathedral, Santa Fe's grandest religious structure, is just a block east of the Plaza on Cathedral Place at San Francisco Street (tel. 982-5619). An architectural anomaly in Santa Fe, it was built between 1869 and 1886 by Archbishop Jean-Baptiste Lamy to resemble the great cathedrals of Europe. French architects designed the Romanesque building—named after Santa Fe's patron saint—and Italian masons assisted with its construction.

The small adobe Our Lady of the Rosary chapel on the northeast side of the cathedral reflects a Spanish look. Built in 1807, it is the only parcel remaining from Our Lady of the Assumption Church, founded with Santa Fe in 1610. The new cathedral was built over and around the old church.

Still in her niche on an 18th-century chapel wall inside the 19th-century cathedral is *La Conquistadora,* "Our Lady of the Conquest." This wooden icon is the oldest existing statue of the Madonna in the United States. Rescued from the church during the 1680 rebellion, it was carried back by Don Diego de Vargas on his peaceful reconquest 12 years later, thus the name. Today *La Conquistadora* plays an important part in the annual Feast of Corpus Christi in June and July.

In 1986 a $600,000 renovation project relocated an early-18th-century wooden statue of St. Francis of Assisi to the center of the altar screen. Around the cathedral's exterior are front doors featuring 16 carved door panels of historic note, a plaque memorializing the 38 Franciscan friars who were martyred in New Mexico's early years, and a large statue of Archbishop Lamy himself.

Visitors are welcome to attend mass six days at 6, 7, and 7:45 a.m. and 5:15 p.m., and on Sunday at 6, 8, and 10 a.m., noon, and 7 p.m.

The **Loretto Chapel,** more properly called the Chapel of Our Lady of Light, adjoins the Best Western Inn at Loretto on the Old Santa Fe Trail near Water Street (tel. 984-7971). In 1873 Lamy appointed the same French architects and Italian masons who were constructing his cathedral to build this chapel for the Sisters of Loretto, who had established a school for young ladies in Santa Fe in 1852. The chapel was patterned after a famous Paris church, Sainte-Chapelle.

The chapel is especially notable for its remarkable spiral staircase: it makes two complete 360° turns with no central or other visible support! (A railing was added later.) Legend has it that the building was nearly finished in 1878 when workers realized the stairs to the choir loft wouldn't fit. Hoping for a solution more attractive than a ladder, the sisters made a novena to St. Joseph—and were rewarded when a mysterious carpenter appeared astride a donkey and offered to build a staircase. Armed with only a saw, a hammer, and a T-square, the master constructed this work of genius by soaking slats of wood in tubs of water to curve them, and holding them together with wooden pegs. Then he disappeared without waiting to collect his fee.

The admission fee for modern visitors is 50¢. Entry is through the Inn at Loretto. The chapel, maintained by the Historic Santa Fe Foundation, is open daily from 9 a.m. to 5 p.m.

Farther south along the Old Santa Fe Trail, at East De Vargas Street, is the **Mission of San Miguel** (tel. 983-3974). It is one of the oldest churches in America, having been raised within a couple of years of the founding of Santa Fe. Tlaxcala Indians, servants of early Spanish soldiers and missionaries, may have used fragments of a 12th-century pueblo on this site in its construction. Severely damaged in the 1680 revolt, it was almost completely rebuilt in 1710, and has been altered numerous times since.

The mission and a nearby house—today a gift shop billed as "The Oldest House," though there's no way of knowing for sure—were bought by the Christian Brothers from Archbishop Lamy for $3,000 in 1881, and the order still operates both structures. Among the treasures in the mission are the San José Bell, reputedly cast in Spain in 1356 and brought to Santa Fe via Mexico several centuries later; and a series of buffalo hides and deerskins decorated with Bible stories for Indian converts.

The mission is open daily in winter from 11:30 a.m. to 4 p.m. (on Sunday from 1 to 4:30 p.m.). Summer hours start earlier. Mass is said at 5 p.m. There's no admission charge, but donations are welcomed.

The **Santuario de Nuestra Señora de Guadalupe,** 100 Guadalupe St. at Agua Fria (tel. 988-2027), is believed to be the oldest shrine in the United States honoring the Virgin of Guadalupe, patroness of Mexico. It was built at the end of El Camino Real, the main trail from Mexico, by Franciscan missionaries between 1795 and 1800.

The sanctuary's adobe walls are almost three feet thick, and the deep-red plaster wall behind the altar was dyed with oxblood in traditional fashion when the church was restored earlier this century. The church today is administered as a museum by the nonprofit Guadalupe Historic Foundation.

Within the sanctuary is a famous oil painting, *Our Lady of Guadalupe,* created in 1783 by renowned Mexican artist José de Alzibar. Painted expressly for the church, it was brought from Mexico City by mule caravan.

Admission to the sanctuary is 50¢. It is open from 9 a.m. to 4 p.m. Tuesday through Friday, 10 a.m. to 3 p.m. on Saturday, and on numerous other occasions for religious art shows, chamber music concerts, flamenco dance programs, dramas, and lectures.

Also notable, but hardly ancient, is the **Cristo Rey Church,** a huge modern adobe structure located where Upper Canyon Road meets Camino Cabra (tel. 983-8528). This Catholic church was built to commemorate the 400th anniversary of Coronado's exploration of the Southwest. Parishioners did most of the construction work on the building, even making adobe bricks from the earth where the church stands.

Architect John Gaw Meem designed the building, in mission style, as a place to keep some magnificent stone reredos (altar screens) created by the Spanish during the colonial era and restored in the mid-20th Century.

OTHER ATTRACTIONS

Many New Mexicans think of their **State Capitol,** at Paseo de Peralta and Old Santa Fe Trail (tel. 984-9589), as "The Roundhouse." Built in 1966 in the shape of a Pueblo Indian *zia,* it symbolizes the Circle of Life: the four winds, four seasons, four directions, and four sacred obligations. Surprisingly, perhaps, it's the only round capitol building in America.

Surrounding the Capitol is a lush 6½-acre garden boasting more than 100 varieties of plants—roses, plums, almonds, nectarines, Russian olive trees, and sequoias among them. Benches are placed around the grounds for the enjoyment of visitors.

Footsteps Across New Mexico, inside the Inn at Loretto at 211 Old Santa Fe Trail (tel. 982-9297), features an impressive multimedia introduction to the state. From pre-Hispanic Pueblo culture to the landing of the space shuttle at White Sands, slides, music, and a sculptured, three-dimensional map combine to tell the New Mexico story. Showtime is every half hour from 9:30 a.m. to 6 p.m. Monday through Saturday, to 5:30 p.m. on Sunday. Admission is $3 for adults, $2.25 for kids 6 to 16. There's also a fine bookstore for browsing before or after the show.

HISTORIC WALKING TOURS

THE PLAZA: The Plaza has been the heart and soul of Santa Fe life since it was established with the city in 1610. It has been the location of innumerable festivals and other historical, cultural, and social events, and for many years was a dusty hive of activity as the staging ground and terminus of the Santa Fe Trail.

Originally designed as a meeting place, the Plaza has undergone many changes. For a while it was a tree-shaded park surrounded with a white picket fence. It had an incarnation as a Mexican-style *zócalo*, with a gazebo at its center. Today those who sit around its central fountain are afforded the best people-watching in New Mexico.

A block east of the Plaza at 125 E. Palace Ave., **Sena Plaza** offers a quiet respite from the busy streets with its park-like patio. La Casa Sena restaurant is the primary occupant of what was once the 31-room Sena family adobe hacienda, built in 1831. The Territorial legislature met in the upper rooms of the hacienda in the 1890s. Next door, at 113 E. Palace Ave., **Prince Plaza** was a former governor's home. This Territorial-style structure, which now includes the Shed restaurant, had huge wooden gates to keep out Indian attacks. There are several 18th-century hacienda buildings in the 300 block of West San Francisco Street, notably the **Ortiz House.**

The **Delgado House** is at 124 W. Palace Ave.; an 1890 Victorian mansion, it now belongs to the Historic Santa Fe Foundation. The foundation's offices are in the **Tully House,** 136 Grant Ave., built in 1851 in the Territorial style. Across the street at 135 Grant Ave., the **Bergere House** (circa 1870) hosted U.S. President Ulysses S. Grant and his wife during an 1880 visit to Santa Fe.

North of the Plaza, the **Padre de Gallegos House,** 227-237 Washington Ave., was built in 1857, also in the Territorial style. It now houses the Santacafe restaurant. Padre de Gallegos was a priest who, in the eyes of newly arrived Bishop Lamy, kept too high a social profile and was defrocked in 1852. Gallegos later represented the Territory in Congress and eventually became the federal superintendent of Indian affairs.

THE BARRIO DE ANALCO: The Barrio de Analco, now East De Vargas Street, is beyond question one of the oldest continuously inhabited streets in the United States. Spanish colonists and their Mexican-Indian servants built homes here in the early 1600s when Santa Fe was founded, and some of them survive to this day.

It's questionable whether or not the **Oldest House,** across from the Mission of San Miguel, is really that. But it is certainly quite old. Located on East De Vargas just east of the Old Santa Fe Trail, it is among the last of the poured-mud adobe houses—and may have been built by Pueblo Indians. It's sad that modern graffiti has defiled some interior walls. The Christian Brothers maintain it. Entrance is through a gift shop.

Don't plan on entering the other historic homes in this area —they're all private residences, although most do have interpretive historical plaques on their outer walls facing the street. They include the **Tudesqui House,** 129 E. De Vargas, with wisteria growing over adobe walls; the pueblo-cum-Territorial-style **Gregorio Crespin House,** no. 132, of which records date at least to 1747 (when it was sold for 50 pesos); the **Boyle House,** no. 327, a mid-18th-century hacienda; the circa-1830 **José Alarid House,** no. 338, now an art gallery; and the **Adolph Bandelier House,** no. 352, home of the archeologist who unearthed the prehistoric ruins at Bandelier National Monument.

CANYON ROAD: Just six blocks southeast of the Plaza is Canyon Road. Extending about two miles from the Paseo de Peralta to Camino Cabra, this quaint and narrow road today is lined with art galleries, shops, and restaurants—but it once was an Indian trail across which Pueblo Indians came to launch their 1680 insurrection against the Spanish colonists. Historic buildings include the **Juan José Prada House,** 519 Canyon Rd., dating from about 1760, and **El Zaguan,** a hacienda at 545 Canyon Rd. (Galleries will be discussed in some detail in the next chapter.)

PARKS AND REFUGES

The **Randall Davey Audubon Center,** on Upper Canyon Road (tel. 983-4609), is of special interest to those who prefer outdoors to indoors. Named for the late Santa Fe artist who willed his home to the National Audubon Society as a wildlife refuge, it occupies 35 acres at the mouth of Santa Fe Canyon. More than 100 species of birds and 120 types of plants live here, and a variety of mammals—including black bears, mule deer, mountain lions, bobcats, raccoons, and coyotes—have been spotted. The center is open daily from 9 a.m. to 5 p.m.; admission for nonmembers of the Audubon Society members is $1. Tours of the historic home can be arranged by appointment.

Santa Fe has two city parks of special note. **Santa Fe River State Park** winds along the midtown stream for about four miles, roughly from St. Francis Drive to Camino Cabra at the east end of Canyon Road. It's a nice spot for an early-morning jog, a midday walk beneath the trees, or perhaps a sack lunch at a picnic table.

Old Fort Marcy Park overlooks the northeast corner of downtown, marking the 1846 site of the first U.S. military reservation in the Southwest. Only a few mounds remain. But the Cross of the Martyrs, at the top of a winding brick walkway from

Paseo de Peralta near Otero Street, is a popular spot for bird's-eye photographs. The cross was erected in 1920 by the Knights of Columbus and the Historical Society of New Mexico to commemorate Franciscans killed in the Pueblo Revolt of 1680. It has since played a role in numerous religious processions. The cross and park are accessible by vehicle off Artist Road.

SPECIAL EVENTS

FIESTA DE SANTA FE: This is an exuberant combination of spirit and history, music and general merrymaking. Held each year over three days starting the Friday after Labor Day, it is the oldest continuous community festival in the United States. Established in 1712, it celebrates the peaceful reconquest of the city by Don Diego de Vargas in 1692, a dozen years after the Spanish had been routed in the Pueblo Revolt of 1680.

Fiesta has two "shining stars." *La Conquistadora,* a carved Madonna described earlier in the section on the St. Francis Cathedral, was credited by the Spanish with their victory over the Indians. Now accorded a place of honor in St. Francis Cathedral, *La Conquistadora* is carried twice in candlelight procession from the cathedral to the Plaza at the beginning and conclusion of the Fiesta.

Zozobra, sometimes called Old Man Gloom, was the creation of early-20th-century artist Will Shuster. A 40-foot-tall effigy of wood and canvas painted to resemble a Hispanic nobleman, he is burned on Friday at dusk to symbolically rid the community of past disappointments and revitalize it for a joyous Fiesta and future success. Tens of thousands of people turn out for the spectacular cremation, then stay to dance the night away in the Plaza.

Fiesta also features musical offerings, from bands and mariachis to choral groups; street dances; an arts-and-crafts fair; a carnival, with local citizens dressed in 17th-century costumes; and a plethora of outdoor booths selling regional ethnic (and not-so-ethnic) food. A Fiesta pageant sees the crowning of a queen and her court, and the knighting of a new Don Diego de Vargas accompanied by a 17-member retinue.

Telephone the Fiesta Line (tel. 505/988-7575) for direct information.

THE INDIAN MARKET: If there's a more crowded time to be in Santa Fe than Fiesta, that time is the Indian Market. Held annually (since 1922) over the third weekend of August, this is the largest all-Indian market in the country. About 800 of the Southwest's finest native artisans set up rows of booths in the streets around the

Plaza, displaying their baskets and blankets, jewelry and pottery, woodcarvings and rugs, sand paintings and sculptures. Sales are already brisk by shortly after dawn on Saturday, and they continue throughout the weekend.

There are always more Indians who wish to participate in Indian Market than there's space for. Winners are determined in a jury competition. The artisans must prove the authenticity and originality of their work, and a ten-member "evaluator" team constantly patrols the market to verify this. Exhibitors' fees help fund $20,000 worth of annual scholarships and grants through the Southwest Association of Indian Arts.

Browsers can converse with artists and craftspeople about their work and purchase traditional or contemporary work directly from the creators. Costumed Indian dancing and crafts demonstrations are normally scheduled in the afternoons on the patio of the Palace of the Governors.

If you're planning to attend Indian Market, it's essential to make reservations months in advance. For more information about the event, call 505/983-5226.

THE SPANISH MARKETS: Held during the last full weekend of July, they include the **Traditional Market** (annual since 1952) and the **Contemporary Market** (since 1985). About 100 craftspeople—all of whom must be at least one-quarter Hispanic —are chosen to exhibit by the Spanish Colonial Arts Society from an applicant list of several hundred.

The Traditional Market is held under the portal of the Palace of the Governors; the Contemporary Market is in the palace courtyard. Look for carved wooden santos (Catholic icons), retablos (altar paintings), embroidery, textiles, weavings (especially rugs from Chimayo or Truchas), straw appliqués, tinwork, hand-painted tiles, filigree jewelry, ceramics, and wrought-iron and handmade furniture.

For more information, write the **Spanish Colonial Arts Society,** P.O. Box 1611, Santa Fe, NM 87501.

SANTA FE FESTIVAL OF THE ARTS: Held annually the third week of October, this festival showcases the visual arts and artists of New Mexico in general and Santa Fe in particular. It includes major exhibitions of early regional works or selections from private local collections, and highlights the work of newer, relatively unknown artists in painting, sculpture, and photography. Also a part of the festival are a series of lectures and demonstrations on the visual arts. The festival, founded in 1977, takes place at the Sweeney Convention Center, West Marcy Street and Grant

Avenue. For information, contact the **Santa Fe Festival Foundation,** 628 Paseo de Peralta, Santa Fe, NM 87501 (tel. 505/988-3924).

RODEO DE SANTA FE: The four-day Rodeo de Santa Fe is held annually in early July, usually over the weekend after the Fourth. It starts with a western parade on Thursday morning and ends with a Rodeo Dance; in between are 8 p.m. performances on Thursday, Friday, and Saturday and a 2:30 p.m. Sunday matinee.

Between 300 and 350 cowboys from all over the Southwest typically compete in this mid-size rodeo, first held in 1948. A total purse of around $30,000 is offered for such events as Brahma bull and bronc riding, calf roping, steer wrestling, and barrel racing. There's also trick riding, cowgirl contests, clown and animal acts, and a local version of bullfighting in which neither bull nor matador is intended to be hurt.

A covered grandstand seats about 5,500 spectators, but the seats are hard—bring a cushion and/or backrest. Tickets and information can be obtained at the La Fonda Hotel or at the "rodeo wagon" in the Plaza during rodeo weekend. The rodeo grounds are on Rodeo Road off Cerrillos Road, about 5½ miles from the center of town. Call 505/471-4300 for information.

OTHER SANTA FE EVENTS: A benefit for the Palace of the Governors, the **Mountain Man Rendezvous and Buffalo Roast** brings the early 19th century back to life for one weekend in mid-July, usually a week after the rodeo. Black-powder shooting, blacksmith forging, knife and tomahawk throwing, and primitive music lend flavor to the event, which also includes lectures, films, and other presentations. A two-day trade fair of artifacts, weapons, clothing, and other articles precedes the actual rendezvous, and a Mountain Man's Dinner climaxes it. Information can be obtained by writing P.O. Box 2087, Santa Fe, NM 87504 (tel. 505/827-6473 or 827-6474).

The **Santa Fe Banjo and Fiddle Contest,** first held in 1975, brings big-name folk musicians and accomplished locals to the rodeo grounds on the Sunday before Labor Day. Guitars and mandolins add to the oldtime band and bluegrass competitions. Many enthusiasts camp overnight on the grounds and start their Sunday with a full country breakfast served on-site. More information is available by writing P.O. Box 5851, Santa Fe, NM 87502 (tel. 505/982-8548).

Winterfestival is Santa Fe's annual retreat from the midwinter doldrums. Usually held over four days the third weekend of February, it appeals to skiers and nonskiers alike, with events in the city and at the Santa Fe Ski Area. Highlights include the Great Santa Fe Chile Cookoff, the Governor's Cup and Santa Fe Cup ski races, snow sculpture contests, snowshoe and obstacle course races, and hot-air balloon rides. For information, call 505/983-8200 or toll free 800/982-SNOW.

Not so much an annual event as a season is horse racing at **The Downs at Santa Fe.** Races are held from Memorial Day through September at the track, located on U.S. 85 (Cerrillos Road) en route to La Cienega, 11 miles south of downtown. Post time for 10-race cards is 3:30 p.m. on Wednesday and Friday; for 12-race cards, 1:30 p.m. on Saturday and Sunday, plus Memorial Day, the Fourth of July, and Labor Day. General admission is $1; prices escalate from there to $8 for Jockey Club admission. The Downs has a closed-circuit TV system to show instant replays of each race's final stretch run, as well as transmission of out-of-state races for legal betting.

OUTDOOR ACTIVITIES

Santa Fe is the focus of a region that attracts outdoor sports enthusiasts from all over America. Santa Fe National Forest, which extends right to the city's eastern limits, contains 900 miles of hiking trails, 39 recreation sites (including 24 campsites) accessible by road, and a major ski area. The mountain rivers and streams attract both fishermen and whitewater rafters; others, from hunters to bicyclists, rockhounds to golfers, likewise find their perfect terrain.

DOWNHILL SKIING: There's something for all ability levels at the **Santa Fe Ski Area,** 16 miles northeast of Santa Fe via Hyde Park (Ski Basin) Road. Beginners can test their mettle on Easy Street and Lower Broadway, while experts tackle runs with names like Desperado, Parachute, and Muerte. One thing all have in common is plenty of light, dry powder.

Depending on snow conditions, the season can last from Thanksgiving to Easter. Built on the upper reaches of 12,000-foot Tesuque Peak, the area has an average annual snowfall of 250 inches and a vertical drop of 1,650 feet. Seven lifts, including a new 5,000-foot triple chair, serve 32 runs and 700 acres of terrain. There are also two double chairs, three Pomas, and a kids' lift for a total capacity of 6,400 skiers per hour.

Base facilities are at the 10,350-foot level of the mountain. They center around La Casa Mall, with a cafeteria, lounge, outdoor grill, sundeck, ski shop, boutique, and Skier Services Desk. Another restaurant, the Sierra Lodge, has a mid-mountain patio; skiers can sip cocktails there or dine indoors.

The ski area is open daily from 9 a.m. to 4 p.m. Rates for all lifts are $24 for adults, $15 for children and seniors, free for kids under 3 feet 10 inches (in their ski boots). Three-day adult passes are $66; five-day passes run $105. Full rentals—skis, boots, and poles—cost $12 a day.

Ski-school rates range from $17 for a half-day group lesson to $68 for a two-hour private lesson. Two-day beginners' packages, including Poma ticket and rentals, are $78. "Chipmunk Corner" is set aside for kids 3 to 6 years old. The ski area also has a nationally handicapped NASTAR racing program for competitive types.

Three-day ski packages, including lodging and lifts, are offered in conjunction with many Santa Fe hotels. Per-person rates start at $102 at the Travelodge and go as high as $248 at the Hilton. Check with the Santa Fe Central Reservation Service (tel. 505/983-8200, or toll free 800/982-SNOW) for details.

More information on the ski area can be obtained by contacting the Santa Fe Ski Area, 1210 Luisa St., Suite 10, Santa Fe, NM 87501 (tel. 505/982-4429 or 983-9155).

NORDIC SKIING: Cross-country enthusiasts find seemingly endless miles of snow to track through the **Santa Fe National Forest.** A favorite place to start is at the Black Canyon campground, nine miles from downtown en route to the Santa Fe Ski Area. In the same area are the Borrega Trail and the Aspen Vista Trail. Also recommended are the Pecos Wilderness and Windsor Trail in the national forest's Pecos district (tel. 505/757-6121), Peralta Canyon Road and the Valle Grande in the Los Alamos district (tel. 505/667-5120), and Fenton Hill and Jemez Falls in the Jemez Springs district (tel. 505/829-3535).

Overnight trips are often planned by the **New Mexico Ski Touring Club** in Albuquerque (tel. 505/255-1954).

Basic nordic ski lessons, telemarking instruction, backcountry tours, and overnight packages are all offered by Bill Neuwirth's **Tracks,** P.O. Box 173, Santa Fe, NM 87504 (tel. 505/982-2586). Cross-country trips of a half day ($28) or a full day ($45) can also be arranged through **Santa Fe Detours** at the La Fonda Hotel (tel. 505/983-7262, or toll free 800/DE-TOURS).

RIVER RAFTING: Although Taos is the real rafting center of New Mexico, several companies serve Santa Fe during the April-to-October whitewater season.

Southwest Wilderness Center, P.O. Box 2840, Santa Fe, NM 87501 (tel. 505/982-3126), takes thrill-seekers on full-day ($55) and half-day ($35) trips from Rio Grande Gorge State Park, as well as eight-hour excursions through the notorious Taos Box

($65 weekdays, $70 weekends). Two- and three-day overnighters in the Chama Canyon Wilderness run $150 to $210.

Rio Bravo River Tours, 1412 Cerrillos Rd., Santa Fe, NM 87501 (tel. 505/988-1153, or toll free 800/451-0708), also offers the full- and half-day Rio Grande journeys, as well as expeditions through White Rock Canyon to Bandelier National Monument. Rates are similar.

New Wave Rafting, Route 5, Box 302A, Santa Fe, NM 87501 (tel. 505/984-1444), takes adventurers down the Rio Grande, Chama, and other rivers.

If you're going rafting, be sure to bring warm clothes (especially early in the season) and a change of clothes at any time, plus camping gear (including a sleeping bag) if you're going overnight. Round-trip transportation from Santa Fe is provided on all trips, and lunches are included except on half-day excursions.

HORSE TRIPS: The **Mountain Mama Packing & Riding Co.,** Route 3, Box 95, Santa Fe NM 87505 (tel. 986-1924), takes riders on one- to five-day trips through the Sangre de Cristo, with burros or mountain ponies packing all gear including food and equipment. Rates are $50 per day per person, or $65 for singles. Shorter trail rides or riding lessons can be arranged at a rate of $12 an hour, or $9 for children under 12.

Enchanted Trail Rides, whose trips are booked with Santa Fe Detours at La Fonda, charge $50 for full days, $25 for half days, $125 for overnights. A morning ride with brunch is $35.

Double Arrow Stable, Old Santa Fe Trail (tel. 983-1561); **Camel Rock Riding Stables,** on the Taos Hwy. (tel. 505/983-6565, or toll free 800/338-6877), and **Caballeros de la Mancha,** N.M. 14 near Cerrillos (tel. 473-4474), also offer hourly and overnight rates. Also popular are two local resorts, **Bishop's Lodge** and **Rancho Encantado** (see Chapter III).

HIKING AND BACKPACKING: While it's hard to decide which of the 900 miles of nearby national forest trails to tackle, three wilderness areas are especially attractive.

Nearest to Santa Fe is **Pecos Wilderness,** which takes in 223,000 acres of the magnificent Sangre de Cristo range. Within the wilderness are Truchas Peak, second highest in New Mexico at 13,102 feet; the headwaters of the Pecos River; and more than 150 miles of streams and lakes. Fishing and hunting are excellent, and botanists thrill at the many rare species of wildflowers.

Tiny (5,200 acres) **Dome Wilderness,** adjacent to Bandelier National Monument, contains rugged canyon terrain and many prehistoric ruins. Several trailheads along Forest Road 289 penetrate the wilderness, whose elevations range from 5,800 to 8,200 feet. (The adjoining national monument is a terrific spot for hiking; see Chapter XII.)

West of Los Alamos, **San Pedro Parks Wilderness** comprises a moist plateau, 10,000 feet high. Rolling mountaintops—there are no jagged peaks or rocky cliffs—alternate with dense spruce forest and open meadows where cattle graze. Fishing is good in this 41,000-acre preserve, and the trail system is well developed.

Detailed information on these wilderness areas can be obtained from the head office of **Santa Fe National Forest,** 1220 St. Francis Dr. (P.O. Box 1689), Santa Fe, NM 87504 (tel. 505/988-6940), or from any of its district offices in Coyote, Cuba, Espanola, Jemez Springs, Las Vegas, Los Alamos, or Pecos. You'll need a permit, especially for an overnighter; it's free, but helps restrict use for the sake of the environment.

Day hikes with an emphasis on nature studies are frequently organized by the **Southwest Wilderness Center,** 815 Dunlap St., Santa Fe, NM 87501 (tel. 505/982-3126 or 983-7262). The **Santa Fe Sierra Club,** 1709 Paseo de Peralta, Santa Fe, NM 87501 (tel. 505/983-2703), also puts together day and overnight backpacking trips.

FISHING AND HUNTING: Before you start, get a license and specific information on game and seasons from the **New Mexico Game and Fish Department,** State Capitol, Santa Fe, NM 87503 (tel. 505/827-7882).

Rainbow trout are the favorite fish for most high-lakes anglers, who head for the hills as soon as the season opens on April 1 (it continues through December). Mule deer and elk are taken by hunters in the Pecos Wilderness and Jemez Mountains, as well as occasional black bear and bighorn sheep. Wild turkey and grouse are frequently bagged in the uplands, geese and ducks at lower elevations.

BICYCLING: Bicycle rentals are expensive in Santa Fe—around $25 a day from dealers—but if you've brought your own, the **Santa Fe Bicycling Club,** 1417 Galisteo St. (tel. 471-6845), can help you out with a free "Scenic Bicycle Map of Santa Fe." The **Sangre de Cristo Cycling Club** organizes weekend training rides; contact Pedal Power at 1331 Cerrillos Rd. (tel. 982-0664).

GOLF: There are three golf courses in the vicinity, including the **Santa Fe Country Club,** on Airport Road (tel. 471-0601). The 18-hole course is open for play from May to November, with play time based on availability. Memberships from other country clubs are honored.

Advance reservations are suggested at the Robert Trent Jones–

designed **Cochiti Golf Course** (tel. 465-2239), 35 miles south of Santa Fe near Cochiti Lake; and the **Los Alamos Golf Course** (tel. 662-8139) in Los Alamos.

TENNIS: Nearest to downtown are the courts at the city-run **Fort Marcy Sports Complex** (tel. 984-6725), five blocks north of the Plaza. There are also courts at the **Santa Fe Country Club** (tel. 471-3378), the **Club at El Gancho** on the Old Las Vegas Hwy. (tel. 988-5000), and the **Bishop's Lodge** (tel. 983-6377).

BALLOONING: Wind River Balloons, P.O. Box 983, Santa Fe, NM 87504 (tel. 505/983-8714), offers lessons and champagne breakfasts in hot-air balloons.

SPORTING GOODS STORES: Gardenswartz Sportz, 2860 Cerrillos Rd. (tel. 473-3636), probably has the city's most complete range of equipment for all recreational endeavors. **Santa Fe Sporting Goods Co.,** 2105 Cerrillos Rd. (tel. 471-2233), specializes in hunting and fishing gear, while **Base Camp,** 121 W. San Francisco St., caters to backpackers and mountaineers.

SPAS: A common stop for skiers en route down the mountain road from the Santa Fe Ski Area is **Ten Thousand Waves,** a Japanese-style health spa 3 miles northeast of Santa Fe on Hyde Park Road (tel. 988-1047 or 982-9304). This serene retreat, nestled in a grove of piñon, offers hot tubs, saunas, and cold plunges, plus a variety of massage and other bodywork techniques.

Bathing suits are optional in the ten-foot communal hot tub, where you can stay as long as you want for $7.50. Eight private hot tubs cost $12 to $17 an hour. (Seniors and children under four feet tall are half price.) Kimonos and sandals, soap and shampoo, towels, hairdryers, and lockers are provided. Massages—take your pick from Swedish, shiatsu, deep-tissue, reflexology, or a combination of all techniques—run $20 a half hour, $35 an hour. You can also get aromatherapy, acupuncture, or Rolfing work ($60 for 1 hour).

Ten Thousand Waves is open daily: on Sunday, Monday, Wednesday, and Thursday from 12:30 p.m. to 9:30 p.m., on Friday and Saturday to 11 p.m., and on Tuesday from 4:30 to 9:30 p.m. Reservations are recommended, especially on weekends.

Massages are also available at the **SunRise Springs Resort** (see Chapter III) and the **New Mexico Academy Wellness Center,** 501 Franklin Ave. at Agua Fria (tel. 982-6271). Swedish and deep-tissue massage, reflexology, polarity therapy, energy balancing, and acupressure are done by appointment Monday through

Saturday from 9 a.m. to 6 p.m. One-hour treatments cost $25 to $50. Student massages on Friday and Saturday cost $10 and $15.

AFTER DARK

Santa Fe isn't known for a wild nightlife. Aside from a hand-ful of nightclubs, lounges in the major hotels, and the usual com-plement of movie theaters and bowling alleys, it's rather tame. Most visitors prefer to enjoy a leisurely dinner and return to their hotel rooms to prepare for another full day of shopping or sight-seeing.

Several programs help inject more excitement into the sum-mer season. The City of Santa Fe and the chamber of commerce co-sponsor a series of free concerts, lectures, and other events, known as **Santa Fe Summerscene,** mid-June through August. Concerts, held at 7 p.m. on Tuesday and Thursday on the Plaza, or in Fort Marcy Park or Amelia White Park (Old Santa Fe Trail at Camino Corrales), run the gamut from classical to rock. There's also a wide-ranging Noon Concert Series on Tuesday and Thurs-day on the Plaza. Call 983-7317 for more information.

The **Santa Fe Summer Concert Series,** held at Paolo Soleri Outdoor Amphitheatre on the Santa Fe Indian School campus on Cerrillos Road, has brought such name performers as Frank Zappa, Kenny Loggins, and B.B. King. More than two dozen con-certs and special events are scheduled each summer.

Daily events schedules can be found in the "Pasatiempo" sec-tion of Friday's *New Mexican* newspaper; the "Daily Calendar" of the *Albuquerque Journal* (North Section); and the "Day by Day" section of the *Santa Fe Reporter,* published Wednesday.

NIGHTCLUBS: The hot spot in downtown Santa Fe is **Club West,** 213 W. Alameda St. (tel. 982-0099). There's live music here nightly except Monday, and it runs the gamut from rock 'n' roll to Latin salsa, blues to bluegrass. You might catch a national act like jazz/classical trumpeter Wynton Marsalis or reggae artist Burning Spear, or a regional favorite like the Broadway Elks or 1-800. The décor is undistinguished, but a big dance floor and a long bar satisfy patrons. Cover charge is usually $2 to $5, ranging upward to $16 and more for name performers.

Other contemporary rockers head for the long bar at **The Rafters,** 550 Montezuma St. (tel. 988-1080), for rhythm-and-blues dance music (cover charge is about $3); **The Bull Ring,** 414 Old Santa Fe Trail (tel. 983-3328), where rock groups are pre-ceded by a classical guitarist during happy hour; **Chelsea Street Pub,** in Villa Linda Mall (tel. 473-5105), which tends to draw a younger suburban crowd (cover is $2); or **Las Quinellas,** 9885

Cerrillos Rd. (tel. 471-1925), across I-25 from the race track, for top-40 bands.

Santa Fe's No. 1 country-and-western scene, and its biggest dance floor, is at **Mr. R's,** 2911 Cerrillos Rd. (tel. 473-4138), next to the Ramada Inn. Dance music plays nonstop seven days a week from 5 p.m. to 1:30 a.m.; the cover charge is never more than $3. If you don't know how to two-step, you can learn during free Monday-evening lessons.

Jazz fans enjoy the offerings at **Take Five,** in Las Tres Gentes Marketplace, 418 Cerrillos Rd. (tel. 986-3483).

LOUNGES: Most of the major hotel lounges have music. The variety includes swing and Latin dance music at La Fiesta Lounge in **La Fonda Hotel,** 100 E. San Francisco St. (tel. 988-5511); jazz and Latin ballads at the **Sheraton de Santa Fe,** 750 N. St. Francis Dr. (tel. 982-5591); easy-listening piano and guitar at the **Eldorado Hotel,** 309 W. San Francisco St. (tel. 988-4455); a piano bar at the **Best Western Inn at Loretto,** 211 Old Santa Fe Trail (tel. 988-5531); light jazz and vocals in La Cantina at the **Howard Johnson Plaza Hotel,** 4048 Cerrillos Rd. (tel. 473-4646); and live rock 'n' roll at Mad Dog's Lounge in the **Ramada Inn,** 2907 Cerrillos Rd. (tel. 471-3000).

In local restaurants, the show-tune troubadours at **La Casa Sena,** 125 E. Palace Ave. (tel. 988-9232), are touted. There's folk and jazz at **Babe's,** 731 Canyon Rd. (tel. 983-3512); a piano bar at the **Carriage Trade Cantina,** 724 Canyon Rd. (tel. 982-3541); light jazz at **Comme Chez Vous,** 116 W. San Francisco St. (tel. 984-0004); ethnic folk and jazz at **El Farol,** 808 Canyon Rd. (tel. 983-9912); jazz piano at the **Ore House on the Plaza,** 50 Lincoln Ave. (tel. 983-8687), and **The Palace,** 142 W. Palace Ave. (tel. 982-9891); Latin rock at **Tiny's,** St. Francis Drive and Cerrillos Road (tel. 983-9817); and a vaunted piano bar, featuring Doug Montgomery, at **Vanessie of Santa Fe,** 434 W. San Francisco St. (tel. 982-9966). Call ahead for days and times.

CHAPTER VI

THE ARTS OF SANTA FE

□ □ □

Above all else, Santa Fe is a city committed to the arts: music, dance, theater, painting, sculpture, and more. No fewer than 24 performing arts groups flourish in Santa Fe, and artists' galleries and studios are legion—well over 100 and multiplying. With each passing year more creative individuals from other parts of America and the world discover Santa Fe and resettle here, while an increasing number of young New Mexicans are also entering the field, particularly Native Americans and Hispanics.

While galleries are open year round, many performing arts are seasonal. The internationally acclaimed Santa Fe Opera, for instance, has a two-month summer season: July and August. Also active only in summer are the Santa Fe Desert Chorale, the Santa Fe Chamber Music Festival, and Estampa Flamenca. But numerous other groups, including the symphony and orchestra, the Santa Fe Concert Association, and the New Mexico Repertory Theatre, concentrate their seasons October through May.

PERFORMING ARTS

OPERA: Even if your visit isn't timed to coincide with the **Santa Fe Opera** season, you shouldn't miss seeing its open-air amphitheater. Located on a wooded hilltop seven miles north of the city off U.S. 84/285, the sweeping curves of this serene structure seem perfectly attuned to the contour of the surrounding terrain. At night, the lights of Los Alamos can be seen in the distance under clear southwestern skies.

Many who know rank the Santa Fe Opera behind only the Metropolitan Opera of New York as the finest company in the United States today. Established in 1957 by John Crosby, still the opera's artistic director, it consistently attracts famed conductors, directors, and singers, the list of whom has included Igor Stravinsky. At the height of the season the company is 500 strong, including the skilled craftspeople and designers who work on the sets.

The opera is noted for its performances of great classics (Puccini's *Madama Butterfly* in 1987, Johann Strauss's *Die Fledermaus* in 1988); little-known works by classical European composers (Richard Strauss's *Feuersnot und Friedenstag* in 1988, for instance); and American premières of 20th-century works (Shostakovich's *Nose* in 1987, Penderecki's *The Black Mask* in 1988).

The nine-week, 37-performance opera season typically runs from July 1 through the last Saturday of August. All performances begin at 9 p.m. Ticket prices range from $12 to $55 Monday through Thursday, $17 to $60 on weekends. Standing-room tickets, at $5, go on sale at 8 p.m. the night of the performance. The opera box office (tel. 982-3855) is open from 10 a.m. to 5 p.m. Monday through Saturday from June 1 (when rehearsals start) throughout the season. On performance days it's open through the first intermission. Tickets are also available at the Galisteo News & Ticket Office, at Galisteo and Water Streets in Santa Fe.

A pre-opera buffet, at $20 per person, is offered at the theater at 6:30 p.m. before each performance. Backstage tours are offered at 2 p.m. Monday through Saturday, June through August, for those with reservations 24 hours in advance. Tickets are $3 for adults, $1.50 for children.

For more complete information and a list of the coming season's calendar, contact the opera at P.O. Box 2408, Santa Fe, NM 87504 (tel. 505/982-3851).

CHORAL GROUPS: The **Santa Fe Desert Chorale,** in its seventh season in 1989, performs from the third week of June to the second week of August at the venerable Santuario de Guadalupe, noted for its superb acoustics. The 24- to 30-voice professional choral ensemble, selected in nationwide recruiting, performs an eclectic blend of Renaissance melodies and modern avant-garde compositions. Concerts begin at 8 p.m. (at 6 p.m. on Sunday). Tickets are $12.50. For more information, contact P.O. Box 2813, Santa Fe, NM 87504 (tel. 505/988-2282 or 988-7505).

Among other local vocal groups, the **Chorus of Santa Fe** is of special note for the Native American and Third World influence it introduces to contemporary tunes. The chorus also performs classical works. Scheduled between September and June are several chamber concerts and full-scale choral productions, as well as community events. Call for more information (tel. 988-2922 or 982-3708).

The **Sangre de Cristo Chorale** is a 25-member ensemble whose repertoire ranges from classical, baroque, and Renaissance works to more recent folk music and spirituals. Much of it is presented a cappella. The group gives fall and spring concerts at the Santuario de Guadalupe, and its Christmas dinner concert is avidly attended. Call for information (tel. 662-9717 evenings).

The **Santa Fe Women's Ensemble** offers classical works during the spring and fall seasons, either a cappella or with accompaniment. Concerts of these 12 semiprofessional singers are held in St. Francis Auditorium, with an additional four Christmas concerts at Loretto Chapel. Call for information (tel. 982-9385).

ORCHESTRAL MUSIC: The **Santa Fe Chamber Music Festival,** whose six-week season runs from the second week of July through the third week of August, has been held in beautiful St. Francis Auditorium (at the Museum of Fine Arts) since its founding in 1973. Performances, which are taped by the National Public Radio system for national broadcast, include selections by great classical and contemporary composers and a week of baroque music on original instruments. Also part of the festival is a Music of the Americas series, emphasizing the traditions of a different Western Hemisphere culture each year (in 1988, Brazil). A noted composer and a string quartet are invited to be "in residence" each season. Ticket prices for most performances run $15 to $25 and can be purchased at the festival office at 640 Paseo de Peralta. For more information, contact P.O. Box 853, Santa Fe, NM 87504 (tel. 505/982-2075, or toll free 800/962-7286).

The oldest musical organization in northern New Mexico is the **Santa Fe Concert Association.** Founded in 1938, its mid-October to early-May season includes more than 20 events annually, among them a distinguished artist series featuring renowned instrumental and voice soloists and ensembles; a youth concert series; a Sunday-afternoon recital series by local performers; a master class for vocalists; and a special Christmas Eve concert. All performances are at the historic St. Francis Auditorium at the Museum of Fine Arts. For information, call or write P.O. Box 4626, Santa Fe, NM 87502 (tel. 505/984-8759).

The Orchestra of Santa Fe, which enters its 16th season in 1989, is best known for its holiday productions of Handel's *Messiah* and its January/February Bach or Mozart festivals. William Kirschke conducts all performances, held in the Lensic Theatre on San Francisco Street. The late August to early May season typically comprises 12 to 15 concerts, with guest artists often engaged in the classical, baroque, and contemporary programs. For more information, call or write P.O. Box 2901, Santa Fe, NM 87504 (tel. 505/988-4640).

The Ensemble of Santa Fe is the orchestra's outreach group. The professional chamber music ensemble performs nine times between September and May in Loretto Chapel or St. John's College. Its Christmas Eve and Easter Week concerts are especially well attended. For information, contact P.O. Box 8427, Santa Fe, NM 87504 (tel. 505/988-4640).

The Santa Fe Symphony, under the direction of Stewart Robertson, has grown rapidly in stature since its founding in 1984. Matinee performances of classical and popular works are presented at Sweeney Center in October, December, January, March, and May. The symphony orchestra also conducts evening lectures and concerts during its Beethoven festival the week prior to Christmas, and offers a series of four midday concerts in Santa Fe and Los Alamos in the midst of its season. For information, contact P.O. Box 9692, Santa Fe, NM 87504 (tel. 505/983-3530).

OTHER MUSIC: The **Santa Fe School of Contemporary Music** has teacher/student ensembles specializing in original and adapted jazz and jazz fusion. Year-round performances are scheduled at various locations around northern New Mexico. Visitors are welcome to attend a series of half-day summer workshops by noted American and European jazz musicians. For information, call 982-3719.

The **Santa Fe Guitar Society** hosts a series of solo virtuoso performances by internationally famed and/or locally accomplished guitarists at the Santuario de Guadalupe. The society is a nonprofit association whose monthly meetings are open to the public. For information, contact P.O. Box 4421, Santa Fe, NM 87504 (tel. 984-0214).

Musica Antigua de Albuquerque is a professional ensemble which specializes in medieval, Renaissance, and early baroque music. Group members, who offer four Santa Fe concerts annually, accompany themselves on traditional instruments like gamba, oud, psaltery, and recorder. For information, call 842-9613.

The **Theatre of Music,** in its tenth year in 1989, specializes in winter and spring productions of Broadway revues and musicals. For full information, call 982-2221.

DANCE: The **Pajarito Ballet Theatre,** the only professional regional ballet company in New Mexico, opens its season in mid-April with a week-long regional dance festival. The rest of the calendar includes several repertory performances during June, an original or contemporary ballet premiering in October, and a series of performances of Tchaikovsky's *The Nutcracker* during the Christmas season at various locations throughout northern New

Mexico. In residence at the Ballet Academie de Santa Fe, Pajarito has toured from California to Louisiana.

Ticket prices range from $10 to $25. For information, contact 560 Montezuma Ave., Suite 103, Santa Fe, NM 87501 (tel. 505/984-1345).

Estampa Flamenca, an offshoot of the Maria Benitez Spanish Dance Company, performs from mid-June to mid-September at the Sheraton de Santa Fe. True flamenco is one of the most thrilling of all dance forms, displaying the inner spirit and verve of the gypsies of Spanish Andalusia with rapid footwork and clacking castanets. For information, call 505/982-1237, or toll free 800/325-0759 in New Mexico.

The 12-member **Santa Fe Dance Company** interprets modern dance forms several times a year between May and October. Guest artists frequently join the company during its summer season. The group tours the state in spring. For information, call 983-9456.

The **New Mexico Dance Coalition** showcases the work of regional choreographers in professional productions. For information, call 983-5742.

THEATER: The **New Mexico Repertory Theatre** was founded in 1983 as the state's sole resident professional company. Already it is developing a solid reputation for its innovative productions of classical works and contemporary American and European plays. At least one work annually is penned by a New Mexico writer.

Seven productions are scheduled in an October-to-April season. (The 1988 schedule included Philip Barry's *Holiday,* Mark Medoff's *The Homage That Follows,* David Richard Jones's adaptation of Dickens's *A Christmas Carol,* Eduardo Machado's *Once Removed,* Molière's *Tartuffe,* Athol Fugard's *The Road to Mecca,* and William Inge's *Bus Stop.*)

Each production opens with a two-week run at the Rep's stage in a renovated church at 217 Johnson St. in Santa Fe, then moves to the KiMo Theatre in downtown Albuquerque. Ticket prices range from $10 to $18.50. The company also tours statewide and conducts theater workshops in outlying districts. For further information, contact P.O. Box 9279, Santa Fe, NM 87504 (tel. 505/983-2372, or 984-2226 for the box office).

The **Santa Fe Community Theatre** is the oldest theater group in New Mexico, having been founded in the 1920s. Well-received dramas and comedies are performed from October to April in a historic adobe theater at 142 E. De Vargas St. (in the Barrio de Analco). Most popular is the annual Fiesta Melodrama in January and February: this series of one-act melodramas calls upon the public to boo the sneering villain and swoon for the damsel in distress. For information, contact P.O. Box 2084, Santa Fe, NM 87504 (tel. 505/988-4262).

The **Greer Garson Theatre,** on the campus of the College of Santa Fe, has four student productions annually, with five performances each, from October to April. Typically, a comedy, a drama, a musical, and a classic are chosen for presentation. For information, contact the college's Performing Arts Department, St. Michael's Drive, Santa Fe, NM 87501 (tel. 505/473-6511 or 473-6439).

ARTS CENTERS: If any one site can be said to be the heart and soul of theater and the arts in the Santa Fe area, that site is the **Armory for the Arts,** 1050 Old Pecos Trail (tel. 988-1886). The theater and gallery host local, regional, and national artists and productions ranging from the classics to avant-garde and stand-up comedy. Lily Tomlin's Tony Award–winning *Search for Signs of Intelligent Life in the Universe* premiered here in 1985. The armory sponsors an innovative dance program, the Santa Fe Children's Museum, a Children's Theatre Project, and a photograph collaborative known as Center of the Eye.

The **Center for Contemporary Arts,** 291 E. Barcelona St. (tel. 982-1338), schedules events and exhibits throughout the year that cover the gamut of the Santa Fe art scene. There are film and video screenings an average of twice a week; seven annual exhibitions of painting, sculpture, and photography; poetry readings; music and dance concerts in a 143-seat theater; and a variety of other events. Studios and rehearsal facilities are provided for every medium.

The **Santa Fe Council for the Arts** schedules an eclectic variety of concerts (ranging from classical to ethnic to jazz), lectures, and youth workshops, many of which are free and open to the public. For information, call 988-1878, 10 a.m. and 2 p.m. Tuesday through Friday.

CINEMA: Ever since *The Santa Fe Trail,* a splashy western starring Errol Flynn, Olivia de Havilland, Ronald Reagan, and Raymond Massey, premiered in Santa Fe in 1940, northern New Mexico has been a prime site for major studio movie productions. Films like *Butch Cassidy and the Sundance Kid* (1968), *Easy Rider* (1968), *Billy Jack* (1970), *Silverado* (1984), and *Young Guns* (1988) have become big national hits. In fact an estimated 500 movies have been shot in this region since 1900.

The industry is growing too: in 1987, $31 million was spent in the state in the production of 33 motion pictures, TV movies, commercials, and other film projects. That was about four times as much as in 1984.

Many of the latest New Mexico films are presented to the public each year in the **Santa Fe Film Festival** at several locations in the area. For information, contact the festival office at 1050 Old Santa Fe Trail (tel. 827-8580).

FINE ARTS

The Santa Fe art scene dates from the first two decades of this century. The climate and landscape, the unusual depth of the desert light, and the fascinating Hispanic and Indian cultures combined to draw some 15 artists to the area from the East Coast and beyond by 1921.

Will Shuster (1893–1969) emerged as the most prominent member of the group. Though poverty-stricken in the 1920s, he helped found Los Cinco Pintores, a group of five avant-garde painters who put Santa Fe on the world art map. The others were Fremont Ellis, Jozef Bakos, Willard Nash, and Walter Mruk: search them out at local galleries. Shuster also helped to create the Fiesta de Santa Fe, still the city's most popular celebration.

Today the number of full-time professional artists in the Santa Fe area exceeds 700, and thousands more dabble in the arts. Their studios and galleries are spread throughout the valley and surrounding hills, but there are two prime areas for art aficionados to browse—downtown Santa Fe and Canyon Road.

Most of the downtown shops are open seven days a week; on Canyon Road, many galleries close Monday and all but a few hours on Sunday afternoons. Other artists show their work by appointment only.

Following is a listing of many of the city's fine-arts outlets. Many galleries have a varied selection of works, but they are listed here by their primary specialties:

CONTEMPORARY ART: Adeline's Art Atrium, 1590B Pacheco St. (tel. 982-5579). Oil and watercolor landscapes by Adeline Meyer.

Allman Ricks Fine Art & Framing, 812 Canyon Rd. (tel. 983-9767). Western oils and acrylics, elaborate frames.

Altura Fine Contemporary & Southwestern Art, 943 Canyon Rd. (tel. 989-9633). Regional artists.

Artists' Gallery, 228 Galisteo St. (tel. 988-2582). Cooperative of about 30 artists with a wide range of media represented.

Claude Bentley Studio/Gallery, 227 E. Palace Ave. (tel. 982-9920). Abstract-impressionist oils and collages.

Howard Bobbs Gallery, 651 Canyon Rd. (tel. 983-5672). Landscape watercolors; modern sculpture.

Marilyn Butler Fine Art, 225 Galisteo St. (tel. 988-5387). Paintings, sculptures, mixed media work by 25 artists.

Concepts Gallery, 656 Canyon Rd. (tel. 988-3743). Cooperative of abstract painters, sculptors, and photographers.

The Creative Eye, 656 Canyon Rd. (tel. 982-4982). Jim Harrison watercolors.

Frank Croft Fine Art, 616A Canyon Rd. (tel. 984-2220). Paula Narbutovskih oils, pastels, and watercolors.

Phil Daves Studio/Gallery, 669 Canyon Rd. (tel. 982-4867). Colorful, classical oils.

Dubin Fine Arts, 325 W. San Francisco St. (tel. 982-6234). Mexican and Japanese graphics and paintings.

Linda Durham Gallery, 400 Canyon Rd. (tel. 988-1313). Abstract painting and sculpture by emerging artists.

El Taller Gallery, 235 Don Gaspar Ave. (tel. 988-9298). Southwestern art of many media, featuring Amado Pena.

Enthios Gallery, 1111 Paseo de Peralta (tel. 988-1505). Painters, printmakers, ceramicists, weavers.

Father Sky/Mother Earth Gallery, 227 Don Gaspar Ave. (tel. 988-5118). Daniel Valdes scratchboard, Connie Valdes clay sculptures.

Mell Feltman Studio, 1838 Sun Mountain Dr., by appointment (tel. 988-9127). Watercolors and graphics.

Fenn Galleries, 1075 Paseo de Peralta (tel. 982-4631). Taos School, Georgia O'Keeffe, Norman Rockwell, Thomas Hart Benton, other American greats.

Galeria Capistrano, 409 Canyon Rd. (tel. 984-3024). Mixed-media southwestern themes.

The Gallery Wall, 50 E. San Francisco St. (tel. 988-4168). Dan Namingha acrylics, Allan Houser stone and bronze sculptures.

Gondeck Gallery, 225 Canyon Rd. (tel. 988-3580). Mixed-media southwestern themes.

Gordon Galleries, 415 Canyon Rd. (tel. 983-9776). Acrylics, watercolors, lithographs, metal sculptures, jewelry.

Elaine Holien, P.O. Box 4673, Santa Fe, NM 87502 (tel. 988-5078). Abstract southwestern watercolors.

Elaine Horwitch Galleries, 129 W. Palace Ave. (tel. 988-8997). Oils, acrylics, etchings, sculptures, and ceramics, mainly of southwestern themes.

The Jamison Galleries, 111 E. San Francisco St. (tel. 982-3666). Major Santa Fe and Taos artists of past and present.

Janus Gallery, 110 Galisteo St. (tel. 983-1590). Paintings, sculpture, and mixed media with international focus.

Laurel Jones Gallery, 729 Canyon Rd. (tel. 984-3029). Traditional and modern southwestern themes.

Juanita's Collections, 727 Canyon Rd. (tel. 982-0336). Paintings, jewelry, artifacts, antiques.

Keats Gallery and Antiques, 644 Canyon Rd. (tel. 982-6686). Abstract collages and assemblages; also jewelry, rugs, furniture.

La Roche Gallery, 706 Canyon Rd. (tel. 982-1186). Acrylics and pottery by Carole La Roche.

Edith Lambert Gallery, 707 Canyon Rd. (tel. 984-2783). Paintings, silver jewelry, ceramics, fiber arts.

Janet Lippincott Studio/Gallery, 1270 Upper Canyon Rd. (tel. 983-2171). Non-objective oils, acrylics, and monoprints.

H. Love Gallery, 308 Johnson St. (tel. 988-1953). Oils, watercolors, and sculptures, mainly southwestern in theme.

Maitland Gallery, 109 E. Palace Ave. (tel. 471-3473). Richard Maitland's surrealistic paintings and sculptures.

The Marcus Gallery, 207 W. San Francisco St. (tel. 982-9363). Paintings, sculptures, handcrafts, and fiber art.

John Massee Studio, P.O. Box 0, Galisteo, NM 87540 (tel. 988-4519). Steel sculpture.

Nedra Matteucci Fine Art, 300 Garcia St. at Canyon Road (tel. 983-2731). Classics by the Taos School and early Santa Fe artists, plus modern sculpture.

Ernesto Mayans Gallery, 601 Canyon Rd. (tel. 983-8068). Regional classics and abstract oils.

Linda McAdoo Gallery, 503 Canyon Rd. (tel. 983-7182). Impressionist painters and sculptors.

Meyer Gallery, 225 Canyon Rd. (tel. 983-1434). Bronze sculpture, paintings, jewelry, handcrafts.

Linda Miner-Wickes Water Sculpture Studio, Bishop's Lodge Road, Tesuque, by appointment (tel. 988-3172). Bronze fountain sculptures.

Studio of Ann Moul, 468 Arroyo Tenorio (tel. 982-5954). Abstract regional landscapes.

Munson Gallery, 225 Canyon Rd. (tel. 983-1657). Southwestern-theme paintings and limited-edition prints.

Joanna Nedboy Studios & Gallery, 821 Canyon Rd. (tel. 983-9662). Paintings and hand-painted fabrics of southwestern themes.

New Trends Gallery, 228 Old Santa Fe Trail (tel. 988-1199). Hand-dyed apparel, oils, watercolors, sculpture, paper art, jewelry.

Night Sky Gallery & Studio, 826 Canyon Rd. (tel. 982-1468). Paintings, ceramics, blown glass, original prints.

Owings-Dewey Fine Art, 74 E. San Francisco St. (tel. 982-6244). Deceased western artists, including Charles Russell and Georgia O'Keeffe.

Gerald Peters Gallery, 439 Camino del Monte Sol (tel.

988-8961). Taos School and other classical artists; modern oils, watercolors, ceramics.

Presden Gallery, 134 W. Water St. (tel. 983-1014). Paintings, ceramics, mixed media, unusual modern "folk art."

Realist Gallery, 28 Burro Alley (tel. 989-7422). Social realism and expressionism in paintings and graphics.

C. G. Rein Galleries, 122 W. San Francisco St. (tel. 982-6226). Eclectic selection of paintings, sculptures, woodcuts, mixed-media assemblages.

Rettig y Martinez Gallery, 418 Montezuma Ave. (tel. 983-4640). Surrealist to non-objective paintings, sculptures, lithographs, photography.

I. Ringelmann Studio, by appointment (tel. 983-2791). Western-theme oils.

David Roe Studios, 825 Early St., by appointment (tel. 983-9212). Surrealist oils and lithographs.

Francisco Sanabria Studio, by appointment (tel. 989-8820). Acrylics of modern folk-art theme.

Santa Fe East, 200 Old Santa Fe Trail (tel. 988-3103). Classic paintings; jewelry.

Savage Galleries, 102 E. Water St. (tel. 982-1640). Realistic modern western paintings.

Scott's Studio/Gallery, 1127 Paseo de Peralta (tel. 983-3913). Bronze and porcelain sculptures, paper works, neon art, bisque dolls.

Sena Galleries East, 125 E. Palace Ave. (tel. 982-8181). Modern southwestern paintings and sculpture.

Sena Galleries West, Plaza Mercado, 116-118 W. San Francisco St. (tel. 982-8805). Avant-garde painters and sculptors.

Shidoni Gallery, Bishop's Lodge Road, Tesuque (tel. 988-8008). Sculpture garden, bronze casting.

The Small Gallery, 622 Canyon Rd. (tel. 984-2220). Surrealist and classic oils, watercolors, lithographs, and engravings.

Stiha Gallery, La Fonda Hotel (tel. 983-6145). Vladan Stiha joyous oils; several area sculptors.

Carol Thornton Gallery, 211 Old Santa Fe Trail (tel. 988-4659). Paintings and sculptures of western theme.

Variant Gallery, 114 Old Santa Fe Trail (tel. 984-1109). Impressionist and abstract paintings, sculptures, and ceramics.

Ventana Fine Art, Inn at Loretto (tel. 983-8815). Oils, pastels, watercolors, graphics, ceramics.

David Vigil Studio, 821A Canyon Rd. (tel. 983-4210). Expressionist oils of regional theme.

Joe Wade Fine Arts, 102 E. Water St. (tel. 988-2727). Southwestern realist and impressionist paintings and sculpture.

Wadle Galleries, 128 W. Palace Ave. (tel. 983-9219). Modern realist and impressionist paintings, ceramics, and bronzes.

Waxlander Gallery, 622 Canyon Rd. (tel. 984-2202). Oils, pastels, watercolors, woodcuts.

Wolf Hoggan, 133 W. Water St. (tel. 983-8597). Wall art of various media from leading local artists.

Woodrow Wilson Fine Arts, 319 Read St. (tel. 983-2444). High-profile Taos and Santa Fe artists, plus modern impressionism and realism.

Star Liana York Studio/Gallery, Route 4, Box 60B, Santa Fe, NM 87501 (tel. 983-1647). Bronze sculpture.

Zaplin-Lampert Gallery, 651 Canyon Rd. (tel. 982-6100). Classical western oils, watercolors, and prints.

NATIVE AMERICAN ART: Joshua Baer & Company, 116 E. Palace Ave. (tel. 988-8944). 19th-century Navajo blankets, pottery, jewelry, tribal art.

Balink's Studio, 832 Old Santa Fe Rd. (tel. 982-0286). Portraits by Henry C. Balink Sr. (1882–1963), artifacts, woodcarvings.

Blue Gem Shop & Gallery, 100 E. San Francisco St. (tel. 988-2488). Pottery, jewelry, handcrafts.

Kenneth Canfield / Barbara Burgdorf, 414 Canyon Rd., by appointment (tel. 988-4199). Antique Indian art.

Cristof's, 106 W. San Francisco St. (tel. 988-9881). Modern Navajo textiles and handcrafts of various southwestern Indians.

Dewey Galleries Ltd., 74 E. San Francisco St. (tel. 982-6244). Textiles, jewelry, historical pottery.

Discover Santa Fe Indian Arts & Crafts, 130B W. Palace Ave. (tel. 984-8484). Modern jewelry, pottery, other handcrafts.

El Parian de Santa Fe, Plaza Mercado, 112 W. San Francisco St. (tel. 984-3150). Pueblo and Navajo painters.

Fading Sun Gallery, 235 Don Gaspar Ave., no. 5 (tel. 989-8200). Regional native artists.

Gallery 10, 225 Canyon Rd. (tel. 983-9707). Museum-quality pottery, weavings, basketry.

The Givingness Gallery, 309 W. San Francisco St., in the Clarion Eldorado Hotel (tel. 988-4721). Unique hand-painted gourds of Robert Rivera; paintings and sculptures of Yellowman.

Frank Howell Gallery, 54 E. San Francisco St. (tel. 984-1053). Thematic American Indian portraits.

Indian Trader West, 204 W. San Francisco St. (tel. 988-5776). Navajo rugs, Pueblo pottery, other handcrafts.

Kachina House & Gallery, 236 Delgado St. (tel. 982-8415). Outstanding collection of kachina dolls, native oils.

John J. Kania, 652 Canyon Rd. (tel. 982-8767). Fine baskets, pottery, beadwork.

Alan Kessler, 305 Camino Cerrito at Canyon Road (tel. 986-1017). Antique art.

Benson L. Lanford / Robert W. Gilmore, 859 Camino Ranchitos, by appointment (tel. 988-1321). Pottery, other handcrafts.

Morning Star Gallery, 513 Canyon Rd. (tel. 982-8187). North American Indian artifacts.

Native American Artifacts, P.O. Box 503, Santa Fe, NM 87504 (tel. 473-5161). Rare artifacts and literature.

Robert F. Nichols Americana, 419 Canyon Rd. (tel. 982-2145). Prehistoric pottery, country antiques.

Prairie Edge, El Centro, 102 E. Water St. (tel. 984-1336). Plains Indian art, artifacts, jewelry.

The Rainbow Man, 107 E. Palace Ave. (tel. 982-8706). Kachinas, pottery, basketry, jewelry, folk art.

Raven Gallery, 622 Canyon Rd. (tel. 984-2202). Northwest Coast Indian art.

Rio Grande Gallery, 80 E. San Francisco St. (tel. 983-2458). R. C. Gorman paintings, Miguel Antonio bronzes.

Christopher Selser, P.O. Box 9328, Santa Fe, NM 87504, by appointment (tel. 984-1481). Pottery, silverwork, artifacts.

Silver Sun, 656 Canyon Rd. (tel. 983-8743). Turquoise and silver work.

Smoky Ridge Gallery, 201 Canyon Rd. (tel. 988-4357). Michael Atkinson watercolors.

Richard Solomon, by appointment (tel. 986-0436). Mixed-media assemblages of ancient tribal themes.

Streets of Taos, 200 Canyon Rd. (tel. 983-8268 or 983-4509). Navajo rugs, Pueblo jewelry, pottery, and baskets.

Taylor's Gallery, 113 E. San Francisco St. (tel. 982-4562). Western paintings and sculpture, Indian jewelry and pottery.

Thunderbear Gallery, 129 W. San Francisco St. (tel. 988-2268). Indian paintings, sculpture, beadwork.

21st Century Fox Fine Art, 201 Galisteo St. (tel. 983-2002). Major native artists, including R. C. Gorman and Kevin Red Star; prints and posters.

HISPANIC AND FOLK ART: **Arte Primitivo,** 125 E. Palace Ave. (tel. 983-2535). Spanish colonial art and furniture.

Channing-Dale-Throckmorton, 53 Old Santa Fe Trail (tel. 984-2133). Rare tribal antique arts and crafts.

Davila, Route 5, Box 296AA, Santa Fe, NM 87501, by appointment (tel. 455-2962). Snake carvings.

Economos Works of Art, 225 Canyon Rd. (tel. 982-6347). Horacio Valdez death-cart carvings.

Folklorico, 652 Canyon Rd. (tel. 983-6699). Spanish colonial religious art.

Galeria Lara, 108 Galisteo St. (tel. 983-1942). Latin American masks and folk art.

Gallery Tiqua, 216 Old Santa Fe Trail (tel. 984-8704). Spanish colonial art, American Indian artifacts.

David Mather Folk Art Gallery, 141 Lincoln Ave. (tel. 983-1660 or 988-1218). New Mexican animal woodcarvings and Mexican folk art.

Native Market, 555 Canyon Rd. (tel. 983-6535), and **Native Market Country Store,** 330 Old Santa Fe Trail (tel. 982-8006). Mexican rugs, folk arts.

Origins, 135 W. San Francisco St. (tel. 988-2323). Modern and prehistoric folk art from around the world.

Tom Riggs Gallery, 943 Canyon Rd. (tel. 982-9377). Art of primitive and exotic cultures.

Santa Fe Store, 211 Old Santa Fe Trail, in the Inn at Loretto (tel. 982-2425). Local and imported folk art.

Shop of the Frightened Owl, 1117 Canyon Rd. (tel. 983-7607). Spanish colonial art and furniture.

Richard Worthen Galleries, 510 Galisteo St. (tel. 988-2460). Spanish colonial art and antiques.

CONTEMPORARY CRAFTS: Arius American Art Tile Gallery, 114 Don Gaspar Ave. (tel. 988-1196). Limited-edition and custom tiles.

Bellas Artes, Garcia Street and Canyon Road (tel. 983-2745). Ceramic and textile art.

The Contemporary Craftsman, 100 W. San Francisco St. (tel. 988-1001). Ceramics, furniture, jewelry, fiber art, and glass by artists selected nationwide.

Doolings of Santa Fe, 525 Airport Rd. (tel. 471-5956). Southwestern country furniture.

Expressions of Don Freedman, 136 W. Water St. (tel. 982-5611). Woodcarvings and tapestries.

Gian Andrea Studio/Gallery, 626 Canyon Rd. (tel. 982-0054). Modern religious art in many media by Andrea and Gian Bacigalupa.

Handwoven Originals, 211 Old Santa Fe Trail, in the Inn at Loretto (tel. 982-4118). Clothing and accessories.

Paula James, by appointment (tel. 988-2682). Porcelain vases and bowls.

La Mesa of Santa Fe, 225 Canyon Rd. (tel. 984-1688). Handcrafted dinnerware, furniture, household objects.

Charles Miner Art Glass, Bishop's Lodge Road, Tesuque (tel. 988-2165). Glasswork.

Nambe Mills, Inc., 924 Paseo de Peralta at Canyon Road (tel. 988-5528) and 112 W. San Francisco St., Plaza Mercado (tel. 988-3574). Exquisite alloy is sandcast and handcrafted to create cooking, serving, and decorating pieces.

The Nambe Shop, Route 5, Box 360FF, Santa Fe, NM 87501 (tel. 455-2731). Nambe ware seconds outlet.

Chris O'Connell Spider Woman Designs, 225 Canyon Rd. (tel. 984-0136). Weaving and design studio, antique furniture.

Plaza Gallery, 80 E. San Francisco St. (tel. 983-2448). Pottery, bronze sculpture, stone fetishes.

Rabbit Artworks, Route 14, Box 216X, La Cienega (tel. 471-3671). Painted porcelain ware by Robert Brodsky and Cristina Davila.

Jennifer Roche Tile Art Gallery, 118 E. San Francisco St., Plaza Mercado (tel. 989-8478). Limited and unlimited editions.

Running Ridge Gallery, 640 Canyon Rd. (tel. 988-2515). Ceramics, fiber and paper art, glasswork.

Paul White, Route 10, Box 88N, Santa Fe, NM 87501 (tel. 473-0379). Glass fetishes.

JEWELRY: Antony/Williams Designers, 211 Old Santa Fe Trail, in the Inn at Loretto (tel. 982-3443). Original gold designs.

The Golden Eye, 115 Don Gaspar Ave. (tel. 984-0040). Use of rare and exotic gemstones.

Handcrafters Gallery, 227 Galisteo St. (tel. 982-4880). Michael Bondanza platinum jewelry.

Jett, A Gallery of Designer Jewelry, 110 Old Santa Fe Trail (tel. 988-1414). Innovative designs.

The Passionate Eye, 235 Don Gaspar Ave. (tel. 984-1606, or toll free 800/468-8962). Handmade sterling-silver jewelry, lapidary pieces, Stan Bentall bronze sculptures.

Frank Patania, 119 E. Palace Ave. (tel. 983-2155). Indian-style silversmithing, Papua New Guinean primitive art.

James Reid Ltd., 114 E. Palace Ave. (tel. 988-1147). Silver-smithing, gold jewelry, Indian artifacts, furniture, stone sculpture.

Talisman Contemporary Arts, by appointment (tel. 983-8240). Custom lapidary and designs.

Things Finer, 100 E. San Francisco St., in the La Fonda Hotel (tel. 983-5552). Russian objets d'art, silverwork.

Tresa Vorenberg Goldsmiths, 656 Canyon Rd. (tel. 988-7215). Handcrafted jewelry.

HOME FURNISHINGS: Dell Woodworks, 1326 Rufina Circle (tel. 471-3005). Handcrafted Santa Fe–style furniture.

Ken Figueredo & Associates, 607 Old Santa Fe Trail (tel. 984-8430). Country pine and primitive pieces, antiques.

Kailer-Grant Designs, 143 Lincoln Ave. (tel. 983-6449). Interior and custom design.

Mudd-Carr Gallery, 924 Paseo de Peralta (tel. 982-8206). Southwestern furniture, Indian pottery and textiles.

The Sombraje Collection, 403 Canyon Rd. (tel. 988-5567). Custom-designed furniture and crafts.

Southwest Spanish Craftsmen, 116 W. San Francisco St., Plaza Mercado (tel. 982-1767, or toll free 800/777-1767). Spanish colonial- and Spanish provincial-style furniture, doors, accessories.

Willow Gallery, 821 Canyon Rd. (tel. 989-8130). Custom willow shutters and furniture.

ANTIQUES: Jeffrey Adams Antiques, 555 Canyon Rd. (tel. 982-1922). English, Hispanic, southwestern items.

Claiborne Gallery, 558 Canyon Rd. (tel. 982-8019). Original Spanish colonial furniture.

Mary Corley Antiques, 518 Old Santa Fe Trail (tel. 984-0863). French country articles.

William S. Dutton Rare Things, 125 E. Palace Ave., Suite 10A (tel. 982-5904). Northern New Mexican and Pueblo art and artifacts.

Hansen Gallery, 923 Paseo de Peralta (tel. 983-2336). American, European, and Oriental furniture, porcelain, silver, paintings.

O'Meara Gallery, P.O. Box 369, Santa Fe, NM 87504 (tel. 982-2997). 19th- and 20th-century American art.

Scarlett's Antique Shop & Gallery, 225 Canyon Rd. (tel. 983-7092). Early American articles.

PHOTOGRAPHY: Canyon Road Photographs, 652 Canyon Rd. (tel. 984-8311). Modern southwestern scenes.

Bob Kapoun Vintage Photograph Gallery, 107 E. Palace Ave. (tel. 982-8706). Early works.

Santa Fe Photo Graphics, 113 Old Santa Fe Trail (tel. 988-5400). Edward Curtis originals, limited-edition photogravures.

Scheinbaum & Russek, 615 Don Felix St. (tel. 988-5116). Rare and modern photography, prints, and limited-edition portfolios.

Andrew Smith Gallery, 76 E. San Francisco St. (tel.

984-1234). Classic photography, including Ansel Adams and Alfred Stieglitz; new mixed-media photographers.

PRINTS AND POSTERS: American Print & Fine Art Gallery,
112 W. San Francisco St. (tel. 984-3211). Engravings, etchings, lithographs, including John James Audubon and Currier and Ives.

Graphics House, 702 Canyon Rd. (tel. 983-2654). Limited-edition etchings, engravings, silkscreens, and lithographs.

Hand Graphics, 418 Montezuma Ave. (tel. 988-1241). Limited-edition fine-art graphics.

Margolis and Moss, 129 W. San Francisco St. (tel. 982-1028). Early-20th-century prints, rare books.

Posters of Santa Fe, 644 Canyon Rd. (tel. 983-9697). Reproduced works of major southwestern artists.

Santa Fe Print Gallery, 112 W. San Francisco St., Plaza Mercado (tel. 984-3211). Antique maps, prints, paintings.

William R. Talbot, P.O. Box 2757, Santa Fe, NM 87504, by appointment (tel. 983-7144). Antique maps, natural history paintings and prints.

White Hyacinth Gallery, 137 W. San Francisco St. (tel. 983-2831). Southwestern posters, Ken Peterson serigraphs.

IMPORTS: Artesanos Imports, 222 Galisteo St. (tel. 983-5563). Mexican furniture, tiles, metalwork.

Counter Point Tile, P.O. Box 2132, Santa Fe, NM 87504 (tel. 982-1247). Colorful Mexican household designs.

The Gamut, 54 E. San Francisco St. (tel. 983-4929). Clothing, jewelry, folk crafts from around the world.

Jackalope Pottery, 2820 Cerrillos Rd., and downtown at Alameda and Galisteo Street (tel. 471-8539). Latin American imports.

The Little Shop, 138 W. Water St. (tel. 984-1050). Oriental art.

World Arts, 836 Canyon Rd. (tel. 986-1446). Textiles, furnishings, artifacts from around the world.

Yazzie Mohammed and Muldoon, 227 Don Gaspar Ave. (tel. 982-4556). Eclectic collection of mainly Asian artifacts.

MISCELLANEOUS: Colors of the Wind, 321 W. San Francisco St. (tel. 982-8235). Custom flags, kites, wind socks.

Mineral and Fossil Gallery of Santa Fe, 116½ Don Gaspar Ave. (tel. 984-1682). Fossils, meteorites, lapidary items.

Toys for Big Boys, 720 Canyon Rd. (tel. 983-8049). Antique weapons and coins, Indian artifacts.

CHAPTER VII

GETTING TO KNOW TAOS

□ □ □

If Santa Fe commands, "Look what I am; love me," Taos says, "Here's what I am; take me or leave me."

Situated where the western flank of the Sangre de Cristo range meets the semi-arid high desert of the upper Rio Grande Valley, Taos combines nature and culture, history and progress. There's a much less artificial atmosphere here than in the state capital: though the architecture might not be as aesthetically pleasing, it somehow seems more appropriate to the rough-and-ready setting.

Located just 40 miles south of the Colorado border, 70 miles north of Santa Fe, and 130 from Albuquerque, Taos is best known for its thriving art colony, its historic Indian pueblo, and its nearby ski area, one of the most highly regarded in the Rockies. It also has several fine museums and a wide choice of accommodations and restaurants for visitors.

About 4,800 people consider themselves Taoseños (permanent residents of Taos) today. They carry on a legacy of habitation that may have begun as long as 5,000 years ago; prehistoric ruins more than a millennium old exist throughout the Taos Valley.

The Spanish first visited in 1540 and colonized the area in 1598, putting down three rebellions at the Taos Pueblo in the last two decades of the 17th century. Through the 18th and 19th centuries Taos was an important trade center: New Mexico's annual caravan to Chihuahua, Mexico, couldn't leave until after the annual midsummer Taos Fair. French trappers began attending the fair in 1739, and by the early 1800s Taos had become a headquarters for American "mountain men." The most famous of them was Kit Carson, who made his home in Taos from 1826 to 1868.

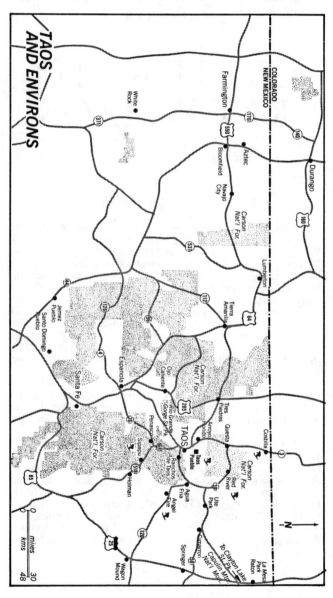

TAOS AND ENVIRONS

Taos was firmly Hispanic, and stayed loyal to Mexico during the Mexican War of 1846. The city rebelled against its new land-lord in 1847, killing newly appointed Gov. Charles Bent in his Taos home. Nevertheless it became a part of the Territory of New Mexico in 1850. It fell into Confederate hands for just six weeks during the Civil War, at the end of which time Carson and two other statesmen raised the Union flag over Taos Plaza and guarded it day and night. Since then Taos has had the honor of flying the flag 24 hours a day.

When the railroad bypassed Taos for Santa Fe, the popula-tion dwindled. But in 1898 two eastern artists—Ernest Blumenschein and Bert Phillips—discovered the dramatic light changes in the Taos Valley and put them on canvas. By 1912 the Taos Society of Artists had placed the town on the international cultural map. Today, by some estimates, more than 10% of the townspeople are painters, sculptors, writers, musicians, or other-wise earn income from an artistic pursuit.

Most of the galleries today are located on or near the Plaza, which was bricked over several years ago, and along neighboring streets.

ORIENTATION

The Plaza is a short block west of Taos's major intersection— where U.S. 64 **(Kit Carson Road)** from the east joins N.M. 3 and N.M. 68. South of the intersection, N.M. 3/68 is known as **South Santa Fe Road or Paseo del Pueblo Sur;** N.M. 68 is the primary route to Santa Fe. North of the intersection, N.M. 3 and U.S. 64 coincide as **North Pueblo Road or Paseo del Pueblo Norte.** Camino de la Placita (Placitas Road) circles the west side of downtown, passing within a block of the other side of the Plaza. Many of the streets that join these thoroughfares are winding lanes lined by traditional adobe homes, many of them 100 years old or more.

The town of Taos is merely the focal point of rugged 2,200-square-mile Taos County. Two features dominate this sparsely populated region: the high desert mesa, split in two by the 650-foot-deep chasm of the Rio Grande; and the Sangre de Cristo range, which tops out at 13,161-foot Wheeler Peak, New Mexico's highest mountain. From the forested uplands to the sage-carpeted mesa, the county is home to a great variety of wildlife. The human element includes the native Indians, still at home in ancient pueb-los, and Hispanic farmers who continue to irrigate their farmlands by centuries-old methods.

THE ABC'S OF TAOS

Here are quick answers to some of the requests most fre-quently made by visitors:

AIRPORT: The **Taos Airport** (tel. 758-9501) is about eight miles northwest of the town on U.S. 64, en route to the Rio Grande Gorge Bridge. **Mesa Airlines** (tel. 758-9677, or toll free 800/MESA AIR) has numerous daily flights during ski season (Thanksgiving to Easter) connecting Taos with Albuquerque and Colorado Springs. **Mountain Air Charter** (tel. 758-9382 or 758-4995) provides local Cessna 310 services to communities and national parks of the region.

ART GALLERIES: There are several dozen in town, many of them focused in the Plaza area and along U.S. 64. For more information, turn to Chapter XI.

AUTOMOBILE RENTALS: With offices at the airport plus in-town pickup and delivery, **Rich Ford Rental Cars** (tel. 758-9501), is reliable and efficient. **Hertz** rentals are handled by the Sagebrush Inn, South Santa Fe Road (tel. 758-2254); **Taos Motors,** on South Santa Fe Road (tel. 758-2286), also has vehicles available.

BANKS: Most banks are open from 9 a.m. to 3 p.m. Monday through Thursday, to 6 p.m. on Friday. **Banquest/First State Bank of Taos** (tel. 758-4242) is on the Plaza. **Centinel Bank of Taos** (tel. 758-4201) has two branches on Santa Fe Road, while **Western Bank Taos** (tel. 758-8100) has one.

BARBERS AND BEAUTY SALONS: The **Hair Saloon,** directly behind the Plaza on Ranchitos Road (tel. 758-0750), and **Helen's,** at the Kachina Lodge on North Pueblo Road (tel. 758-8727), welcome drop-ins of either sex. There are numerous other shops in town.

BICYCLES: The **Bicicletas Corp.,** next to the bus station on Cruz Alta at South Santa Fe Road (tel. 758-3522), rents Klein and Trek mountain bikes at $10 for all day. All you need is a credit card. The store is open from 9 a.m. to 6 p.m. daily except Sunday.

BOOKSTORES: The **Taos Book Shop,** 114 Kit Carson Rd. (tel. 758-3733), founded in 1947, is the oldest general bookstore in New Mexico. **Moby Dickens Bookshop,** 23 Bent St. (tel. 758-3050), has a children's as well as an adult collection. **Fernandez de Taos Bookstore** is located on the Plaza and offers a complete magazine collection as well as regional books. **Higher Ground Metaphysical Book Store,** 33 Bent St. (tel. 758-9251), and

Good News Christian Book Store, on South Santa Fe Road (tel. 758-1923), appeal to spiritual interests.

BUSES: The **bus station** is on South Santa Fe Road at Cruz Alta, a couple of miles south of the Plaza. **Greyhound** (tel. 758-1144) and **Texas, New Mexico & Oklahoma Coaches** (tel. 758-1144) both arrive and depart from this depot.

    Moreno Valley Transit (tel. 377-3737) and **Faust's Transportation** (tel. 758-3410, or toll-free 800/345-3738) provide shuttlebus service to and from Albuquerque as well as Red River, Angel Fire, and other resort towns.

    Pride of Taos (tel. 758-8340) meets incoming Mesa Airlines flights at the Taos Airport. It also offers shuttlebus service three times daily in winter between city hotels and Taos Ski Valley. The fare is $5 round trip. A night bus ($10) brings skiers staying at the ski valley into town for dinner at 5:30 p.m., returning them to their lodgings about 10 p.m.

    Pride of Taos plans an hourly shuttle through Taos during the summer months. Scheduled to operate from 9 a.m. to 10 p.m. at a charge of $5, it would run from the Kachina Lodge to the Sagebrush Inn.

CHIROPRACTORS: Try Dr. Janet Lewis at **El Centro Chiropractic,** South Santa Fe Road (tel. 758-2944).

CLIMATE: Only 50 feet lower than Santa Fe in elevation, Taos is similar in climate to the state capital. Summer days are dry and sunny, except for frequent afternoon thunderstorms; winter days are often bracing, with snowfalls frequent but rarely long-lived. Average summer temperatures range from lows of 50° to highs of 87°, with 9.1 inches annual precipitation. Average winter temperatures vary between lows of 9° and highs of 40°, with 35 inches annual snowfall in town (and 300 inches annually at Taos Ski Valley, elevation 9,207).

DENTISTS: Several dentists are listed in the telephone directory. Three of them have offices at 650 N. Pueblo Rd.: **Dr. Larry J. Cook** (tel. 758-9777), **Dr. Tom Simms** (tel. 758-8303), and orthodontist **Dr. William A. Schackel** (tel. 758-2087).

DOCTORS: Members of the **Taos Medical Group,** on Weimer Road (tel. 758-2224), are highly respected. Also good are **Family Practice Associates of Taos,** on Don Fernando Street (tel. 758-3005), a short distance west of the Plaza.

EMERGENCY: Dial 911 for police, sheriff, fire department, or ambulance.

FIRE DEPARTMENT: The city fire station is on Placitas Road north of the Plaza (tel. 758-3386 for non-emergencies). There's also a station at Taos Ski Valley (tel. 776-8118).

GASOLINE: Look for Chevron, Exxon, Gulf, Phillips 66, Shell, Texaco, and cut-rate operators, mainly along N.M. 68 north and south of town.

GLASSES: Taos Eyewear, in Cruz Alta Mall near the bus depot (tel. 758-8758), handles most needs between 10 a.m. and 5 p.m. Monday through Friday. It also has emergency service.

HOSPITAL: The **Holy Cross Hospital,** on South Santa Fe Road (tel. 758-8883), is a 33-bed unit with 24-hour emergency service. Serious cases are transferred to Santa Fe or Albuquerque.

LAUNDRY AND DRY CLEANING: The **Peralta Laundro-mat,** on South Santa Fe Road (tel. 758-0239), a couple miles south of downtown, is open daily. **La Bell One Hour Cleaners,** on Kit Carson Road (tel. 758-3382), one block east of the Plaza traffic light, covers dry-cleaning needs.

LIBRARIES: The two public libraries are both associated with museums. Most prominent is the **Harwood Library and Muse-um,** on Ledoux Street near the Plaza (tel. 758-3063). The **Kit Car-son Foundation Research Center,** on Los Cruces Road (tel. 758-9898), also opens its shelves to the public.

LIQUOR LAWS: As in Santa Fe, bars must close by 2 a.m. Mon-day through Saturday, and can open only between noon and mid-night on Sunday.

LITERATURE: Taos's best-known modern writer is John Nichols, whose book *The Milagro Beanfield War* was turned into a movie by Robert Redford in 1988. The first of a trilogy, it sets the scene for understanding much of the Hispanic lifestyle of the sur-rounding area. For a glimpse of the early heyday of the Taos arts community, see *Lorenzo in Taos,* Mabel Dodge Luhan's 1932 book about novelist D. H. Lawrence. The best historical overview of Taos can be found in *A Taos Mosaic,* written by one of the founders of the Taos Book Shop, Claire Morrill, and now available in a paperback edition.

LOST PROPERTY: Check with police (tel. 758-2216).

MAPS: The chamber of commerce office, near downtown on South Santa Fe Road, has free city maps.

NEWSPAPERS: The *Taos News,* published from an office on the Plaza (tel. 758-2241), appears weekly on Thursday. The *Albuquerque Journal* and *Tribune, The New Mexican* from Santa Fe, and the *Denver Post* are easily obtained daily at the Fernandez de Taos Bookstore on the Plaza.

PHARMACIES: The **Taos Pharmacy,** in Piñon Plaza on South Santa Fe Road (tel. 758-3342 or 758-3507), located next door to Holy Cross Hospital, is open from 9 a.m. to 7 p.m. weekdays and 9 a.m. to 5 p.m. on Saturday.

PHOTOGRAPHY: **Plaza Photo,** 202½ North Plaza (tel. 758-3420), handles most shutterbugs' needs, including one-day processing. Repairs usually must go to Santa Fe and require several days.

POLICE: In case of emergency, dial 911. All other inquiries should be directed to **Taos Police** in the Old Armory Building on Placitas Road (tel. 758-2216). The **Taos County Sheriff,** with jurisdiction outside the city limits, is located in the county courthouse on South Santa Fe Road (tel. 758-3361).

POSTAL SERVICES: The main **Taos Post Office** is on North Pueblo Road (tel. 758-2081), on your left as you head north, shortly before the turnoff to the Taos Pueblo. There are smaller offices in **Ranchos de Taos** (tel. 758-3944) and at **El Prado** (tel. 758-4810). The ZIP Code for Taos is 87571.

RADIO AND TELEVISION: There's TV reception from Albuquerque and Santa Fe. In local radio, listen to **KKIT-AM** (1340) for news, sports, and weather (tel. 758-2231); and **KTAO-FM** (101.7), which broadcasts an entertainment calendar at 6 p.m. daily (tel. 758-1017).

RELIGIOUS SERVICES: As in many communities of the heavily Hispanic Southwest, Roman Catholicism is the predominant faith. The town's religious focus is **Our Lady of Guadalupe Church,** west of the Plaza on Placitas Road (tel. 758-9208). Visitors often enjoy attending a service at the famous **San Francisco de Asis Church,** four miles south of the Plaza in Ranchos de Taos (tel. 758-2754). Masses are mainly in English, but each church has a Sunday-morning Spanish-language mass.

Other denominations active in Taos include Assemblies of God, Baptist, Brethren, Church of Christ, Foursquare Gospel, Friends, Jehovah's Witnesses, Methodist, and Presbyterian; Church of Jesus Christ of Latter-Day Saints (Mormon); Baha'i; and Eckankar.

ROAD CONDITIONS: Information on conditions in the Taos/Eagle Nest area can be obtained from the **State Police** (tel. 758-8878), or by dialing 1-983-0120.

SENIOR DISCOUNTS: Many establishments offer discounts of 10% or more to card-carrying members of the American Association of Retired Persons (AARP).

SHOE REPAIRS: The **Line Camp Boot Service,** on North Pueblo Road (tel. 758-8361), has a convenient location.

STORE HOURS: Most businesses are open from 9 a.m. to 5 p.m. Monday through Friday. Some may open as early as 8 a.m. or close at 6 p.m. Many also open on Saturday mornings, and some art galleries and antique dealers are even open all day on Saturday and Sunday, especially during peak summer and winter tourist seasons. Call shops for specific hours.

TAXES: New Mexico state sales tax on all merchandise and services is 5.625%. There is a lodger's tax of 3% on hotel rooms in Taos County.

TAXIS: Faust's Transportation (tel. 753-3410) provides local service. It is difficult to hail a taxi from the street, so it is best to call.

TELEPHONES: The area code for New Mexico is 505. For directory assistance within the state, dial 411; for outside the state, dial 1, followed by the area code and 555-1212.

TIME: Mountain Standard Time is one hour ahead of the West Coast and two hours behind the East Coast. Daylight Saving Time is in effect from April to October.

TIPPING: It's appropriate to leave 15% to 20% of your bill for waiters and waitresses in restaurants and lounges.

TOUR OPERATORS: Damaso and Helen Martinez's **Pride of Taos Tours,** P.O. Box 1192, Taos, NM 87571 (tel. 505/758-8340), has several packages. The Taos tour lasts 3 to 3½ hours and takes in the Plaza, Taos Pueblo, Millicent Rogers Museum, Martinez Hacienda, and more, for $20. Scenic sunset tours in an army safari truck descend to a hot springs at the bottom of the Rio Grande Gorge, with a half-mile hike to a campfire dinner. They run June to October and cost $50.

Taos Historic Walking Tours (tel. 758-3861), conducted by Char Graebner, are offered for 1½ hours Monday through Saturday. Most other tour operators working in the area are based in Santa Fe.

TOURIST INFORMATION: The **Taos County Chamber of Commerce,** P.O. Drawer I, Taos, NM 87571 (tel. 505/758-3873, or toll free 800/732-TAOS), is a quarter-mile walk or drive south of the Plaza area on South Santa Fe Road, next door to the Indian Hills Inn.

More information on specific destinations elsewhere in Taos County is available from the **Angel Fire / Eagle Nest Chamber of Commerce,** P.O. Box 547, Angel Fire, NM 87710 (tel. 505/377-6353); and the **Red River Chamber of Commerce,** P.O. Box 868, Red River, MN 87558 (tel. 505/754-2366).

USEFUL TELEPHONE NUMBERS: Battered women's hotline (tel. 785-9888). . . . New Mexico Environmental Improvement Division (tel. 1-827-9329). . . . Poison Control Center (tel. toll free 800/432-6866). . . . Rape Crisis Center hotline (tel. 758-2910). . . . Sangre de Cristo mental health hotline (tel. 758-1444). . . . Taos County offices (tel. 758-8834). . . . Time and temperature (tel. 758-1122).

CHAPTER VIII

WHERE TO STAY IN TAOS AND THE SKI VALLEY

□ □ □

Accommodations in Taos are generally rustic, emphasizing the town's Indian, Hispanic, and frontier roots. Most hotels and motels are located on N.M. 68, with a few scattered just east of the city center along U.S. 64 (Kit Carson Road). During the peak seasons, visitors without reservations may find no space in any of the 1,000 rooms in the 40 hotels, motels, bed-and-breakfasts, or other establishments in and near town. **Taos Central Reservations,** P.O. Box 1713, Taos, NM 87571 (tel. 505/758-9767, or toll free 800/821-2437), might be able to help.

There are another 300-plus rooms in 13 accommodations at or near the Taos Ski Valley. If they're full, the **Taos Valley Resort Association,** P.O. Box 85, Taos Ski Valley, NM 87525 (tel. 505/776-2233, or 800/992-SNOW), frequently knows of unadvertised condominium vacancies.

Unlike Santa Fe, there are two high seasons, with winter (Christmas-to-Easter ski season) usually busier and sometimes more expensive than summer. Spring and fall are shoulder seasons, often with lower rates. The period between Easter and Memorial Day is notoriously slow in the tourist industry here, and many restaurants and other businesses take their annual vacations at this time. Book well ahead during ski holiday periods (especially Christmas) and during the annual arts festivals (late May to mid-June and late September to early October).

HOTELS AND MOTELS IN TAOS

In this listing, "Upper Bracket" hotels are those with high-season doubles ranging from $75 to $100 a night; "Moderate," $45 to $75; and "Budget," less than $45. Deluxe accommodations, with price tags above $100 a night, can be found at Taos Ski Valley. All prices are subject to a state tax of 5.625% and a county lodgers' tax of 3%.

A Taos Sheraton and a Holiday Inn are scheduled to open in late 1989. For more information contact Holiday Inn (toll free 800/465-4329) or Sheraton Hotels (toll free 800/325-3535.)

UPPER-BRACKET CHOICES: The sports-oriented **Quail Ridge Inn,** Ski Valley Road (N.M. 150; P.O. Box 707), Taos, NM 87571 (tel. 505/776-2211, or toll free 800/624-4448), bills itself as a family resort and conference center. Tennis and skiing are the recreations of note at this contemporary pueblo-style hotel, which spreads across several acres of open sagebrush about four miles north of Taos and three-quarters of a mile east of U.S. 64, en route to the ski area 14 miles distant.

Guests in the 110 units can hone their racquet abilities on six outdoor or two indoor tennis courts, or on four racquetball courts. A volleyball pit is used in summer; there's also a heated 20-meter swimming pool, and two hot tubs and saunas much beloved by sore-muscled skiers.

Five room options are available at the Quail Ridge Inn, which was built in 1978. Smallest are "hotel rooms," which can sleep four on a queen-size bed and queen-size sleeper sofa. Next are studios, actually semi-suites with full kitchens and patios or balconies. One-bedroom suites, the most popular accommodations, consist of a studio with a connecting hotel room. A dozen separate "casitas" contain spacious two- and three-bedroom suites of about 1,600 square feet each.

Each well-lit, carpeted room, no matter the size, has a big fireplace, color TV/radio with local reception and pay satellite attachment, free local phone service, huge closets with mirrored doors, reading lamps over the beds, and full shower/baths with private hot-water heaters. Décor is breezy southwestern pastel, with light woods, dried-flower arrangements in handcrafted pottery, and various pieces of local art and artifacts on the walls. Continental breakfasts are included in all room rates.

Studio kitchenettes are fully stocked and include a stove, refrigerator, microwave oven, and dishwasher. There's plenty of seating around the dining room table, breakfast bar, and living-room coffee table, and additional sleeping space on a sofa sleeper and Murphy bed.

Rates vary according to season, from $55 to $90 (single or

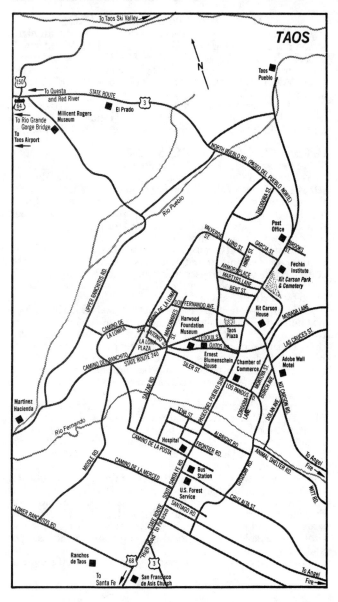

double) for a hotel room, $65 to $105 for a studio, $110 to $185 for a one-bedroom suite for up to four people. In the casitas, units housing up to six at the same cost include two-bedroom suites for $150 to $250 and three-bedroom suites for $175 to $275. High season is February 4 to March 31 and December 16 to January 1; low season is April 10 to May 26 and October 9 to November 23. Midsummer rates, and those of other shoulder seasons, strike a middle ground.

A 2% gratuity is added to all rates. Children under 18 stay free in a room with their parents, but there is a $5-per-night charge for cribs. Coin-op laundry facilities are on the premises.

Carl's French Quarter restaurant (tel. 776-8319) is one of the most popular in the Taos area, especially during its frequent amateur musical dinner-theater presentations. Breakfasts are served to hotel guests here, and lunches are strictly group affairs, but dinners are when Carl's bounces like Basin Street. Diners are encouraged to start with an authentic New Orleans cocktail, such as a mint julep or Hurricane ($3.50), and follow it with an appetizer of seafood filet gumbo ($3) or shrimp and artichoke bisque ($3). Entrees include shrimp Créole ($14), blackened chicken ($11), and a ten-ounce Cajun prime rib ($15). Dessert favorites are key lime pie ($2.50) and chocolate marquise cake ($3.50). There's also a kids' menu with all meals priced between $7 and $9.

MODERATELY PRICED ACCOMMODATIONS: The last century of Taos history is alive and well within the walls of the atmospheric **Taos Inn,** North Pueblo Road (P.O. Drawer N), Taos, NM 87571 (tel. 505/758-2233, or toll free 800/TAOS-INN). An adobe structure stood on this site, just one block north of the main Taos Plaza, in the mid-17th century. By the early 1800s a community of five residences was focused around a small plaza containing the town well, where citizens exchanged news and gossip. Frontiersman Kit Carson and others used the two-story courtyard as a fortification and lookout against Indian raids.

Dr. T. Paul Martin bought the complex when he settled in Taos in 1895. He was Taos County's first physician, and for most of the years until his death in 1935, he was the only one. Martin's wife, Helen, was the sister-in-law of painter Bert Phillips; it was in the Martins' dining room in 1912 that Phillips and fellow artist Ernest Blumenschein hatched the concept of the Taos Society of Artists, now world-famous. As the society burgeoned, many of the small houses owned by the Martins were rented to artists and writers.

After the doctor's death in 1935, his widow enclosed the plaza, installed indoor plumbing, placed a neon art deco "thunderbird" sign over the front door, and opened the Hotel Martin in 1936 (later renamed the Taos Inn). The plaza became the hotel lobby. In 1981–1982, the inn was restored; it is now listed on the state and national Registers of Historic Places, and is a member of the Association of Historic Hotels of the Rocky Mountain West.

Today hotel visitors find an inn of hospitality and charm, combining 20th-century elegance with 19th-century touches like adobe fireplaces, wrought-iron railings, and traditional hand-crafted furniture. The two-story lobby has interior balconies over-looking the town well, reborn as a tiered and tiled fountain. Above it rises a stained-glass cupola. Large *vigas* are set in the ceiling, Pueblo Indian rugs hang on the walls, and Taos-style furniture faces a sunken fireplace in one corner of the room.

No two guest rooms are alike. While all 40 are furnished in regional style, they differ in size, shape, and antique craft items—and thus each has a distinct personality. All rooms contain Taos-style furniture built by local artisans and original Indian, Hispanic, and New Mexican arts. All have custom hand-loomed wool Zapotec Indian bedspreads. And 31 rooms have fireplaces designed by Carmen Velarde, a famed Taos Pueblo *enjarradora* or adobe sculptress. (There's a daily supply of firewood in cool weather.) All rooms have phones, tiled baths, and cable color TVs with HBO. Rooms for the handicapped and nonsmokers are available.

Year-round room rates are $45 to $75 single, $50 to $95 double. The most expensive rooms can sleep five, although there's an extra $10 charge for cribs or rollaways. Lower prices are reserved for rooms above the lounge, all with queen-size beds, mostly without fireplaces. Special packages are available for those on ski vacations.

An outdoor courtyard surrounds a swimming pool, open seasonally, and a year-round Jacuzzi in a greenhouse.

Doc Martin's Restaurant occupies what was once the home, office, and delivery room of the good doctor. One of Taos's leading dining establishments, it serves three meals daily of regional specialties, nouvelle cuisine, and fresh seafood in a traditional southwestern setting. In summer, diners can eat on an outdoor patio. Breakfast favorites include stuffed sopaipillas (with eggs, onions, cheese and chiles; $4.75) and piñon nut waffles ($3.75). Lunches include a guacamole-seafood salad ($7.50), New Mexican cassoulet with duck and lamb ($6.25), and a shrimp burrito ($8). Dinners range from artist's-choice pasta (vermicelli with chicken, cashews, scallions, and a peach vinaigrette; $7 and $13) to a buffalo steak entree with chapotle sauce ($19.50). Espresso coffee drinks ($1.50 to $4) add a finishing touch to meals. Doc Martin's wine list has been praised by *Wine Spectator* magazine.

The inn's intimate Adobe Bar, popular among Taos artists and other locals, features northern New Mexico's only shrimp and oyster bar. There's live entertainment on weekends, and a late-night food menu. A favorite drink is the Cowboy Buddha—tequila, Cointreau, and lime, giving it a "rugged yet serene nature," according to the menu.

The Taos Inn has always been at the vanguard of the Taos arts movement. Its highest-profile contribution is the "Meet the Artist" series, a semi-annual event held in the spring (May 15 to June 21, coinciding with the spring arts celebration) and autumn (October 15 to December 15).

Georgia O'Keeffe, probably the most famous artist to have worked extensively in the Southwest, lived and painted for six months in the 1930s in a third-story room at the **Sagebrush Inn,** South Santa Fe Road (P.O. Box 557), Taos, NM 87571 (tel. 505/758-2254, or toll free 800/428-3626). The artistic legacy persists in the rare antiques, pottery, Navajo rugs, and painted masterpieces that adorn many walls of this venerable lodge.

Originally called the Chamisa Inn, the hotel was built in Pueblo Mission style in 1929 by native Taoseños, three miles south of the Plaza near Ranchos de Taos. The men made the adobe blocks and transported logs from the mountains for the huge *vigas* (beams) in the ceilings; the women laid the adobe in two-foot-thick walls and stuccoed both sides.

The Sagebrush has 82 rooms, including 19 condominium suites referred to as "Sagebrush Village." Most of the spacious, well-kept units face either an open grass courtyard, the outdoor swimming pool, or the stables. The traditional *viga* décor is complemented by earth-patterned décor and standard furnishings. Rooms have cable TV/radio and free local phone connections. Singles are $32 to $35; doubles, $55 to $75.

Condo suites, priced at $95 a night, have *kiva* fireplaces and beautiful hand-carved furnishings. There's a king-size bed in the bedroom, a Murphy bed in the main living area, two full baths, and charcoal drawings of local Indians on the walls.

In addition to the pool, the hotel has two Jacuzzis and tennis courts. A complimentary full breakfast is served daily from 7 to 11 a.m. in the Sagebrush Dining Room.

The Los Vaqueros Room is open for dinner from 5:30 to 10 p.m. daily. Most meals run between $8.50 and $15, although beef-and-seafood specials are considerably higher. The standard steak-and-seafood fare is supplemented by a handful of Mexican and Chinese stir-fry dishes. A children's menu is priced at $3.50 to $6 for full meals.

The lobby bar is open from 3:30 p.m. to midnight. Beginning at 9 p.m. there's live entertainment, sometimes featuring name entertainers like local singer-guitarist Michael Martin Murphey of "Wildfire" fame.

A three-foot-high Hopi *kachina* doll welcomes new arrivals to the lobby of the **Best Western Kachina Lodge,** North Pueblo Road (P.O. Box NN), Taos, NM 87571 (tel. 505/758-2275, or toll free 800/528-1234). If you like what you see, look further into the Kachina Art Gallery, connecting the lobby to the lodge's restaurants. It has a changing exhibit of paintings and other works from the Taos Gallery. Many additional artifacts are for sale in glass cases in the lobby.

The Kachina Lodge, established for more than 25 years, is due to renovate its 122 rooms. They are decorated with rust-colored carpets, southwestern-motif bedspreads, and standard furnishings. All rooms have cable TV and phones; local calls are 25¢. The hotel has a guest laundry and an outdoor swimming pool. In season (May 30 to September 30, December 15 to January 1, and February 15 to March 31) singles are $55 to $65 and doubles run $65 to $75; $20 less the remainder of year.

A large Navajo-theme living room and a separate, spacious reading room adjoin the lobby.

The Hopi Dining Room, resplendent in a turquoise-and-red color pattern with stylized sculpted-tin chandeliers, serves dinner entrees priced from $8 (avocado steak, chicken Kachina stuffed with broccoli) to $12 (T-bone steak, 12-ounce prime rib). The Kiva Coffee House is more appealing for breakfasts (a stack of corn pancakes is $2), lunches (bowl of green chile stew at $2.50), and full Mexican dinners ($6 and $7). The Zuñi Lounge offers cabaret-style Hispanic or country-and-western weekend entertainment, sometimes involving name talents like the Desert Rose Band.

Four more *kachina* dolls rest in a niche over the fireplace in the Hopi Dining Room. According to legend, Sun Kachin represents the creative force, Corn Maiden symbolizes increase and regeneration; Cow Kachina bestows good health and safety; and Crow Maiden grants wisdom and intuition. "Our Kachinas," says the management, "grant a special benediction for our guests."

Just across North Pueblo Road from the Kachina Lodge is **El Pueblo Lodge,** P.O. Box 92, Taos, NM 87571 (tel. 505/758-8641, or toll free 800/433-9612). The outstanding feature here, aside from well-kept rooms, is the nicely landscaped 2½-acre grounds, complete with fir trees, rose gardens, a barbecue pit, lawn furniture, and a slide for children. Throw in a year-round outdoor swimming pool and hot tub and it's no surprise that this motel is popular with families.

El Pueblo has 38 units and four condominium units in five

separate buildings, at least one of which dates to 1910. All the brightly colored rooms have refrigerators, hand-carved furniture, *viga* ceilings, Taos art on the walls, and screen doors. All have cable TV with HBO, direct-dial phones (free local calls), clock radios, and full baths. Many rooms have furnished mini-kitchens with microwave and hot pot; 12 have *kiva* fireplaces or Franklin stoves.

All guests are served complimentary continental breakfast and have access to free laundry facilities. The management goes out of its way to pick up arrivals from the airport.

Rates are $32 to $39 single, $45 to $65 double, and $5 to $7 for a third guest in the same room. Rates are highest June 24 to September 9 and December 16 to April 2.

The four condos all have three bedrooms (each with its own bath and TV) on two floors, full kitchens with dishwashers and all utensils, and walk-in closets. Three have fireplaces. The units, which accommodate six to eight guests, run $75 to $150 in the low season, $95 to $195 in the high season.

Art from the Cowboys and Indians Gallery on the Taos Plaza adorns the lobby of the **Ramada Inn Taos,** South Santa Fe Road and Frontier Road (P.O. Box 6257), Taos, NM 87571 (tel. 505/758-2900, or toll free 800/2-RAMADA). A large adobe-style building with a traditional belltower, it frequently features working artists. The gallery effect extends to art prints on the walls of all 124 guest rooms.

Each clean, spacious room has a king-size bed or two queen-size beds and other standard furnishings, including a vanity table for women guests, a TV/radio with the Movie Channel featured on cable and direct-dial phones (local calls are 50¢). Beige walls and carpets are accented by striped pastel bedspreads. Twelve rooms are specifically set aside for women travelers; no-smoking rooms are also available. The hotel has a courtesy van, the largest indoor swimming pool in Taos, a Jacuzzi, and a sundeck.

Rates, depending on season, are $50 to $70 single, $60 to $80 double, and $10 more per additional person up to four. High season runs from December 19 to April 15. Seniors may get discounts of up to 25%. Children under 18 are free with a parent.

Café Fennel, which perhaps has more green than any other restaurant in Taos, is open every day from 6 a.m. to 2:30 p.m. and 5:30 to 10 p.m. Omelets are $4 to $5 for breakfast; lunches, such as sandwiches and Mexican dishes, are priced $4.50 to $6. Full dinners run $11 to $12.50 and include an appetizer, house salad, dessert, coffee or tea, and after-dinner cordial. Champagne brunches on Sunday and fresh seafood buffets on Friday cost $13. The Fireside Lounge has complimentary hors d'oeuvres during its daily 4 to 7 p.m. happy hour. Solo or duo contemporary pop or country-and-western musicians entertain Thursday through Saturday nights.

Century-old cottonwood trees stand in a park-like picnic area, complete with barbecue grills and children's playground, outside the **El Monte Lodge,** Kit Carson Road (P.O. Box 22), Taos, NM 87571 (tel. 505/758-3171). This very friendly motel, which dates from the 1930s, is four blocks east of the Plaza. It's old-fashioned but homey, built in traditional adobe style with protruding *vigas,* painted yellow and framed by flower gardens.

The 13 units, many with fireplaces, occupy eight small buildings. The eclectic décor features considerable Southwest Indian art. Standard furnishings include a sofa bed, cable TV with HBO, alarm clock, and direct-dial phones (local calls are 25¢). Four rooms have fully stocked kitchenettes with refrigerator-freezers, four-burner stoves, toasters, and (in most cases) microwaves. There's also a free guest laundry. Year-round rates are $38 to $49 single, $49 to $65 double.

Easily overlooked, because it's well off the beaten track, is the **San Geronimo Lodge,** Witt Road at San Geronimo Road (P.O. Box 2491), Taos, NM 87571 (tel. 505/758-7117). Owned by the same family as the El Monte, this recently renovated two-story adobe lodge has the original *vigas* used in its construction about 1880. It's located half a mile south of Kit Carson Road, about 1½ mile east of the Plaza.

The extended three-room lobby area comprises an expansive art gallery. Complimentary continental breakfasts are served here each morning. Adjoining is a large tent containing a kidney-shaped swimming pool (open year round), a sauna, and hot tub.

The 18 rooms, most of them upstairs with shared balconies, have standard furnishings, regional art on the walls, cable TV with HBO, and direct-dial phones (local calls are 25¢). Unlimited wood is provided to the six rooms with fireplaces. Year-round rates are $38 to $65 single, $49 to $85 double.

The **Rodeway Inn,** South Santa Fe Road at Santiago Street (P.O. Box 2319), Taos, NM 87571 (tel. 505/758-2200), has 99 rooms, priced $34 to $44 for singles and $41 to $51 for doubles. The 11 king-size units have coffee makers and oversize easy chairs. All have turquoise-toned bedspreads and standard room furnishings, including cable TV, phones (local calls are 50¢), and silk-screen impressions on the walls. Two suites ($95 to $105) have kitchenettes. High season here is November 27 to April 10 and June 11 to September 10.

The Rodeway has an outdoor swimming pool and a gift shop with sundries and ski items. Carson National Forest, a short trek east, is nearer than the Plaza, two miles north. The attractive Aspen Café is open daily from 6 a.m. to 1:30 p.m. and 5:30 to 9:30

p.m.; the daily luncheon buffet is popular among locals. Light pop music is played in the lounge on weekends.

La Fonda de Taos, South Plaza (P.O. Box 1447), Taos, NM 87571 (tel. 505/758-2211), is an oldtime, family-owned hotel that hosted many of Taos's most glamorous guests in the 1950s and 1960s. The only lodging on the Plaza, it frankly has seen better days. Today it's most often visited by drop-ins who want a look at Saki Karavas's fine art collection, displayed on walls throughout the hotel. Ten original nudes by author D. H. Lawrence are sealed away in a private room, and are exhibited for the payment of $1 admission.

The hotel has 24 doubles and twins, gaily decorated with red carpets and blue trim. Furnishings include a dresser and desk, plus telephone (local calls are free). Guests can get their video fix in the television room on the balcony. Singles are $40 to $45; doubles, $50 to $60; and the three suites, $75 to $85.

The adobe **Hacienda Inn,** South Santa Fe Road (P.O. Box 5751), Taos, NM 87571 (tel. 505/758-8610, or toll free 800/345-9158), has an Old West feel with its wooden columns, corbels, and railings. The 51 units have two queen-size beds and other standard furnishings, including cable TV with HBO, direct-dial phones (free local calls), rust-colored carpeting, and R. C. Gorman prints on the walls. There's an indoor swimming pool and hot tub in the grassy central courtyard. Year-round rates are $45 single, $50 double. Children under 12 stay free with a parent. Adjoining the hotel is the Far West Club, a weekend country-and-western lounge, and Magdalena's coffeeshop.

THE BUDGET RANGE: The **Adobe Wall Motel,** 415 Kit Carson Rd. (P.O. Box 1081), Taos, NM 87571 (tel. 505/758-3972), was once a stagecoach stop. Its 20 cozy older units have king- or queen-size beds, handmade Mexican furniture, leather-upholstered chairs, original Hispanic oils on the walls, and cable TVs with HBO. All rooms have showers; some also have baths. There are no private phones, but guests can use a pay phone in the lobby, where there's also a 24-hour desk with complimentary coffee, tea, and cider. Two units have kitchenettes. Rooms are $26 to $34 single, $34 to $40 double. Seniors get 10% discounts with AARP cards. Special skiers packages are available.

The **Indian Hills Inn,** South Santa Fe Road (P.O. Box 1229), Taos, NM 87571 (tel. 505/758-4293), shares space with the chamber of commerce, five to ten minutes' walk from the Plaza. The renovated adobe building has 50 well-lit units with a king-size bed or two queen-size beds and other standard furnishings, including regional art, cable TV with HBO, and free local phone calls. Rates are $30 to $47 single, $35 to $52 double, June to September; $5 less the rest of the year. Seven kitchen units are priced $10 higher. Behind the hotel are a swimming pool, picnic area, and public mini-golf course (50¢ admission). A spa is planned.

The **Sun God Lodge,** South Santa Fe Road (P.O. Box 1713), Taos, NM 87571 (tel. 505/758-3162), is a friendly family operation. An older white adobe structure with tan-and-brown trim, its 21 rooms have beige carpets, beamed ceilings with fans, double beds, cable TV with HBO and Discovery, phones (local calls are 25¢), and complimentary coffee in each room. Rates are $28 single, $38 double, in the off-season; $35 single, $45 double, in high season. There are outdoor grills and a hot-tub room. The 1½ acres of landscaped grounds have a significant jackrabbit population, attracting a variety of birds including owls. The motel has its own supply of fresh, clean well water. It's quite popular with AARP members.

The **Taos 6 Motel,** 4175 S. Santa Fe Rd. (P.O. Box 729), Ranchos de Taos, NM 87557 (tel. 505/758-2524, or toll free 800/323-6009), is a Spanish Colonial–style building with spiral pillars and corbels and a red-tile roofs. The 28 units are decorated in earth shades with white walls; they have double beds and built-in desk/dressers. All have cable TVs and free phones. An RV park, mini-golf course, laundry, and recreation room are planned. Free coffee is offered in the lobby from 6 a.m. to 11 p.m. Year-round rates are $28.75 to $32 weekdays, $32 to $36 weekends. Kids under 12 stay free in their parents' room, and other special rates apply.

One of Taos's most unusual accommodations is the **Laughing Horse Inn,** North Pueblo Road (P.O. Box 4904), Taos, NM 87571 (tel. 505/758-8350 or 758-0952). Occupying the former home and print shop of one Spud Johnson, a D. H. Lawrence and Alice B. Toklas contemporary who published literary and satiric tracts on his hand-set "Laughing Horse Press" in the 1920s and 1930s, it is an unmistakable white stucco structure with lilac-purple trim.

Guests can choose between bunks in sunny dorm rooms, cozy private rooms ($28 to $40 single, $30 to $45 double), or a deluxe solar-heated penthouse ($75 to $100). The nine private rooms, though small, are unique: beds are on sleeping lofts or carved from adobe, and some have fireplaces, cassette decks, and TVs with VCRs. Bathrooms are shared. The penthouse has a private solar bedroom, a separate enclosed double sleeping loft, a private bath, wood stove, big-screen TV, and video and audio decks.

The inn has a common room around a big fireplace, a games room, a video parlor, and a breakfast café where continental breakfasts are served for a modest additional charge. A hot tub is in an outdoor courtyard, and ten-speed touring bikes are free for guests' use.

The **Highland/Taos International Hostel,** on North Pueblo Road near Placitas Road (P.O. Box 613), El Prado, NM 87529 (tel. 505/758-1651 or 758-8340), is a very basic youth hostel. There are four bunks in each of two rooms, plus rollaways. Guests share a single bath and kitchen. Rates are $10 per night, $1 less for those with an International Youth Hostel card.

BED-AND-BREAKFASTS

Some two dozen bed-and-breakfasts are listed with the Taos Chamber of Commerce. The **Taos Bed & Breakfast Association** (tel. 505/758-9767, or toll free 800/821-2437) will provide information and make reservations for member homes. **Old Taos Bed & Breakfast Inns,** P.O. Box Q, Taos, NM 87571 (tel. 505/758-0497, or toll free 800/448-INNS), has a more selective listing.

The following are some of my favorites:

Casa de Las Chimeneas, Cordoba Lane at Los Pandos Road (P.O. Box 5303), Taos, NM 87571 (tel. 505/758-4777), qualifies as Taos's Luxury B&B. Its three rooms, each of them a work of art, look out on a beautifully landscaped private garden. The two-room suite incorporates an old library and two fireplaces; it is furnished with marble-topped antique furniture, lace linen, sheepskin mattress pads, brass bathroom fixtures, and a Mexican pewter chandelier. The Blue Room and Willow Room have their own similar charm. Each room has its own 50-gallon hot-water heater; guests can also use the casa's hot tub. Fine art is for sale in the office area, where a full native breakfast is served daily. Year-round rates are $85 single, $95 double, for the smaller rooms, and $125 for the suite. Three more rooms are planned.

Casa Europa, Upper Ranchitos Road (Los Cordovas Route, Box 157), Taos, NM 87571 (tel. 505/758-9798), is a cream-colored, Mediterranean-style pueblo home built of adobe and *vigas* 200 years ago, and fully renovated in 1983. The five elegant rooms, each with full private bath, vary in furnishings: the Red Room, for example, has a marble whirlpool and enamel wood stove; the Spa Room has a full-size Jacuzzi and fireplace, with glass doors opening onto a courtyard; the Apartment has a full kitchen and a living room with a *kiva* fireplace.

In fact, there are eight fireplaces and 14 skylights in Casa Europa. Regional artwork in the rooms is available for purchase. Smoking is not permitted. Guests often gather in the sitting room for reading and/or conversation. A full or continental breakfast is served each morning; coffee and pastries are offered each afternoon in the sitting room, and après-ski hors d'oeuvres are also available. Rates are $55 to $95 per room for two. Casa Europa is 1.7 miles from the Plaza.

Across the street from the Kit Carson Home and Museum, half a block from the Plaza, is **El Rincon B&B,** 110 E. Kit Carson Rd. (P.O. Drawer Q), Taos, NM 87571 (tel. 505/758-4874 or 758-9188). The former home of 19th-century cultural leader La Dona Luz Lucero de Martinez, this inn has seven rooms in two 100-year-old dwellings separated by a flower-filled courtyard where breakfast is served in warm weather. Fine art and hand-carved furniture are scattered through both houses.

All rooms have private baths, coffee pots, and TVs with VCRs; five have *kiva* fireplaces, and most also have small refrigerators. Hostess Nina Meyers, an artist, has added trim and other decorations in her happy and colorful style. The largest room, No. 1, up a steep spiral staircase in the Hain House, has a sundeck, hot tub, and additional sleeping loft to accommodate up to six guests. In the Lucero home, No. 6 is an adobe room with a South Asian theme typified by its hand-carved teak woodwork, East Indian paisley linens, and Balinese artifacts. No. 7 in the same building has a frontier theme; its furniture is made of pine logs and barn wood, and the room is filled with oldtime artifacts, including a Franklin stove and clawfoot tub. Adjacent to the B&B is the Original Trading Post of Taos, still run by Rowena Martinez, widow of Indian trader and founder Ralph Meyers.

Rooms are $45 to $55 for two, except No. 1, which is $75 for two, $115 for four. Children are charged the same rate as adults.

La Posada de Taos, 309 Juanita Lane (P.O. Box 1118), Taos, NM 87571 (tel. 505/758-8164), has space for 17 guests in four rooms and a self-contained honeymoon cottage. Each of the small but charming units has a tiled private bath and is decorated with an international array of art and furnishings. La Casa, the cottage, has its own kitchen, fireplace, and double bed in a loft with a skylight. The Beautler Suite has a double bed and two twins, plus a wood stove, a Jacuzzi, and a game table. Two of the other units also have a stove or fireplace. Rates are $46 to $79 double, $8 extra for additional guests. Room charges include a hearty breakfast.

The **Mabel Dodge Luhan House,** Morada Lane (P.O. Box 3400), Taos, NM 87571 (tel. 505/758-9456), is called Las Palomas de Taos because of the throngs of doves (*palomas*) that live in bird condominiums on the property. Like so many other free spirits, they were attracted by the flamboyant Mabel Luhan (1879–1962), who came to Taos in 1916 (after spells in Florence and New York) as "the most common denominator that society, literature, art, and radical revolutionaries ever found," according to a Chicago newspaper.

Mabel and her fourth husband, a full-blooded Pueblo Indian named Tony Luhan, set out to complete the vision of Taos as a creative Eden. She imported writers like D. H. Lawrence and Willa Cather, painters like Georgia O'Keeffe and John Marin, and activists like John Collier. Their headquarters was this 200-year-old home, which Mabel and Tony enlarged to its present 22-room size in the 1920s. Incorporating elements of various cultural traditions, the house's Spanish Colonial–style portal and flagstone placita are hidden behind an adobe wall and shaded by huge hardwood trees. All main rooms have *viga-latilla* ceilings, arched pueblo-style doorways, hand-carved Hispanic doors, *kiva* fireplaces, and dark hardwood floors. The house is a New Mexico state historic site and is listed on the National Register of Historic Places.

Ten rooms are rented out at bed-and-breakfast prices of $55 to $85 per night. Doubles and twins all have antique furnishings. Six rooms have fireplaces; baths are private or shared. Some are named for the well-known arts figures who stayed here.

For much of the year Las Palomas is an educational center, sponsoring workshops and other programs in global education, student leadership, art, and culture. Some courses carry college credit. During workshop periods, B&B rooms are generally reserved for attendees.

Other preferred B&Bs include the **American Artist Gallery House,** Frontier Road (P.O. Box 584), Taos, NM 87571 (tel. 505/758-4446); the **Brooks Street Inn,** 207 Brooks St. (P.O. Box 4964), Taos, NM 87571 (tel. 505/758-1489); **Hacienda del Sol,** P.O. Box 177, Taos, NM 87571 (tel. 505/758-0287); **The Suite Retreat,** La Loma Plaza (P.O. Box 85), Taos, NM 87571 (tel. 505/758-3960); and **Two Pipe,** Box 52, Talpa Route, Ranchos de Taos, NM 87557 (tel. 505/758-4770). All have rooms priced between $40 and $70.

ACCOMMODATIONS IN TAOS SKI VALLEY

The ski area, 18 miles from the town of Taos at 9,207 feet elevation, has numerous accommodations both at the foot of the slopes and along the approach road.

DELUXE CHOICES: The **Hotel Edelweiss,** Taos Ski Valley, NM 87525 (tel. 505/776-2301), is a quiet, elegant hotel offering family-style accommodations directly on the ski slopes. French cuisine is offered for breakfast and lunch. The 20 units are priced from $125 to $150 a night, double.

Kandahar Condominiums, Taos Ski Valley, NM 87525 (tel. 505/776-2226), have the highest location on the slopes—and with it, ski-in/ski-out access. Facilities include an exercise room, steamroom, Jacuzzi, professional masseur, TVs in all rooms, and laundry. There are 27 units at $98 to $180 double, nightly.

The two-story **Twining Condominiums,** P.O. Box 696, Taos Ski Valley, NM 87525 (tel. 505/776-8648), have fireplaces, color TVs, fully equipped kitchens with dishwashers, and a hot tub. The main lift area is just a three-minute walk away. The 18 studios and two-bedroom units are priced at $110 to $235.

The pueblo-style **Hacienda de San Roberto,** P.O. Box 5751, Taos, NM 87571 (tel. 505/776-2218), is off Ski Valley Road about eight miles toward Taos. Each unit has a fully furnished kitchen with microwave oven, fireplace with firewood provided, queen-size beds, and color TV. There are outdoor hot tubs and daily maid service. The 13 units are $80 to $240.

THE UPPER BRACKET: An International Jazz Festival is hosted annually for three weeks in January by the **Thunderbird Lodge,** P.O. Box 87, Taos Ski Valley, NM 87525 (tel. 505/776-2280). Located 150 yards from the slopes on the north ("sunny") side of the valley, its extras include a sauna and Jacuzzi, a superb restaurant with a huge wine cellar, and nightly entertainment in the bar. Packages are available. The rate of $94 to $116 double for its 32 units includes three meals daily.

Rio Hondo Condominiums, Taos Ski Valley, NM 87525 (tel. 505/776-2646), have two- to four-bedroom, two-bath apartments with fully equipped kitchens, living rooms with fireplaces, TV, and stereo. They have ski-in/lift-out access and ski storage. The 16 units, priced at $85 to $120, are also open in the summer at discount rates.

Sierra del Sol Condominiums, P.O. Box 84, Taos Ski Valley, NM 87525 (tel. 505/776-2981, or toll free 800/523-3954), are just a two-minute walk from the lifts. Each of the 32 condo units has a fully equipped kitchen, fireplace, TV, and balcony. Two hot tubs and saunas are on the premises. Two-bedroom units sleep up to seven; one-bedrooms and studios are also available. Rates run $84 to $120.

Austing Haus, Taos Ski Valley Road (P.O. Box 8), Taos Ski Valley, NM 87525 (tel. 505/776-2649 or 776-2629), has a hot tub, satellite TV in the lobby, and house phone for guests' use, as well as a restaurant. There are 14 units priced at $75.

The **Anizette Inn,** Taos Ski Valley Road (P.O. Box 756), Taos, NM 87571 (tel. 505/776-2451, or toll free 800/233-8958), has a hot tub and redwood sauna, color TV, tanning deck, and full-service restaurant. The 12 units, priced at $57 to $139, are open in winter only.

MODERATELY PRICED ACCOMMODATIONS: You'll
get the lowest rates on the mountain in casual, comfortable accommodations at the **Innsbruck Lodge & Condos,** Taos Ski Valley, NM 87525 (tel. 505/776-2313). There are TVs in all 24 rooms, and other facilities include a games room, exercise room, and whirlpool. The Ski School meeting place is 400 yards away; the main lifts are about half a mile. Rates vary between $57 and $89.

Taos East Condominiums, Ski Valley Road (P.O. Box 657), Taos Ski Valley, NM 87525 (tel. 505/758-1708, or toll free 800/238-7669), have 11 year-round units priced from $63. Each condo has a color TV, fireplace, phone, full kitchen with microwave, and daily maid service. There's also a laundry and hot tub.

BUDGET CHOICES: The name itself entices many younger
people to the **Abominable Snowmansion Skiers' Hostel,** Taos Ski Valley Road (P.O. Box 3271), Taos, NM 87571 (tel. 505/776-8298). Located in the small community of Arroyo Seco, about eight miles from Taos and ten miles from the ski resort, this seasonal lodging is clean and comfortable for those happy with dormitory-style accommodation. Lavatories, shower rooms, and dressing rooms are segregated by sex. A two-story lodge room focuses around a circular fireplace, and features a piano and games area. The price, $15 to $28 per person, includes home-cooked meals. Capacity is 75.

CAMPGROUNDS / RV PARKS
Four privately owned facilities are located within easy reach of Taos. They are:

Sierra Village Campground, east in Taos Canyon on U.S. 64 (Rte. 1, Box 12), Taos, NM 87571 (tel. 505/758-3660). Cost is $8.

Taos Mid-Town RV Park, South Santa Fe Road (P.O. Box 3273), Taos, NM 87571 (tel. 505/758-1327). There are 25 units behind a Taco Bell restaurant. Rates are $8 to $12.

Taos Wagons West, 12 miles east on U.S. 64 (P.O. Box 1803), Taos, NM 87571 (tel. 505/758-1088). Price is $13.

Taos Valley RV Park, 1,000 feet east of N.M. 68 on Este Es Road (P.O. Box 200), Ranchos de Taos, NM 87557 (tel. 505/758-4469). Sites cost $9.75 to $12.75.

Information on nearby public forest sites can be obtained from **Carson National Forest,** P.O. Box 558, Taos, NM 87571 (tel. 505/758-6200), or the **Bureau of Land Management,** P.O. Box 6168, Taos, NM 87571 (tel. 505/758-8851).

There are nine national forest campsites within 20 miles of

Taos, all opening in April or May and remaining open—depending on snow conditions—until September, October, or November. Largest of them, and the only fee area ($5), is **La Sombra,** with 13 sites at 7,800 feet elevation eight miles east of town on U.S. 64 en route to Angel Fire. There are two other recreation areas with campsites along U.S. 64, four and seven miles from Taos; five small campgrounds between 12 and 20 miles from town along Taos Ski Valley Road (N.M. 150); and another, **Cebolla Mesa,** on the Rio Grande, off N.M. 3 near Questa, 14 miles north of Taos. Contact the national forest office for more details.

CHAPTER IX

THE RESTAURANTS OF TAOS

□ □ □

Some, but not all, of Taos's best restaurants are in its hotels. Certainly **Doc Martin's,** in the Taos Inn, ranks among the best, as do **Carl's French Quarter** at the Quail Ridge Inn and **Café Fennel** in the Ramada (see Chapter VIII). Here are others, categorized as nearly as possible by type of cuisine, that stand on their own merits.

REGIONAL CUISINE: Under the same ownership for 35 years, **La Cocina de Taos,** North Plaza (tel. 758-2412), has developed a loyal local following. Old-fashioned fan/lamps hang from the high ceiling, enhancing the room's spacious appearance. Decorative wrought iron and stained glass act as room dividers. Specialties include chicken mole poblano (marinated in chocolate-chile sauce) and carne adovada (pork roast baked in red chile), each $10. Mexican dinners start at $6.50; beef and seafood dishes are priced at $12.50 to $15. Children's dinners—sirloin, fish, or a taco—cost just $4. Luncheon diners enjoy stuffed sopaipillas ($6), green chile omelets ($6.25), or burgers and other sandwiches (from $4.25). La Cocina is open every day but Christmas from 11 a.m. to 9 p.m., with hours extended to 10 p.m. in ski season.

La Parranda Room, a tiled Mexican bar with an entrance off the municipal parking lot on Bent Street, is open daily from 11 a.m. to midnight. A guitarist performs Thursday through Sunday from 6 to 10 p.m.

La Ultima, 704 S. Santa Fe Rd. (tel. 758-3340), is a new gourmet Mexican eatery, casual and elegant, with spiraled pillars, hanging plants in front of big picture windows, glass-top tables, and piped-in mariachi music. Combinations start at $6; specialties like fajitas and camarones (prawns) Vera Cruz are priced about $8.50. Open from 11 a.m. to 9 p.m. on Sunday and Tuesday through Thursday, to 10 p.m. on Friday and Saturday; closed Monday.

Chile Connection, Ski Valley Road, one mile east of N.M. 3 (tel. 776-8787), is a sprawling pink adobe building with a large outside patio, next to the Quail Ridge Inn. Meals are priced from $6; house specials such as crab rellenos, shrimp chimechangas, and pollo borracho or "drunken chicken" (char-broiled half chicken in a sauce of wine, ham, capers, olives, and raisins), are each $10. Margarita pie, the house favorite at $3.50, is made with tequila, Cointreau, and fresh lime juice. There's a full bar with weekend entertainment. Dinner is served from 6 to 10 p.m. nightly except Christmas.

NOUVELLE CUISINE: Classical and baroque music pervades the four elegant adobe rooms of the **Apple Tree Restaurant,** 26 Bent St., one block north of the Plaza (tel. 758-1900). Original paintings by Taos masters overlook the candlelit, white-linen service.

Daily specials supplement a standing menu. Featured appetizers are spinach piñon salad ($2.50 and $4.50) and smoked trout with sun-dried tomatoes ($5). Entrees include New Mexican meals like chicken avocado tacos in blue-corn tortillas ($7.50), continental dishes like shrimp provençal ($12); fresh seafood like Utah trout in a spinach-mushroom-cream sauce ($13.25), and desert lamb in red wine sauce with pasta ($17). Vegetarians are catered to with such meals as tofu and steamed vegetables in Szechwan peanut sauce ($8) and pasta Liguria ($8). There's a limited children's menu. There are homemade desserts, featured wines, and cappuccinos. Meals are served daily from 11:30 a.m. to 3 p.m. and 7:30 to 9 p.m.

STEAKS AND SEAFOOD: On East Plaza, **Ogelvie's Bar & Grill** (tel. 758-8866) has the same menu and style as Ogelvie's in Santa Fe and Albuquerque. A casual restaurant with rich wood décor, it serves lunch, dinner, and a late-night bar menu. Homemade soups start at $2.25; burgers and other sandwiches, from $4; huevos de casa Ogelvie's, $4.75. Dinners, placing emphasis on regional preparations of poultry, steak, and seafood, go for $9.50 to $14.50. The restaurant is open daily in summer from 10 a.m. to 4 p.m. and 5 to 10:30 p.m.; in winter, 11 a.m. to 4 p.m. and 5 to 10 p.m.

Floyd's Restaurant, South Santa Fe Road (tel. 758-4142), has steak dinners from $8.50 and Mexican lunches from $4.75.

It's a casual spot, with rich red décor and wood-paneled walls. There's live music here weekend and other nights. Open daily from 8:30 a.m. to 11:30 p.m.

Sam's Smokehaus, South Santa Fe Road (tel. 758-2357), prides itself on its Texas-style barbecued meats. "Don't mess with Texas!" proclaims a sign on the wall. All meats are smoked, all foods homemade. Beef rib plates run $7 with beans, corn on the cob, and potato salad. A New Braunfels sausage roll is $3.75. There's also chicken, ham, and more. Sam's occupies a former square-dance hall built in 1941 of railroad ties and plaster; today the music is piped-in country-and-western. Diners can sup in front of the big flagstone fireplace, or eat outside in summer. Open from 11 a.m. to 9 p.m. Monday through Saturday.

CONTINENTAL: The **Brett House,** on Taos Ski Valley Road at N.M. 3 (tel. 776-8545), is one of Taos's exclusive restaurants. Artist Dorothy Brett (1883–1977), a confidante of D. H. and Frieda Lawrence, lived here for the last 31 years of her life. Today original art and photography share space on stuccoed walls with hanging vines, under a beamed ceiling. Classical guitar music mellows diners as they absorb a spectacular sunset view of the Sangre de Cristo range.

The menu varies according to the fresh ingredients available. Appetizers typically include escargots in a phyllo nest with spinach ($6.25) and pasta Alfredo with New Zealand mussels ($6.25). Entrees, with soup and salad, may feature a fish dish like baked orange roughy with shrimp sauce ($14.25), Colorado rack of lamb with piñon-mint sauce ($23), roast Muscovy duck breast with tangerine glaze and dried apricots ($17), or skewered pork tenderloin with tomatillo salsa ($15). An extensive list of fine wines is offered.

Lunch is served mid-June to October only, from 11:30 a.m. to 2 p.m. daily; dinner is offered year round from 6 to 9 p.m., daily except Monday and during April and two weeks of November. Sunday brunch (11:30 a.m. to 2:30 p.m.) is popular. Patio dining is a summer option. Reservations are recommended. Nonsmokers beware: there's no special section set aside.

ITALIAN: The **Casa Cordova,** on Taos Ski Valley Road in Arroyo Seco, 4½ miles east of N.M. 3 (tel. 776-2200), is a little out of the way—except for skiers returning to town—but it's the Taos area's most popular restaurant featuring northern Italian cuisine. Steaks, seafood, and poultry dinners, including pasta side dishes, are priced between $15 and $25. The wild mushroom appetizer is regionally famous. A children's menu is available.

Casa Cordova is open from 6 to 9:30 p.m. Monday through Saturday (Thursday through Saturday only, in April and May);

closed Sunday, November 15 to December 15, and Christmas Day. Cocktail service begins at 4:30 p.m. Reservations are advised.

In town, you'll get Mediterranean food at **Joe Mama's,** in Pueblo Alegre Mall on South Santa Fe Road near the chamber of commerce (tel. 758-7200). Midday meals include Greek salads from $4, homemade soups at $1.75 a bowl, and Italian steak sandwiches at $3.75. Eggplant parmesan is $5; calzone, $5.75; spinach pie, $4.25; pastas, no higher than $6. Full veal, scampi, chicken, or fish dinners are priced between $6.50 and $10. Open from 11 a.m. to 9 p.m. daily.

BUDGET DINING: A few blocks north of the Plaza on North Pueblo Road, **Michael's Kitchen** (tel. 758-4178) is a throwback to earlier days. Between its hardwood floor and *viga* ceiling, from which hang ornate fans, are various knickknacks on posts, walls, and windows: a deer head here, a Tiffany lamp there, several scattered antique wood stoves. A painted mural of rural theme occupies the back wall. Seating is at booths and tables.

Meals, too, are old-fashioned, if you consider quality and quantity for price to be other than the norm today. Breakfast, served all day long, might be a tortilla renanada (diced ham and scrambled eggs with chives, wrapped in a flour tortilla and covered with green chile and cheese; $5.25) or pecan pancakes ($3.75). Luncheon sandwiches run $2.25 to $6.50. Dinners, with soup or salad, vegetable, and roll, include fish and chips ($6.25), pork chops ($6.75), and an 11-ounce New York steak ($9.75). There's a kids' menu with lunches from $1.75; dinners, from $4. Open daily from 7 a.m. to 8:30 p.m.

Dori's Bakery & Café, on North Pueblo Road next door to the Taos Post Office (tel. 758-9222), offers breakfasts, including eggs, pancakes, or granola and yogurt, served all day. Deli sandwiches are popular lunch fare. French pastries are homemade daily. Open weekdays from 7:30 a.m. to 2:30 p.m., on Saturday to noon, and on Sunday from 9 a.m. to 1 p.m. for brunch.

El Taoseno Restaurant, South Santa Fe Road (tel. 758-9511), is a long-established local diner-style café with a jukebox in the corner and a games room for kids. Breakfast burritos and huevos rancheros are just $3; daily lunch specials like barbecued chicken or a tamale plate cost $3.75; full dinners are priced under $6. Open daily from 5:30 a.m. to 9 p.m.

The **Mainstreet Bakery,** 1½ blocks from the Taos Plaza in Guadalupe Plaza, Placitas Road (tel. 758-9610), has become possibly Taos's biggest counterculture hangout. That image is fostered by the cuisine—strictly vegetarian and seafood—and the wide selection of newspapers, magazines, and other reading material advocating alternative lifestyles.

Whatever your lifestyle, the food is good and healthy. Fare includes sandwiches like smoked salmon ($5.50), an avocado melt ($4.75), and a tempeh burger ($4). The Mainstreet salad ($4) is a potpourri of carrots, red cabbage, broccoli, tomato, red onion, sunflower seeds, lettuce, and sprouts. Black-bean/green-chile soup with cornbread is $3.50 a bowl; stir-fried tofu and vegetables with brown rice, $4.75. Vegetarian tostadas, burritos, and enchiladas are priced at $4. Fresh fruit juices and coffee are also offered. Meals are served from 7:30 a.m. to 2 p.m. daily except Saturday; the bakery end of the operation is open until 5 p.m.

FAST FOOD: Fast-food junkies will be pleased to know Taos has its fair share of drive-throughs and the like, mainly on South Santa Fe Road. They include two outlets of Blake's Lota Burger and one each of Arby's, Kentucky Fried Chicken, McDonald's, Sonic, Taco Bell, and Tastee Freez.

Mount Wheeler Pizza on Placitas Road (tel. 758-1922), has a good reputation for take-outs; there are also a Pizza Hut and Big Cheese Pizza in town.

CHAPTER X

WHAT TO SEE AND DO IN TAOS

□ □ □

With a history steeped in the influences of pre-Columbian civilization, Spanish colonialism, and the Wild West, an array of outdoor activities ranging from ballooning to world-class skiing, and a healthy portion of modern culture, Taos has something to offer almost everybody.

THE SIGHTS

THE TAOS PUEBLO: No other site is as important or as famous in Taos as the Taos Pueblo. It has been the home of Tiwa Indians for more than 900 years. The northernmost of New Mexico's 19 pueblo communities, its two massive, multistoried adobe structures appear much the same today as they did when a regiment from Coronado's expedition first saw them in 1540. The distinctive, flowing lines of shaped mud with a straw-and-mud exterior plaster are typical of pueblo architecture everywhere throughout the Southwest.

Though the Tiwa were essentially a peaceful agrarian people, they are better remembered as having spearheaded the only (temporarily) successful rebellion by Native Americans in United States history. The revolt launched here in 1680 succeeded in driving the Spanish from Santa Fe until 1693, and from Taos until 1698. Despite the bloodshed, native culture and religion have persisted.

Today the tiny Rio Pueblo de Taos still trickles through the pueblo. The community has a population of 1,500, and is located about three miles north of Taos via a turnoff to the east just to the north of the Kachina Lodge. Arts and crafts and other tourism-related businesses support the economy, along with government services and ranching and farming. Despite the inflow of funds, however, the pueblo still does without electricity and running water.

Visitors to the pueblo are asked to check in at the **Taos Pueblo Visitor Center** (tel. 758-9593) upon arrival. You'll be assessed an admission fee of $6 per vehicle or $2 per person, and there is an additional charge to carry a camera: $5 for a still camera, $10 for a video camera, and a $25 charge for sketching or painting. The pueblo is open daily from 8:30 a.m. to 6 p.m. in summer, 9 a.m. to 4 p.m. in winter.

In the center are exhibits of traditional dress and home life of the pueblo, plus historic photographs from the late 19th century to more recent times.

As you explore the pueblo and absorb insights into its people's lifestyle, you can visit artists' studios, munch on homemade oven bread, look into the new San Geronimo Chapel, and wander past the fascinating ruins of the old church and cemetery. You're expected to ask permission from individuals before photographing them; some ask a small payment, but that's for you to negotiate. *Kivas* and other ceremonial underground areas are out-of-bounds for visitors.

Visitors are invited to attend—but not to photograph—the **seasonal dances** at the pueblo. The most important take place at sundown September 29, on the eve of San Geronimo Day (September 30). San Geronimo is the patron saint of the Taos Pueblo, and his feast day combines Catholic and pre-Hispanic traditions. The San Geronimo Day Trade Fair is a joyous occasion, with foot races, pole climbs, and crafts booths.

Other dances include the Turtle Dance on New Year's Day; the Deer or Buffalo Dance (January 6); and corn dances for Santa Cruz Day (May 3), San Antonio Day (June 13), San Juan Day (June 24), Santiago Day (July 23), and Santa Ana Day (July 24).

The annual **Taos Pueblo Pow Wow,** an Indian dance parade and competition featuring visitors from all over North America, is held the weekend following Fourth of July on reservation land off N.M. 3 north of Taos.

Bonfires are lit throughout the pueblo on Christmas Eve, marking the start of the Children's Corn Dance, the Christmas Day Deer Dance, or the three-day-long Matachina Dance. Procession of the Virgin follows vespers on Christmas Eve.

MUSEUMS: What may be Taos's most interesting collection is housed in the **Millicent Rogers Museum,** four miles north of town off N.M. 3 (tel. 758-2462). The museum was founded in 1953 by family members after the death of Millicent Rogers, a wealthy Taos émigrée who compiled a magnificent array of aesthetically beautiful Native American arts and crafts beginning in 1947. Included are Navajo and Pueblo jewelry, Navajo textiles, Pueblo pottery, Hopi and Zuñi *kachina* dolls, paintings from the Rio Grande Pueblo people, and basketry from a wide variety of southwestern tribes. The collection continues to grow through gifts and museum acquisitions.

Since the 1970s the scope of the museum's permanent collection has been expanded to include Hispanic religious and secular arts and crafts, from Spanish and Mexican colonial to contemporary times. Included are *santos* (religious images), furniture, weavings, *colcha* embroideries, and decorative tinwork. Agricultural implements, domestic utensils, and craftsmen's tools dating from the 17th and 18th centuries are also displayed.

The museum gift shop has a fine collection of superior regional art. Temporary exhibits, classes and workshops, lectures, and field trips are scheduled throughout the year.

The Millicent Rogers Museum is open May 1 to October 1 daily from 9 a.m. to 5 p.m., and November 1 to April 30 Wednesday through Sunday from 10 a.m. to 4 p.m. It's closed Easter, San Geronimo Day (September 30), Thanksgiving, Christmas, and New Year's Days. Admission is $3 for adults, $1 for children 6 to 16 and seniors 65 and older, and $6 for families.

Three historical homes are operated as museums by the **Kit Carson Memorial Foundation** (tel. 758-0505), affording glimpses of early Taos lifestyles. The Kit Carson Home, Ernest Blumenschein Home, and Martinez Hacienda have their individual appeal. Package admissions are available: whereas adults pay $2.50 to see one museum, the price is $4 for two or $5.50 for three. Children 6 to 16 pay $1.50 for one, $2.50 for three; seniors pay $2 for one, $4 for all three. Family and group rates are also available. All three museums are open daily except Thanksgiving, Christmas, and New Year's Days.

Kit Carson Home and Museum of the West, East Kit Carson Road, one block from the Plaza intersection (tel. 758-4741), is the town's only general museum of Taos history. This 12-room adobe home with walls 2½ feet thick was built in 1825 and purchased in 1843 by Carson, the famous mountain man, Indian agent, and scout, as a wedding gift for his young bride, Josefa Jaramillo. It remained their home for 25 years, until both died (a month to the day apart) in 1868.

A living room, bedroom, and kitchen are furnished as they might have been when occupied by the Carsons. The chapel has an interesting collection of Hispanic religious articles. The Indian

Room and Spanish Room contain artifacts of those two cultures; the Early American Room has an array of pioneer items, including a large number of antique firearms and trappers' implements; and the Carson Room presents memorabilia from Carson's unusual life.

The museum bookshop, with a plethora of information on the man and his era, is adjacent to the entry. Hours are 8 a.m. to 6 p.m. (9 a.m. to 5 p.m. in winter).

The **Ernest L. Blumenschein Home & Museum,** 1½ blocks southwest of the Plaza on Ledoux Street (tel. 758-0330), helps recreate the lifestyle of one of the co-founders (in 1915) of the Taos Society of Artists. This adobe home with garden walls and a courtyard—parts of which date to the 1790s—was for the home and studio of Blumenschein (1874–1960) and his family beginning in 1919. Period furnishings include European antiques and handmade Taos furniture in the Spanish Colonial style.

Blumenschein's arrival in Taos in 1898 came somewhat by accident. After having trained in New York and Paris, he and fellow painter Bert Phillips were on assignment for *McClure's* magazine of New York when a wheel of their wagon broke during a mountain traverse 30 miles north of Taos. Blumenschein drew the short straw and carried the wheel by horseback to Taos for repair. He later recounted his initial reaction to the valley he entered: "No artist had ever recorded the New Mexico I was now seeing. No writer had ever written down the smell of this air or the feel of that morning sky. I was receiving . . . the first great unforgettable inspiration of my life. My destiny was being decided."

That spark later led to the foundation of Taos as an art colony. An extensive collection of work by early-20th-century Taos masters is on display in several rooms of the home; changing exhibits are also featured. Among the modern works are paintings by Blumenschein's daughter, Helen Greene Blumenschein, now 80; she still keeps a studio and apartment here. Hours for visiting the home and museum are 9 a.m. to 5 p.m. (10 a.m. to 4 p.m. in winter).

The only remaining colonial Spanish hacienda in the United States is two miles southwest of the Plaza on Ranchitos Road. The **Martinez Hacienda** (tel. 758-1000) was the home of merchant and trader Don Antonio Severino Martinez, who bought it in 1804 and lived there until his death in 1827.

Located on the west bank of the Rio Pueblo de Taos, the hacienda was built like a fortress—with thick adobe walls and no exterior windows—to protect against Plains Indian raids. It had 21 rooms built around two *placitas* (interior courtyards). Most of the rooms open today contain period furnishings: they include the family room, bedrooms, kitchen, storage rooms and pantries, servants' quarters, stables, and even a large party room. Exhibits in one newly renovated room tell the story of the Martinez family and life in Spanish Taos between 1598 and 1821, when Mexico assumed control.

Don Antonio Martinez, who for a time was *alcalde* (mayor) of Taos, owned several caravans which he used in trade on the Chihuahua Trail to Mexico. This business was carried on by his youngest son, Don Juan Pascual, who later owned the hacienda. His eldest son was Padre Antonio José Martinez, northern New Mexico's controversial spiritual leader from 1826 to 1867.

The Kit Carson Foundation is developing a living museum at the museum with weavers, blacksmiths, and other artisans. Currently it's in effect only two weekends of the year—for Spanish arts weekend during the Taos Spring Fair (the second weekend of June), and for the Old Taos Trade Fair (in late September or early October). The latter recalls days when Pueblo, Navajo, and Plains Indians, having completed their harvests, met here to trade with the Spanish, American trappers, and others.

Regular hours at the hacienda are 9 a.m. to 5 p.m. (10 a.m. to 4 p.m. in winter).

Some of the finest works of art produced in or about Taos hang on the walls of the **Harwood Public Library and Museum of Taos Art,** 25 Ledoux St. (tel. 758-3063). A cultural and community center since 1923, the pueblo-style complex is appointed with Spanish Colonial furnishings and adorned with a variety of crafts, paintings, and sculpture.

Eight of the ten founding fathers of the Taos Society of Artists are represented in the museum, along with many of their contemporaries. Among them was Burt Harwood (1857–1922), in whose memory the foundation was established. The Spanish folk-art collection includes more than 80 19th-century *retablos,* or religious paintings on wood, a gift of Mabel Dodge Luhan; and the remarkable woodcarvings of Patrocinio Barela (1908–1964).

The library contains a general collection for Taos residents; a children's library; and special collections on the Southwest and Taos art. Dozens of programs and performances are scheduled throughout the year in the auditorium and adjacent meeting rooms.

The Harwood Library is open from 10 a.m. to 5 p.m. Monday through Friday and 10 a.m. to 4 p.m. on Saturday; closed Sunday and holidays. Admission is free.

The **Governor Bent House Museum,** half a block from the Plaza on Bent Street (tel. 758-2376), was the residence of Charles Bent, New Mexico's first American governor, who was killed in the 1847 Indian and Hispanic rebellion. Containing artifacts and art of the period, it's open daily from 9 a.m. to 5 p.m. in summer, 10 a.m. to 4 p.m. in winter, with admission of $1 for adults, 50¢ for children.

The **Fechin Institute,** on North Pueblo Road (tel. 758-1710), was the home of Russian artist Nikolai Fechin in the 1920s and 1930s. Fechin embellished the adobe house with unusual Russian-style woodcarvings. His art is shown annually for two weeks in September and October; in other months the house is open only from 1 to 5:30 p.m. on Saturday and Sunday, and by appointment. Suggested donation is $3.

OTHER ATTRACTIONS: From N.M. 68 four miles south of Taos, the **San Francisco de Asis Church** in Ranchos de Taos appears as a modernesque adobe sculpture with no doors or windows. It's often photographed and painted (by the likes of Georgia O'Keeffe) from this angle. Visitors must walk through the garden on the west side of this remarkable two-story church to enter and get a full perspective on its massive walls, authentic adobe plaster, and beauty.

On one interior wall is an unusual painting, *The Shadow of the Cross* by Henri Ault (1896). Under ordinary light it portrays a barefoot Christ at the Sea of Galilee; in darkness, however, the portrait becomes luminescent, and the perfect shadow of a cross forms over the left shoulder of Jesus's silhouette. The artist reportedly was as shocked as everyone else. The reason for the illusion remains a mystery.

The church office (tel. 758-2754) and gift shop are just across the driveway to the north of the church. The square is surrounded by several crafts shops.

Visitors may attend mass on Saturday at 5:30 p.m., or on Sunday at 7 a.m. (in Spanish), 9 a.m., or 11:30 a.m.

Kit Carson Park and Cemetery, one block north of the Taos Inn on North Pueblo Road, contains the graves of Carson and his wife, Gov. Charles Bent, the Don Antonio Martinez family, Mabel Dodge Luhan, and many other noted historical figures and artists. Plaques describe their contributions. Major community events are held in the park in the summer.

The impressive **Rio Grande Gorge Bridge,** 650 feet above the river, spans the chasm on U.S. 64 west of the Taos Airport, ten miles northwest of town. If you can withstand the vertigo, it's interesting to come more than once, at different times of day, and observe how the changing light plays tricks with the colors of the cliff walls.

The **D. H. Lawrence Ranch** (tel. 776-2245) might not be on everyone's list of "must" attractions, but it's a pilgrimage site for devotees of the controversial early-20th-century author. Located near San Cristobal, 15 miles north of Taos on N.M. 3 and another 6 miles east into the forested Sangre de Cristo range via a well-marked dirt road, it is operated today by the University of New Mexico as an educational and recreational retreat.

Lawrence's shrine is a short uphill walk from the ranch home. It is littered with various mementoes—photos, coins, messages from fortune cookies—placed by doting visitors. The guestbook is worth a long read. The grave of Lawrence's wife, Frieda, who died in 1956, is outside the shrine.

Lawrence lived in Taos off and on between 1922 and 1925. The ranch was a gift to Frieda from art patron Mabel Dodge Luhan. Lawrence repaid Luhan the favor by giving her the manuscript of *Sons and Lovers*.

SPECIAL EVENTS

The two big arts festivals—Taos Spring Arts Celebration in May-June and the Taos Arts Festival in September-October—are the main occasions of the year. The former, staged in conjunction with the chamber of commerce, tends to be focused more on the contemporary arts; the latter, on the traditional.

The **Taos Spring Arts Celebration** celebrates its seventh year May 26 to June 18, 1989. A three-week survey of contemporary visual, performing, and literary arts in Taos, it has numerous events scheduled daily throughout the town and county. They include gallery openings, studio tours, performances by visiting theater and dance troupes, live musical events, traditional ethnic entertainment, an Indian Market, a film festival, fashion shows, literary readings, and more. Special weekends are set aside for specific topics like Hispanic arts and Native American women's arts. The celebration is held simultaneously with the Santa Fe Festival. For information, contact the Taos Spring Arts Celebration, P.O. Box 1691, Taos, NM 87571 (tel. 505/758-0516).

The **Taos Arts Festival,** scheduled September 22 to October 8, 1989, is in its 15th year of sponsorship by the chamber of commerce. Highlights include "Taos Art Today," a juried exhibition; "Taos Invites Taos," an exhibit by 50 leading Taos artists working in various media; the annual "Art of Taos Pueblo" show at the Millicent Rogers Museum; and an open-air arts-and-crafts show on the Taos Plaza. Also planned are a jewelry exhibit and sale, a "food as art" show, a wool trade fair, gallery openings, studio tours, performing arts productions, lectures, films, concerts, dances, and more. For full information, contact the Taos Chamber of Commerce, P.O. Drawer I, Taos, NM 87571 (tel. 505/758-3873, or toll free 800/732-TAOS).

In conjunction with both arts festivals, a **"Meet the Artist"** series is held annually from May 15 to June 21 and October 15 to December 15 at the Taos Inn on North Pueblo Road (tel. 758-2233). Every Tuesday and Thursday at 8 p.m., visitors and locals meet with nationally known Taos artists to share in their work through demonstrations, slide shows, lectures, and videos.

Other significant annual events in Taos and their 1989 dates include:

Rodeo de Taos, June 23–25. Bronco riding, calf roping, bull riding, barrel racing, and other standard events take place at Sheriff's Posse Rodeo Arena, off South Santa Fe Road behind the Cruz Alta Shopping Center. Many of the West's leading cowboys compete for prize money.

Fiesta de Santiago y Santa Ana, July 21–23. Taos's Anglo, Hispanic, and Native American communities join to celebrate the feast days of Saints Santiago and Santa Ana. The fiesta begins with a Friday-night mass at Our Lady of Guadalupe Church, just west of the Plaza, followed by a candlelight procession to the Plaza, where the fiesta queen is crowned. There's a children's parade on Saturday, the "Historical-Hysterical Fiesta Parade" on Sunday, and all weekend, crafts and food booths in the Plaza and entertainment. For information, contact the Taos Fiesta Council, P.O. Box 3300, Taos, NM 87571 (tel. 505/758-0239).

Paul Bunyan Days, September 2–3. The 16th annual New Mexican chain-saw and loggers championship takes place in Angel Fire, 15 miles east of Taos, with lots of activities for kids. Call 505/377-6401 for details.

Wool Festival, September 30–October 1. Shearing and wool handcrafting demonstrations, spinning and fleecing competitions highlight this event, which runs from 9 a.m. to 5 p.m. both days at Kit Carson Memorial State Park in downtown Taos. Other events include an auction, a fashion show, music and entertainment, booths selling New Mexico and Colorado regional wools and wool products, and exhibitions of sheep, rabbits, goats, and llamas. For information, contact the Wool Festival, P.O. Box 2754, Taos, NM 87571 (tel. 505/758-9650).

The **Old Taos Trade Fair,** September 30 to October 1, coincides with San Geronimo Day at Taos Pueblo. Held at the historic Martinez Hacienda, it is a two-day reenactment of Spanish colonial life of the mid-1820s, with Hispanic and Indian music, dance, foods, weaving and crafts demonstrations and sales, muzzle-loading rifle demonstrations, and "visits" by mountain men. Contact the Kit Carson Foundation, P.O. Drawer CCC, Taos, NM 87571 (tel. 505/758-0505).

Taos Mountain Balloon Rally, October 19–22. In addition

to mass dawn ascensions by about 50 vibrantly colored balloons from Weimer Field, and tethered balloon rides for the public, there are a number of ground events—the foremost of which is a Saturday parade of balloon baskets (in pickup trucks) from Kit Carson Park around the Plaza. Country-and-western cabaret at the Kachina Lodge is big in the evening. Contact the Taos Mountain Balloon Rally Association, P.O. Box 6158, Taos, NM 87571 (tel. 505/758-8100).

A Taste of Taos: A Southwest Culinary Excursion, November 3–12. This event includes food and product fairs, a cooking school at the historic Mabel Dodge Luhan House, restaurant specialties, ice-carving demonstrations, an Epicurian Palette Display and Auction, Indian fry bread demonstrations, chili cookoffs, and creation of the "world's largest burrito." Contact the Taos Chamber of Commerce, P.O. Drawer I, Taos, NM 87571 (tel. 505/758-3873, or toll free 800/732-TAOS).

Yuletide in Taos, December 1–15. The Taos Spring Arts Celebration stages this pre-Christmas event, emphasizing New Mexican traditions, culture, and arts with Christmas carols, festive classical music, Indian and Hispanic songs and dance, historic walking tours, and more. The Taos Inn concludes its "Meet the Artist" series during the Yuletide celebration.

A variety of seasonal events are also held at Taos Pueblo and Taos Ski Valley (see "Outdoor Activities"). See the appropriate entries for details.

OUTDOOR ACTIVITIES

Taos County's 2,200 square miles embrace a great diversity of scenic beauty, from New Mexico's highest mountain, 13,161-foot Wheeler Peak, to the 650-foot chasm of the Rio Grande Gorge. Kit Carson National Forest, which extends right to the eastern city limits of Taos and cloaks a large part of the county, has hundreds of miles of hiking trails through the Sangre de Cristo range and contains several major ski areas.

Recreation sites are mainly in the national forest, where pines and aspen provide refuge for abundant wildlife (48 sites are accessible by road, including 38 with campsites). There are also sites on the high desert mesa, carpeted by sagebrush, cactus, and (frequently) wildflowers. Both terrains are favored by hunters, fishermen, and horseback riders. Two wilderness areas—Wheeler Peak and Latir Peak—are within a short drive of Taos. For full information, contact **Carson National Forest,** 112 Cruz Alta Road (P.O. Box 558), Taos, NM 87571 (tel. 505/758-6201), or the **Bureau of Land Management,** also on Cruz Alta Road (P.O. Box 6168), Santa Fe, NM 87571 (tel. 505/758-8851).

Reliable paved roads lead to takeoff points for side trips up poorer forest roads to many recreation sites. Once you get off the main roads, you won't find gas stations or cafés. Four-wheel-drive vehicles are recommended on snow and much of the otherwise unpaved terrain of the region. If you're doing some off-road adventuring, it's wise to go with a full gas tank, extra food and water, and warm clothing—just in case. At the more than 10,000-foot elevations of northern New Mexico, sudden summer snowstorms are not unusual. Outside the national forest, you may find yourself driving through small villages, so be sure to watch out for children, livestock, and others while observing the daily rituals of traditional rural life.

THE ENCHANTED CIRCLE: Access to many outdoor-recreation sites in the Taos area is via the 90-mile "Enchanted Circle" through Questa, Red River, Eagle Nest, and Angel Fire. This route, which incorporates portions of U.S. 64 and N.M. 3 and 38, can be driven in two hours round trip from Taos—but most folks take a full day, and many use several days, to accomplish it.

Traveling north from Taos via N.M. 3, it's a 24-mile drive to **Questa,** most of whose residents are employed at a molybdenum mine five miles east of town. En route north, the highway passes near **San Cristobal,** where a side road turns off to the D. H. Lawrence Ranch, and **Lama,** site of an isolated spiritual retreat.

If you turn west off N.M. 3 onto N.M. 378 about three miles north of Questa, you'll descend 11 miles on a gravel road into the gorge of the Rio Grande to **Rio Grande Gorge National Recreation Site.** Here, where the Red River enters the gorge, is the most accessible starting point for river-rafting trips through the infamous Taos Box. Some 48 miles of the river, south from the Colorado border, are protected under the national Wild and Scenic River Act of 1968. Information on geology and wildlife, as well as hikers' trail maps, can be obtained at the Visitors Center here. River-rafting trips can be booked in Taos, Santa Fe, Red River, and other communities (see below).

The village of **Costilla,** near the Colorado border, is 20 miles north of Questa. This is the turnoff point to the state's newest ski resort, Ski Rio, and for four-wheel-drive jaunts into Valle Vidal, a huge U.S. Forest Service–administered reserve with 42 miles of roads.

Red River

Turn east at Questa onto N. M. 38 for a 12-mile climb to Red River, a rough-and-ready 1890s gold-mining town which has parlayed its Wild West ambience into a popular resort village. Especially popular with families from Texas and Oklahoma, this community at 8,750 feet is a center for skiing and snowmobiling, fishing and hiking, off-road driving and horseback riding, river rafting, and other outdoor pursuits. Frontier-style celebrations, honky-tonk entertainment, and even staged shootouts on Main Street are held throughout the year.

The **Red River Chamber of Commerce,** P.O. Box 868, Red River, NM 87558 (tel. 505/754-2366, or toll free 800/348-6444), lists more than 40 accommodations, including lodges and condominiums. Some are open winters or summers only. Among the year-round inns are **Lifts West Condominium Hotel,** P.O. Box 318, Red River, NM 87558 (tel. 505/754-2778, or toll free 800/221-1859), with rates of $69 to $199 in winter, $39 to $159 in summer; **Ponderosa Lodge,** P.O. Box 338, Red River, NM 87558 (tel. 505/754-2988, or toll free 800/336-RSVP), with rates of $49 to $115 in winter, $46 to $107 in summer; the **Red River Inn,** P.O. Box 818, Red River, NM 87558 (tel. 505/754-2930), with rates of $44 to $78 in winter, $36 to $58 in summer; **Alpine Lodge,** P.O. Box 67, Red River, NM 87558 (tel. 505/754-2952), with rates of $36 to $114 in winter, $34 to $100 in summer; and **Redwood Lodge,** P.O. Box 182, Red River, NM 87558 (tel. 505/754-2951), with rates of $30 to $82 in winter, $20 to $72 in summer.

Leading restaurants in Red River include **Texas Red's Steakhouse and Lost Love Saloon,** Main Street at Jacks & Sixes Trail (tel. 754-2964); the **Bull Pen,** Main Street at the east end of town (tel. 754-6445), serving three meals daily; **Jalapeño Pete's,** High Street and Golden Treasure Trail, with Tex-Mex cooking; and the **St. Bernard Inn,** Pioneer Road at the river (tel. 754-6404), offering Cajun and southwestern dishes.

Heading the list of special events is **Gold Rush Days,** on Memorial Day weekend, including a fiddling contest, chili cook-off, and trout-fishing jamboree. Also scheduled annually are a **Fourth of July** weekend celebration with a gold-rush parade; the **Enchanted Circle Century Bike Tour** in mid-September, in which some 1,000 cyclists cover a 100-mile circuit; **Aspencade,** a celebration of fall colors in late September and early October with an arts-and-crafts show, German Wurstfest, square and folk dancing, and a four-wheel-drive rally; and **Winterfest** in late January, featuring competitions in dog-sledding, snowmobiling, and cross-country skiing.

In town, kids can play pool or miniature golf, dance, or manipulate video games at the Black Mountain Playhouse, while their parents play tennis or golf, or go square or folk dancing (nightly in summer) at the Red River Community House.

Eagle Nest

About 16 miles east of Red River, on the other side of 9,850-foot Bobcat Pass, is the village of Eagle Nest, resting on the shore of Eagle Nest Lake in the Moreno Valley. There was gold mining in this area as early as 1866, starting in what is now the ghost town of Elizabethtown five miles north; but Eagle Nest itself (pop. 200) wasn't incorporated until 1976. The four-square-mile lake is considered one of the top trout producers in the United States, and attracts ice fishermen in winter as well as summer anglers. Sailboats and sailboards also use the lake, although swimming, waterskiing, and camping are not permitted. The **Laguna Vista Lodge,** P.O. Box 65, Eagle Nest, NM 87718 (tel. 505/377-3522, or toll free 800/572-8500), is the village's best hotel/restaurant.

If you're heading to Cimarron or Denver, proceed east on U.S. 64 from Eagle Nest. But if you're circling back to Taos, continue southwest on N.M. 38 and 64 to Agua Fria and Angel Fire.

Shortly before the Agua Fria junction, you'll see the **DAV Vietnam Veterans Memorial.** It's a stunning structure, its curved white walls soaring high against the backdrop of the Sangre de Cristo range. Consisting of a chapel and underground visitor center, it was built by Dr. Victor Westphall in memory of his son, David, a marine lieutenant killed in Vietnam in 1968. The chapel has a changing gallery of photographs of Vietnam veterans who gave their lives in the Southeast Asian war, but no photo is as poignant as this inscription written by young Westphall, a promising poet: "Greed plowed cities desolate/ Lusts ran snorting through the streets/ Pride reared up to desecrate/ Shrines, and there were no retreats./ So man learned to shed the tears/ With which he measures out his years."

Angel Fire

This full-service resort community, 12 miles south of Eagle Nest, 21 miles east of Taos and 2 miles south of the Agua Fria junction on N.M. 38, dates only from the late 1960s but already has some 30 lodges and condominiums. Winter skiing and summer golf are the most popular activities, but there's also ample opportunity for sailing and fishing on Angel Fire Lake, tennis, racquetball, and horseback riding. The unofficial community center is **The Legends Hotel & Conference Center,** P.O. Drawer B, Angel Fire, NM 87710 (tel. 505/377-6401, or toll free 800/633-7463), a 157-room inn and restaurant with rates starting at $45 double.

For more information and full accommodations listings on the Moreno Valley, contact the **Angel Fire / Eagle Nest Cham-**

ber of Commerce, P.O. Box 547, Angel Fire, NM 87710 (tel. 505/377-6353).

It's 21 miles back to Taos, over 9,100-foot Palo Flechado Pass, down the valley of the Rio Fernando de Taos, and through the small community of Shady Brook.

DOWNHILL SKIING: Five alpine resorts are located within an hour's drive of Taos. All offer complete facilities, including equipment rentals. Although exact opening and closing dates may vary according to snow conditions, it's usually safe to assume that skiing will begin Thanksgiving weekend and continue into early April.

Ski vacationers who can't decide which area to patronize should look into the **Enchanted Circle Explorer,** a discount ticket book containing vouchers for all-day adult lifts at any three of the four Enchanted Circle ski areas—Taos Ski Valley, Angel Fire, Red River, and Ski Rio. Tickets are priced at $65, a discount of nearly 15%. They're not good over the Christmas holidays, President's Day Weekend, or during school vacation week in mid-March. The book is available for purchase at all ski ticket offices.

Ski clothing can be purchased, and ski equipment rented or bought, from several Taos outlets. Among them are **Cottam Ski Shops,** with four locations including the Kachina Lodge (tel. 758-1697) and Taos Ski Valley (tel. 776-8450); **Terry Sports,** in Taos on North Pueblo Road next to the post office (tel. 758-8522) and at Taos Ski Valley next to Thunderbird Lodge (tel. 776-8292); and **Olympic Ski Shops,** with three locations in Taos, including South Santa Fe Road adjacent to Baskin Robbins ice-cream parlor (tel. 758-1167).

DP Chameleon Skis are made in Taos by a unique process that allows them to adjust to particular skiing and snow conditions. The factory is at 211 Cruz Alta Rd. (tel. 505/758-8901, or toll free 800/323-FLEX); visitors are welcome for tours, day or evening, by appointment.

Taos Ski Valley

The preeminent ski resort in the southern Rocky Mountains was founded in 1955 by a Swiss-German immigrant, Ernie Blake. According to local legend, Blake searched for two years in a small plane for the perfect location for a ski resort equal to his native Alps. He found it at the abandoned mining site of Twining, high above Taos.

Today the area is still under Ernie's command, although he now gets assistance from two younger generations of Blakes. The resort has become internationally renowned for its light, dry powder (323 inches annually), its superb ski school, and its personal, friendly manner. *Philadelphia* magazine wrote in 1987: "Taos Ski Valley is the last—and some say the best—of a breed of intimate ski resorts where excellent accommodations, outstanding cuisine, convivial après ski, and uncrowded terrain meld in happy harmony."

Of the 73 trails and bowls, more than half are designated for expert or advanced skiers. But between the 11,800-foot summit and the 9,200-foot base, there are also ample opportunities for novice and intermediate skiers. Don't worry if you find your first look at the slopes frightening; by the end of a week on the slopes, it'll be duck soup.

Blake expects *everyone*—no exceptions—to take lessons. "It's possible to learn to ski, or learn to ski Taos, without instruction," he says. "After all, the Wright Brothers learned to fly without instruction. The thing to consider is that the survival rate is low." Thus most week-long ski vacationers invest in the Ski-BETTER-Week experience, a Saturday-to-Saturday package that includes lifts, lessons, lodging, and meals for prices starting at $580 per person, double occupancy.

Taos Ski Valley has a capacity of 7,000 skiers per hour on its six double chairs, one triple chair, and two surface tows. The lifts run from 9 a.m. to 4 p.m. daily, with one-day tickets priced at $27 for adults, $15 for children 12 and under. Full rental packages are $12 for adults, $7 for kids. Daily lessons start at $17; several choices are available, including the Kinderkafig program for children 3 to 6 years old.

There are two restaurants on the mountain in addition to the expansive facilities of Village Center at the base. A new 35,000-square-foot day lodge, with shops and conference rooms in addition to new restaurants and an elegant bar, opened for the 1988–1989 season.

A winter-long calendar of **events** keeps things lively at Taos Ski Valley. Scheduled each year are a torchlight procession down the slopes on Christmas Eve, the Plymouth All-American Ski Races for amateur recreational skiers during President's Day Weekend, and the season-ending Bump-Bolt-Bike Race (team and individual competition in skiing, running, and biking from the top of the mountain to N.M. 3) in early April.

Ski shuttles between Taos and Taos Ski Valley are provided three times a day between 8 a.m. and 4:30 p.m. by Faust's Transportation (tel. 758-3410), four times daily between 7:30 a.m. and 10 p.m. by Pride of Taos (tel. 758-8340), and seven times each day from 8:50 a.m. to 10 p.m. by Moreno Valley Transit (tel. 377-3737). Fares are $5 round trip.

Detailed information can be obtained from **Taos Ski Valley, Inc.,** Taos Ski Valley, NM 87525 (tel. 505/776-2291), or from the **Taos Valley Resort Association** (tel. 505/776-2233, or toll free 800/992-SNOW). For snow reports, dial 776-2916.

Angel Fire

The 30 miles of ski runs here are heavily oriented to beginning and intermediate skiers. Still, with a vertical drop of 2,180 feet to a base elevation of 8,500 feet, advanced skiers are certain to find something they like.

The area's lifts—four double and two triple chairs, with an hourly capacity of 1,900 skiers—are open from 8:30 a.m. to 4:30 p.m. daily. All-day tickets are $24 for adults, $15 for children. Rental packages run $14 for adults, $11 for kids. Lessons start at $15.

The annual **Winterfest** at Angel Fire begins the last weekend of January and runs through the first week of February. It includes several recreational races, parades, and softball on skis. But the event everyone waits for is the annual **Bob Harney Memorial Shovel Race** down a 1,400-foot course. The event was originated by maintenance crews riding their shovels down the slopes after work; some entrants are now more imaginative.

For more information, contact the **Angel Fire Ski Corp.,** P.O. Drawer B, Angel Fire, NM 87710 (tel. 505/377-6401 or 377-2301, or toll free 800/633-7463).

Red River

Lodgers in Red River, as in Angel Fire, can walk out their doors and be on the slopes. Two other factors make this 30-year-old, family-oriented area special: first, its 27 trails are geared to the intermediate skier, though beginners and experts have their share; and second, good snow is guaranteed early and late in the year by snowmaking equipment which can work on 75% of the runs, more than any other in New Mexico.

There's a 1,500-foot vertical drop here to a base elevation of 8,750 feet. Lifts include four double chairs, a triple chair, and two surface tows, with a skier capacity of 3,000 per hour. They are open from 9 a.m. to 4 p.m., with ticket prices at $23 for adults, $13 for children 12 and under. Rental packages are reasonably priced at $10 a day for adults, $6.50 for children. Lessons start at $15.

Red River's annual four-day **Winter Carnival** is held in mid-January. It includes downhill, cross-country, and snowmobile races, and special events for young children. For more information, contact **Red River Ski Area,** P.O. Box 900, Red River, NM

87558 (tel. 505/754-2223 or 754-2382, or toll free 800/348-6444).

Sipapu

The oldest ski area in the Taos region, founded in 1952, Sipapu Ski Area is 25 miles southeast of Taos on N.M. 3, in Tres Rios Canyon near Peñasco (tel. 505/587-2240). It prides itself on being a small local area, especially popular with schoolchildren.

The lifts—just one triple chair and two tows—are open from 9 a.m. to 4 p.m. Tickets are $17 for adults, $1 for children under 9. The vertical drop is only 865 feet to the 8,200-foot base elevation. There are 18 trails, half classified as intermediate. A bunkhouse provides some overnight lodging.

Ski Rio

Just south of the Colorado border is this new, rapidly expanding ski area. Its 65 runs include the broad, intermediate Cinnamon Bear Bowl and 52 acres of expert trails called 52 Pick Up. A high base elevation of 9,500 feet guarantees that snow is ample and light; the vertical drop is 2,150 feet.

The resort can handle up to 4,500 skiers an hour on its two triple chairs, one double chair, and two surface tows. Lifts are open from 9 a.m. to 4 p.m. daily; tickets are $20 for adults, $17 for children. Rentals run $10 for adults, $8 for youngsters. Lesson prices start at $12.

There's modern lodging for up to 400 people, as well as restaurants, bars, and shops at the base of the slopes. The resort operates a shuttle from Taos Airport for all incoming flights. Further information can be obtained from **Ski Rio,** P.O. Box 59, Costilla, NM 87525 (tel. 505/758-1800, or toll free 800/722-LIFT); for ski conditions, call 758-SNOW.

NORDIC SKIING: There are numerous popular cross-country trails in Carson National Forest, including some so marked en route to Taos Ski Valley. One of the more popular is **Amole Canyon,** off N.M. 3 near Sipapu, where the Taos Nordic Ski Club maintains set tracks and signs along a three-mile loop. It's closed to snowmobiles, a comfort to lovers of serenity.

Just east of Red River, with 18 miles of groomed trails in 600 acres of forest land atop Bobcat Pass, is the **Enchanted Forest Cross Country Ski Area** (tel. 505/754-2374). Full-day trail passes, good from 9 a.m. to 4:30 p.m., are $5 for adults, just $1 for kids 12 and under.

Equipment rentals ($8 for adults, $6.50 for children) and lessons (from $10) are arranged at Millers Crossing ski shop on Main

Street in Red River. Qualified nordic skiers can get further instruction in skating, mountaineering, and telemarking.

The **Southwest Nordic Center,** P.O. Box 3212, Taos, NM 87571 (tel. toll free 800/99X-C SKI) offers lessons ($25) and tours ($40) in various locations around northern New Mexico. It also owns a private Mongolian yurt north of Chama, near the Colorado border, for overnight excursions.

Taos Mountain Outfitters, South Plaza (tel. 758-9292), specializes in cross-country sales, rentals, and guide service.

RIVER RAFTING: Half- or full-day white-water rafting trips down the Rio Grande and Rio Chama originate in Taos and Red River. The wild Taos Box, south of the Rio Grande Gorge National Recreation Area, is especially popular. Early May, when the water is rising, is a good time to go. Experience is not required, but you should wear a lifejacket (provided) and expect to get wet.

One convenient rafting service is **Rio Grand Rapid Transit,** P.O. Box A, Pilar, NM 87571 (tel. 505/758-9700, or toll free 800/222-RAFT). Its headquarters are at the entrance to Rio Grand Gorge State Park, 16 miles south of Taos, where most excursions through the Taos Box exit the river. Several other thrilling serene floats through the Pilar Racecourse start at this point.

Other rafting outfitters in the Taos area include **Big River Raft Trips** (tel. 758-3204); **Embudo Station,** in Embudo (tel. 852-4707); **Far Flung Adventures** (tel. 758-2628); **Los Rios River Runners,** in Red River (tel. 754-6630); and **Sierra Outfitters & Guides,** South Santa Fe Road (tel. 758-9556 or 758-1247). Typical rates are $30 for half-day, $60 for full-day, or $150 and up for overnight excursions.

HORSE AND PACK TRIPS: The **Taos Indian Horse Ranch Co.,** on pueblo land off Ski Valley Road just before Arroyo Seco (tel. 758-3212), offers a variety of riding opportunities. Among the most popular are Sunday Socials Trail Rides, half-day summer rides into the backcountry of Taos Pueblo. For $57.50 per horse, you'll have four hours of riding (10 a.m. to 2 p.m.) and a picnic lunch. Reservations are required. From late November to March the ranch offers evening Russian Sleigh Rides on a ten-passenger sleigh pulled by fast-action draft horses. Adult rates vary from $15 to $27.50, with the higher prices for adult dinner parties.

Lobo Ranch & Taos Equestrian Center, ten miles north of Taos in Arroyo Hondo (tel. 776-8526), has day and overnight horse trips available year round. Rates start at $14 an hour, $66 a day, for five or more riders. Near Red River, the **Bitter Creek Guest Ranch and Stables** (tel. 754-2587) offers horse outfitting and guide services.

Llamas are becoming a favorite pack animal throughout North America. In Taos, **Llama Treks** (tel. 505/758-4696, or toll free 800/552-0070, ext. 822) can arrange backcountry trips with these Andean beasts of burden.

OFF-ROAD VEHICLES: Several companies in Red River rent Jeeps, four-wheel-drives, and snowmobiles as well as conduct tours. They include **High Country Jeep Rentals and Tours** (tel. 754-2441), **Jeep Trailways** (tel. 754-6443), **Roadrunner Tours** (tel. 754-6649), and **T&O ATV Rentals** (tel. 754-2724).

HIKING AND BACKPACKING: There are many hundreds of miles of hiking trails in Taos County's mountain and high-mesa country. They're especially well used in the summer and fall, although nights turn chilly and mountain weather fickle by September.

Maps (at $1 each) and free handouts and advice on all **Carson National Forest** trails and recreation areas can be obtained from the Forest Service Building, 112 Cruz Alta Rd. (tel. 758-6200), or from the Taos Ranger District office, 302 Armory St., downtown (tel. 758-2911). Both are open from 8 a.m. to 4:30 p.m. Monday through Saturday. Detailed USGS topographical maps of backcountry areas can be purchased from **Taos Mountain Outfitters** on the Plaza (tel. 758-9292). This is also the place to rent camping equipment, if you came without your own. Tent rentals are $7.50 a day or $17.50 a weekend; sleeping bags, $6.50 a day or $16 a weekend.

Two wilderness areas within the national forest are close to Taos, and offer outstanding hiking possibilities. They are the 19,663-acre **Wheeler Peak Wilderness,** a wonderland of alpine tundra encompassing New Mexico's highest (13,161 feet) peak; and the 20,000-acre **Latir Peak Wilderness** north of Red River, noted for its high lake country. Both are under the jurisdiction of the Questa Ranger District, P.O. Box 110, Questa, NM 87556 (tel. 505/586-0520).

FISHING AND HUNTING: Fishing season in the high lakes and streams opens April 1 and continues through December, though spring and fall are known as the best times to achieve success. Rainbow, cutthroat, and brown trout, and kokanee, a freshwater salmon, are commonly stocked and caught. The Rio Grande also has pike and catfish.

Out-of-state fishing licenses cost $8.50 for one day, $15 for five days, or $25.50 for the season. The limit is eight trout or kokanee per day.

It's not unusual to take trout of 14 to 20 inches. Many experienced anglers prefer fly fishing, but those who don't recommend using jiggs, spinners, or woolly worms as lures or worms, corn, or salmon eggs as baits.

Hunters in Carson National Forest bag deer, turkey, grouse, and band-tailed pigeons, and elk by special permit. On private land, where hunters must be accompanied by qualified guides, there are also black bear and mountain lion. Hunting seasons vary year to year, so it's important to inquire ahead.

Several Taos sporting-goods shops sell fishing and hunting licenses. Further information on regulations can be obtained by contacting the **New Mexico Game and Fish Department,** State Capitol, Santa Fe, NM 87503 (tel. 505/827-7882).

There are many backcountry guide services in Taos County. They include: **Agua Fria Guide Service,** in Angel Fire (tel. 377-3512); **Deep Creek Wilderness,** in Red River (tel. 776-8423); **Eagle Nest Outfitters,** in Eagle Nest (tel. 377-6941); **The Fish Eagle,** in Eagle Nest (tel. 377-3359); **Los Rios Anglers,** in both Taos and Red River (tel. 758-2798); the **Moreno Ranch,** in Eagle Nest (tel. 377-6931); **Rio Costilla Park,** in Costilla (tel. 586-0542); and the **Taos Fly Shop,** in Taos (tel. 758-0281).

BICYCLING: On Cruz Alta Road next to the bus station, **Bicicletas** (tel. 758-3522) offers bike rentals daily except Sunday, including Klein and Trek mountain bikes at $10 a day.

Taos Mountain Outfitters, South Plaza (tel. 758-9292), also has mountain-bike rentals and sales.

Carson National Forest rangers recommend several mountain-biking trails in the greater Taos area, including Garcia Park and Rio Chiquito for beginner to intermediate bikers, Gallegos and Picuris peaks for experts. Inquire at a U.S. Forest Service office for an excellent handout.

Those who prefer touring shouldn't forget the annual Red River **Enchanted Circle Century Bike Tour** (tel. 754-2366; see above, "Enchanted Circle") or the Bobcat Pass Hill Climb the same mid-September weekend.

GOLF: The 18-hole, par-72 course in **Angel Fire** has been endorsed by the Professional Golfers Association. Surrounded by stands of ponderosa pine, spruce, and aspen, it's one of the highest regulation golf courses in the world at 8,600 feet. It also has a driving range and putting green. Carts and clubs can be rented at the course, and the club pro provides instruction.

A municipal golf course under construction in **Red River** will be slightly higher than that in Angel Fire when completed.

BALLOONING: The Taos Mountain Balloon Rally is held each year the third weekend of October (see "Special Events"). A hot-air balloon workshop is held in Taos the weekend before the rally. Contact the **Taos Mountain Balloon Rally Association,** P.O. Box 6158, Taos, NM 87571 (tel. 505/758-8100), for details.

SPAS: After your day outdoors, **Tubs of Taos,** Pueblo Allegre Mall, South Santa Fe Road (tel. 758-4088), treats the sore muscles of skiers, rafters, and others with hot tubs and massage. It's open daily from noon to 10 p.m.; reservations are recommended, especially evenings. Rates run $9.75 to $11 per hour for outdoor tubs, $8.25 to $9.75 for indoor tubs, $7 to $7.50 for a community tub. A 45-minute massage costs $25; a two-hour intensive, $55.

Ojo Caliente Mineral Springs, Ojo Caliente, NM 87549 (tel. 505/583-2233), is on U.S. 285, 50 miles (a one-hour drive) southwest of Taos. This National Historic Site was considered sacred by prehistoric Indians. When the Spanish explorer Cabeza de Vaca discovered and named the springs in the 16th century, he called them "the greatest treasure that I found these strange people to possess." No other hot spring in the world has Ojo Caliente's combination of iron, soda, lithium, sodium, and arsenic. The resort offers herbal wraps and massages as well as lodging and meals. Summer hours are 8 a.m. to 8 p.m. daily; in winter the springs don't open until 1 p.m. weekdays.

AFTER DARK

You don't come to Taos for the nightlife. But if you're here and yearn for a little evening activity, you'll find it heavily country/western oriented—though not entirely so.

The **Kachina Lodge,** on North Pueblo Road (tel. 758-2275), frequently has top-name country-and-western acts in its cabaret. Saturday night is the big-event night, starting at 9 p.m.; there's typically a $5 cover charge.

The **Sagebrush Inn,** South Santa Fe Road (tel. 758-2254), features country or rock performers nightly throughout the year from 9 p.m. to midnight. Especially popular during ski season is a dinner show by country singer-guitarist Michael Martin Murphey ("Wildfire"). Offered every other Saturday night, the cost is $27.50, with seating at 6 p.m. and the show at 8 p.m.

There's more heavy rock music, and sometimes male strippers, at the Hacienda Inn's **Far West Club,** on South Santa Fe Road (tel. 758-6810). Friday night is party night.

The **Ramada Inn,** South Santa Fe Road at Frontier Road (tel. 758-2900), features solo performers or small combos for dancing in its Hearthside Lounge from 8 p.m. to midnight Friday through Monday.

Floyd's Restaurant, on South Santa Fe Road (tel. 758-4142), frequently has Hispanic performers on Saturday nights.

The **Don Quijote Lounge,** on East Kit Carson Road (tel. 758-1956), well patronized by locals, has a guitarist nightly. **Ogelvie's Bar & Grill,** on the Plaza (tel. 758-8866), and the Taos Inn's **Adobe Bar** (tel. 758-2233) also have live entertainment, mainly on high-season weekends. Mariachi singer-guitarists perform from 6 to 10 p.m. on Friday and Saturday at **La Cocina de Taos,** on the Plaza (tel. 758-2412).

For skiers en route home, **Carl's French Quarter** at the Quail Ridge Inn, Ski Valley Road (tel. 776-8319), features Thursday-night dinner shows, in ski season, by a variety of noted jazz and blues artists and balladeers. The cost is $18, with seating at 7 p.m. and the show at 8 p.m. Musical revues are often presented at other times of year.

Also on Ski Valley Road, the **Chile Connection** (tel. 776-8787) and **Ski Valley Junction** (tel. 776-8891) both have live entertainment in the bars, with dancing at the Junction.

At Taos Ski Valley, there's country music from 8 to 11 p.m. on Wednesday and Thursday at the **Hotel St. Bernard** (tel. 776-2251). The Thunderbird Lodge's **Twining Tavern** (tel. 776-2280) is more eclectic in its tastes: C&W on Wednesday, rock on Thursday, jazz on Friday, and Warren Miller ski movies on Saturday, from 8 p.m. to at least midnight.

Movie lovers will find two cinemas in Taos as well as a film series at 8 p.m. on Wednesday at the **Taos Community Auditorium,** with a charge of $4 for the general public.

CHAPTER XI

THE ARTS OF TAOS

□ □ □

For a town of fewer than 5,000 permanent residents, Taos has a remarkable variety of artistic endeavors taking place.

Warm weather brings artsy folks out of their winter nooks for the Taos Spring Arts Celebration (see "Special Events" in Chapter X). They remain highly visible until the autumn Taos Arts Festival sends them scurrying back to hibernation. In between, the town bustles with creative energy. Throughout the winter, galleries remain open and there are frequent concert and theatrical performances in town and at Taos Ski Valley.

Much of the credit must go to the **Taos Art Association (TAA),** P.O. Box 198, Taos, NM 87571 (tel. 505/758-2052), with headquarters at **The Stables Art Center,** 220 N. Pueblo Rd. The Stables features exhibitions of regional art, crafts, and photography, with an emphasis on contemporary work by Taos artists. Admission is free; open Monday through Saturday from 10 a.m. to 5 p.m. and on Sunday from 1 to 5 p.m.

THE PERFORMING ARTS

At the adjacent **Taos Community Auditorium,** the TAA sponsors local, regional, and national performers in theater, dance, and concerts—Dave Brubeck, Dizzie Gillespie, the American String Quartet, and the American Festival Ballet have performed here—and offers two weekly film series, including one for children. **Local performing groups** supported by the TAA are the Taos Community Orchestra, the Community Chorus, and Taos Repertory Company.

Each summer, the TAA hosts the **Taos School of Music,** the oldest summer chamber-music program in the United States. More than 300 gifted young string and piano students congregate from all over the world for seven weeks of professional instruction between mid-June and early August. Though resident at Taos Ski Valley, they perform weekly concerts of classical and contemporary music in Taos itself. The school was established in the early 1960s.

A complimentary program, the **International Institute of Music,** runs through the month of August. The institute trains child musical prodigies in symphonic music.

In addition, **Music from Angel Fire** (tel. 758-4667), a program of symphonic, folk, and jazz music, has performances weekend nights, mid-June through Labor Day, both in Taos and in the small resort community of Angel Fire, 21 miles east off U.S. 64.

In January, the **Thunderbird Jazz Festival** livens up winter nights at Taos Ski Valley. Leading contemporary jazz musicians perform week-long gigs at the Thunderbird Lodge (tel. 776-2280). Shows start at 8:30 p.m.; admission is $10. Dinner-and-show packages are available.

Aficionados of the literary arts appreciate the annual **SOMOS Taos Poetry Circus** (tel. 758-8977 or 758-0081), held over four days in mid-June. Billed by SOMOS (Society of the Muse of the Southwest) as "a literary gathering and poetry showdown between nationally known writers," it includes readings, workshops, lectures, children's theater, and a banquet. The main event, held at 8 p.m. on a Saturday, is the World Heavyweight Championship Poetry Bout, ten rounds of hard-hitting readings—with the last round extemporaneous.

SOMOS also sponsors a **Summer Writers' Series** at the Stables Art Center, with 8 p.m. readings by noted writers beginning the Thursday after July 4 and continuing to about Labor Day. The 1988 series featured Tony Hillerman and John Nichols.

Be sure to obtain a current listing of "Taos County Events" from the **Taos County Chamber of Commerce,** P.O. Drawer I, Taos, NM 87571 (tel. 505/758-3873, or toll free 800/732-TAOS). The chamber will also provide information on attending the above-listed events and others.

THE FINE ARTS

Taos took its place as a leading light in the world of art when the Taos Society of Artists was founded in 1915. The society disbanded in 1927, having successfully and widely marketed the works of Taos's geographically isolated masters. In doing so, it established a solid foundation for the prolific art community of today.

You'll see works by the society proudly displayed in museums and private collections throughout Taos. Most of the artists are also represented in national museums, including the Metropolitan Museum of Art in New York. The society members, all of whom said they chose Taos as a home because of the remarkable play of light on landscape here, were Kenneth Adams, Oscar Berninghaus, Ernest Blumenschein, Irving Couse, Herbert Dunton, Victor Higgins, E. Martin Hennings, Bert Phillips, Joseph Sharp, and Walter Ufer.

The most noted artist in modern Taos is R. C. Gorman, a Navajo Indian from Arizona who has made his home in Taos for 20 years. Now in his early 50s, Gorman is internationally acclaimed for his bright, somewhat surrealistic depictions of Navajo women. His **Navajo Gallery,** next door to the Blumenschein House at 5 Ledoux St. (tel. 758-3250), is a showcase for his widely varied work: acrylics, lithographs, silkscreens, bronzes, tapestries, hand-cast ceramic vases, etched glass, and more.

"Gorman has been a real inspiration for Indians from all over the country to get into art," says Taos art dealer Philip Bareiss. "In fact, he is a very positive influence on the whole community here. He's very supportive of everyone's art."

Bareiss' gallery, **Philip Bareiss Fine Arts,** 609 N. Pueblo Rd. (tel. 758-4036), features 27 of the leading Taos artists. Among them are sculptor Gray Mercer, noted for his large outdoor horse sculptures, and watercolorist Patricia Sanford, whose striking flower portraits brighten up the studio walls.

Some 60-odd other galleries are located within easy walking distance of the Plaza, and about 20 more are a short drive from town. Most artists display in one or more of the galleries, which are generally open seven days a week, especially in high season. Some artists show their work by appointment only.

Following is a listing of many of the town's fine-arts outlets. Many galleries have a varied selection of works, but they are listed here by their primary specialties:

CONTEMPORARY ART: The **Angels Landing Gallery,** 208 N. Pueblo Rd. (tel. 758-9667). Mixed media, watercolors, fiber arts, sculpture.

Larry Bell Studio (tel. 758-3062). Bell's unique glass sculptures, combining light and form to create illusion. Call for an appointment.

Bryans Gallery, 121C North Plaza (tel. 758-9407). Abstracts, mixed media, sculptures, ceramics, and jewelry by emerging and established artists.

Charles Collins Studio, 131 Los Cordovas Route (tel. 505/ 758-2309, or toll free 800/288-8282). Collins's oils and graphics of Pueblo themes.

Creative Endeavors, Governor Bent House, 16 Bent St. (tel. 758-1180). Abstract oils by Laurie Hill Phelps.

Desurmont-Ellis Gallery, North Plaza (tel. 758-3299). Abstract and impressionist oils and watercolors, sculpture, ceramics, and jewelry.

El Taller Taos Gallery, 119A Kit Carson Rd. (tel. 758-4887). The Amado Pena gallery, with paintings, graphics, sculpture, jewelry, and weavings of southwestern theme, including Noel Hudson-Reidy oils of desert plants.

Fennell Art Gallery, in La Fonda de Taos Hotel, South Plaza (tel. 758-0749). Southwestern-theme paintings.

Alyce Frank, P.O. Box 962, Ranchos de Taos (tel. 758-4446). Serigraphy.

Gallery A, Kit Carson Road (tel. 758-2343). Contemporary and traditional paintings, sculpture, and graphics; features Tom Talbot acrylics.

Gallery 203, Kit Carson Road (tel. 758-4985). Paintings, sculpture, and graphics.

Gallery Elena, 119C Bent St. (tel. 758-9094). Abstract paintings and sculptures, including the work of Veloy Vigil.

Rod Goebel Gallery, Kit Carson Road (tel. 758-2181). Goebel's colorful, internationally acclaimed impressionist paintings.

Grycner Gallery, McCarthy Plaza, east side of Taos Plaza (tel. 758-2215). Paintings, hand-cast paper and ceramic vases, featuring the oils of Peter Van Dusen and the pastels of Miguel Martinez.

La Paloma Gallery, 107 N. Pueblo Rd. (tel. 758-2921). Oils, watercolors, sculptures, and ceramics.

E. S. Lawrence Gallery, 132 E. Kit Carson Rd. (tel. 758-8229). Traditional paintings, sculptures, and ceramics, including the oils of Cary Ennis and Judy Gentry, and the pastels of Valerie Graves.

James Mack Studio/Gallery, 117 Ranchitos Rd. (tel. 758-8517). Abstract acrylics, watercolors, and mixed-media works. Appointment preferred.

Mission Gallery, Sharp House, Kit Carson Road (tel. 758-2861). Leading contemporary paintings and sculptures, and works by Taos masters.

Bren Price Studio, 29A Bent St. (tel. 758-8733). Expressionistic watercolors of primitive, southwestern, and Oriental themes. Appointment requested.

Tally Richards Gallery, 2 Ledoux St. (tel. 758-2731). Modern art, including Donald Anderson's surrealistic landscapes.

Salobra, 6 Bent St. (tel. 758-1128). Paintings, sculpture, ceramics, and jewelry, featuring abstract mixed-media works by Carol Ann Savid.

Spirit Runner Gallery, 800 N. Pueblo Rd. (tel. 758-1132). Imaginative watercolors.

The Taos Gallery / Gallery 2, North Pueblo Road (tel. 758-2475 or 758-7438). Paintings, sculptures, lithographs, serigraphs, and etchings, including Ron Barsano oils.

Total Arts Gallery, 122A Kit Carson Rd. (tel. 758-4667). Paintings from traditional to abstract, including John Axton still-lifes and Walt Gonske impressionistic oils.

Variant Gallery, Northwest Plaza (tel. 758-4949). Paintings, sculpture, ceramics, fiber art, jewelry, and folk art.

NATIVE AMERICAN ART: Burke Armstrong Fine Art,
North Plaza (tel. 758-9016). Historic oils, watercolors, and sculptures, including works by Taos Pueblo sculptor John Suazo.

Broken Arrow Ltd., North Plaza (tel. 758-4304). Paintings, sculpture, ceramics, weaving, jewelry, basketry.

Brooks Indian Shop, Cabot Plaza Mall (tel. 758-9073). Handmade jewelry, pottery, and artifacts.

Casa Craft, John Dunn House, Bent Street (tel. 758-8102). Indian rugs and handmade crafts.

Cowboys and Indians, South Plaza (tel. 758-2188). Western collectibles.

Jordan Gallery T.A.O.S., 415 E. Kit Carson Rd. (tel. 758-7160). Landscapes and sculptures of Southwest Indian theme.

Magic Mountain Gallery, The Plaza (tel. 758-9604). Paintings, sculpture, and traditional pueblo and contemporary pottery and jewelry.

Ouray Meyers Studio, North Pueblo Road (tel. 758-1132). Meyers's contemporary watercolors.

Morgan Gallery, 4 Bent St. (tel. 758-2599). Ed Morgan's embossed prints of Southwest Indian theme.

Navajo Silver Company, North Plaza (tel. 758-3083). Jewelry.

Rainy Mountain Trading Post, South Plaza (tel. 758-4489). Jewelry, pottery, and artifacts.

Reyna's Indian Shop No. 1 and No. 2, Kachina Lodge and Taos Pueblo (tel. 758-2142). Arts and crafts.

Savij Art, 106 N. Pueblo Rd. (tel. 758-4565). Native art.

The Shriver Gallery, North Pueblo Road (tel. 758-4994). Traditional paintings, drawings, and bronze sculpture.

Silver & Sand Trading Co., Northwest Plaza (tel. 758-9698). Collector-quality crafts.

Southwestern Arts, John Dunn House, Bent Street (tel. 758-8418). Navajo weavings and pottery.

Thunder Bow Gallery, Cabot Plaza, Kit Carson Road (tel.

758-8057). Traditional paintings, bronze sculpture, painted Taos drums.

Carmen Velarde Gallery, Ranchos de Taos (tel. 758-4173). Colcha embroidery, santos, adobe art. Call for appointment.

Western Heritage Gallery, South Plaza (tel. 758-4489). Paintings, sculpture, and jewelry of western and southwestern Indian theme.

HISPANIC AND FOLK ART: El Rincon, Kit Carson Road (tel. 758-9188). Spanish and Indian artifacts and jewelry.

Ranchos Ritz, St. Francis Plaza, Ranchos de Taos (tel. 758-2640). Contemporary and traditional designs of regional theme, including paintings, ceramics, jewelry, and many antiques.

Sonrisa Gallery, St. Francis Plaza, Ranchos de Taos (tel. 758-1443). International and local folk art and antiques.

Whitaker Gallery, South Plaza (tel. 758-4541). Southwestern art and fetishes.

CONTEMPORARY CRAFTS: The Clay & Fiber Gallery-Shop, North Pueblo Road (tel. 758-8093). Ceramics, fiber arts, jewelry, custom furnishings.

Kilborn Pottery, N.M. 68 in Pilar, 15 miles south of Taos (tel. 758-0135). Stoneware.

The Market, 125 Kit Carson Rd. (tel. 758-3195). Ceramics and other regional crafts.

Open Space Gallery, Plaza Real, the Plaza (tel. 758-1217). Furniture, fiber art, clothing, clay, original jewelry, and watercolors by Nancy Lee Stewart and Charles A. Stewart.

Taos Artisans Co-op Gallery, Bent Street (tel. 758-1558). Contemporary and traditional fiber arts and jewelry.

Twining Weavers, Arroyo Seco (tel. 776-8367). Handwoven designer items.

Weaving/Southwest, one block south of Taos Plaza (tel. 758-0433). Tapestries, rugs, and apparel by more than 30 New Mexico artists.

JEWELRY: Artwares, The Plaza (tel. 758-8850). Innovative designs. Phil Poirier's one-of-a-kind and limited-edition silverwork.

Emily Benoist Ruffin, 24 Bent St. (tel. 758-1061). Goldsmith. Appointment preferred.

Taos Gems and Minerals, South Santa Fe Road (tel. 758-3910). Gems, jewelry, and crystals.

HOME FURNISHINGS: The Palisander Gallery, 1 Bent St. (tel. 758-3561). Taos-style furniture and southwestern folk art.

Southwestern Arts & Fortner Millworks, John Dunn House, Bent Street (tel. 758-8418). Limited-edition handcrafted furniture; also historic and contemporary Navajo weavings and pueblo pottery.

Taos Mountain Wood Works, Ski Valley Road (tel. 776-8314). Furniture, woodcarving, and wood sculpture.

Wood Design / The Wood Shop (tel. 758-9060). Handcrafted furniture. Call for appointment.

ANTIQUES: Dwellings Revisited, 8 Bent St. (tel. 758-3377).
Mexican and northern New Mexican primitives.

Stewart's Fine Art, Cabot Plaza Mall, 108 Kit Carson Rd. (tel. 758-0049). Historical paintings for collectors.

PHOTOGRAPHY: Gus Foster, Ledoux Street (tel. 758-4007).
Panoramic photographs. By appointment.

PRINTS AND POSTERS: The Taos Company, North Plaza
(tel. 758-1141). Limited-edition prints, posters, and photographs, as well as ceramics, jewelry, and folk art.

IMPORTS: Coyote Pottery, South Santa Fe Road (tel. 758-3030).
Mexican ceramics and other items.

From the Andes, North Pueblo Road (tel. 758-0183 or 758-0485). South American alpaca weavings and sweaters.

CHAPTER XII

DAY TRIPS IN THE PUEBLO COUNTRY

□ □ □

One of the great pleasures of visiting Santa Fe or Taos is the ease with which you can explore the surrounding region. Spectacular scenery, Pueblo communities and ruins, traditional Hispanic farming villages, national and state monuments, a 19th-century narrow-gauge railway, and even the birthplace of the atomic bomb are within two hours' drive of either tourist center.

The following five driving tours incorporate the leading attractions of the Pueblo Country into convenient itineraries.

SANTA FE–TAOS LOOP

This route, about 145 miles round trip, follows the legendary "High Road to Taos" northbound and returns via the Rio Grande.

Leave Santa Fe northbound on U.S. 84/285. It's ten miles to **Tesuque Pueblo** (tel. 505/983-2667), whose most visible signs are the unusual Camel Rock and a large roadside Bingo operation (nightly from 6:30 to 11 p.m.; tel. 984-8414). Despite this concession to the late 20th century, the pueblo dwellers are faithful to traditional religion, ritual, and ceremony. Excavations confirm that there was a pueblo here in 1250 A.D. Many Tesuque women are skilled potters; Ignacia Duran's black-and-white and red micaceous pottery is particularly noted. Visitors are welcomed between 9 a.m. and 5 p.m. daily. San Diego's Feast Day is November 12.

Five miles farther, at the junction of N.M. 4, is **Pojoaque Pueblo** (tel. 505/455-2278). Though small and without a definable village, Pojoaque is important as a center for traveler services.

Indigenous pottery, embroidery, silverwork, and beadwork are available for sale. The annual feast day is December 12, Our Lady of Guadalupe Day.

Drive east on N.M. 4 for three miles, then turn right at the Bureau of Reclamation sign for Nambe Falls. Two miles farther is **Nambe Pueblo** (tel. 505/455-7752 or 455-2304), a modern 700-year-old pueblo at the foot of the Sangre de Cristo range. The scenic highlight here is Nambe Falls, which make a stunning three-tier drop through a cleft in a rock face and tumble into Nambe Reservoir a few miles beyond the pueblo. The recreational site, open from 7 a.m. to 7 p.m. April to October (longer hours in midsummer), offers fishing, boating, camping, and picnicking. The Fourth of July Waterfall Dances and the October 4 San Francisco Feast Day are observed at the sacred falls. Woven belts, beadwork, and black-on-black pottery are impressive crafts. The pueblo has a solar-powered tribal headquarters.

The historic Hispanic weaving center of **Chimayo** is 12 miles farther north, at the junction of N.M. 520 and 76 via N.M. 4. Families like the Ortegas maintain a tradition of hand-woven textiles begun by their ancestors seven generations ago, in the early 1800s, in this small village. **Ortega's Weaving Shop** and **Galeria Ortega** are fine places to take a close look at this ancient craft.

Today, however, many more people come to Chimayo to visit **El Santuario de Nuestro Señor de Esquipulas** (the Shrine of Our Lord of Esquipulas), better known simply as "El Santuario de Chimayo." Attributed with miraculous powers of healing, this church has been the destination of countless thousands of pilgrims since its construction in 1814–1816. Some 30,000 people may participate in the annual Good Friday pilgrimage, many of them walking from as far away as Albuquerque.

Although only the earth in the anteroom beside the altar has healing powers ascribed to it, the entire shrine has a special, serene feeling that's hard to ignore. It's quite moving to peruse the testimonies of rapid recoveries from illness or injury on the walls of the anteroom, and equally poignant to read the as-yet-unanswered entreaties made on behalf of loved ones.

Designated a National Historic Landmark in 1970, the church contains five beautiful reredos, or panes of sacred paintings, one behind the main altar and two on each side of the nave. Each year during the fourth weekend in July, the 9th-century military exploits of the Spanish saint, Santiago, are celebrated in a weekend fiesta, supported by the National Endowment for the Arts, including the historic play *Los Moros y Cristianos* ("Moors and Christians").

Many travelers schedule their drives to have lunch at the

Restaurante Rancho de Chimayo, on N.M. 76 east of the junction (tel. 351-4444). The adobe home, built by Hermenegildo Jaramillo in the 1880s, is approaching its 25th year in the food business. Native New Mexican cuisine, prepared from generations-old Jaramillo family recipes, is served on terraced patios and in cozy dining rooms beneath hand-stripped *vigas.* The restaurant is open from noon to 10 p.m. daily June through August, and noon to 9 p.m. Tuesday through Sunday the rest of the year—except January, when the owners go on vacation.

The Jaramillo family also owns a bed-and-breakfast inn, **Hacienda Rancho de Chimayo,** P.O. Box 11, Chimayo, NM 87522 (tel. 505/351-2222). Once the residence of Epifanio Jaramillo, Hermenegildo's brother, its seven guest rooms all open onto an enclosed courtyard. Each room, furnished with turn-of-the-century antiques, has a private bath and sitting area. Rates are $49 to $86. The office is open daily from 9 a.m. to 9 p.m.; like the restaurant, it's closed in January.

Lovely **Santa Cruz Lake** has a dual purpose: the man-made lake provides water for Chimayo valley farms, but also offers a recreation site for trout fishing and camping at the edge of the Pecos Wilderness. To reach it, turn south four miles on N.M. 503 two miles east of Chimayo.

Just as Chimayo is famous for its weaving, the village of **Cordova,** seven miles east on N.M. 76, is noted for its woodcarvers. Small shops and studios along the highway display *santos* (carved saints) and various decorative items carved from aspen and cedar.

Anyone who saw Robert Redford's 1988 movie production, *The Milagro Beanfield War,* has seen **Truchas.** A former Spanish colonial outpost built at 8,000 feet atop a mesa four miles east of Cordova, it was chosen as the site for filming in part because traditional Hispanic culture remains pervasive. Subsistence *acequia* farming has a high profile here. The scenery is spectacular: 13,101-foot Truchas Peak dominates one side of the mesa, and the broad Rio Grande valley the other. **Rancho Arriba,** P.O. Box 338, Truchas, NM 87578 (tel. 505/689-2374), is a small working farm/bed-and-breakfast for those who seek a little isolation. Three rooms are priced at $35 to $50.

Las Trampas, six miles east of Truchas on N.M. 76, is most notable for its **San José Church,** called by some the most beautiful of all churches built during the Spanish colonial period. It was placed on the National Register of Historic Places in 1966 through the efforts of preservationists who felt it was threatened by a highway project.

Near the regional education center of **Penasco,** 24 miles from Chimayo near the junction of N.M. 75 and 76, is the **Picuris (San Lorenzo) Pueblo** (tel. 505/587-2519). The 270 citizens of this 15,000-acre mountain pueblo, native Tiwa speakers, consider themselves a sovereign nation: their forebears never made a treaty with any foreign country, the United States included. Thus they observe a traditional form of tribal council government. Their annual feast day at San Lorenzo church is August 10.

Still, the people are modern enough to have fully computerized their public showcase, Picuris Tribal Enterprises. Components include the **Picuris Pueblo Museum,** where weaving, beadwork, and the distinctive reddish-brown clay cooking pottery are exhibited from 8 a.m. to 4:30 p.m. Monday through Friday. Guided tours through the old village ruins begin from the museum; camera fees start at $5. **Hidden Valley Restaurant** serves a native Picuris along with an American menu. There's also an information center, crafts shop, grocery, and other shops. Permits ($3 for adults, $2 for children) are available to fish or camp at Pu-Na and Tu-Tah lakes, regularly stocked with trout.

One mile east of Penasco on N.M. 75 is **Vadito,** which early this century was the center for the conservative Catholic brotherhood, the Penitentes. Twenty miles north of Penasco, on N.M. 3 to Taos, is **Talpa,** where excavations being carried out by the Smithsonian Institution have uncovered the prehistoric pit-house settlement of Llano Quemado. It's just two miles from here to Ranchos de Taos.

The return trip from Taos to Santa Fe is a faster, more direct route, without the curves and climbs of the "High Road."

Pilar, a center for many white-water rafting trips on the Rio Grande, is 15 miles south of Taos on N.M. 68. It's adjacent to **Rio Grande Gorge State Park,** whose four major camping areas are open year round. The park has outstanding views of the river, and anglers say this is one of the best spots to fish the Rio Grande.

Nine miles farther south, where Embudo Creek empties into the Rio Grande, are the twin villages of **Embudo** (on N.M. 68) and **Dixon** (a mile east up N.M. 75). Many artists and craftspeople have studios here, and exhibit their works during an annual autumn show sponsored by the Dixon Arts Association. You can follow signs to **La Chiripada Winery** (tel. 579-4437), whose product is surprisingly good. Local pottery is also sold in the tasting room. The winery is open from 10 a.m. to 5 p.m. Monday through Saturday and noon to 5 p.m. on Sunday.

Near Dixon is the **Harding Mine,** a University of New Mexico property where visitors can gather mineral specimens without going underground. If you haven't signed a liability release at the Albuquerque campus, ask at Labeo's Store in Dixon. They'll direct you to the home of a local resident who can get you started fossicking almost immediately.

Two more small villages lie in the Rio Grande Valley at six-mile intervals south of Embudo on N.M. 68. **Velarde** is a fruit-growing center; in season, the road here is lined with stands selling fresh fruit or crimson chile ristras and wreathes of native plants. **Alcalde** is the location of Los Luceros an early-17th-century home planned for refurbishment as an arts and history center. The unique Dance of the Matachines, a Moorish-influenced production brought from Spain by the conquistadors, is performed here on holiday and feast days.

San Juan Pueblo (tel. 505/852-4400) is the largest (pop. 1,700) and northernmost of the Tewa- (not Tiwa-) speaking pueblos and the headquarters of the Eight Northern Indian Pueblos. Located on the east side of the Rio Grande opposite the 1596 site of the first Spanish settlement west of the Mississippi River, it is reached via N.M. 74, a mile off N.M. 68, two miles south of Velarde and four miles north of Española.

Past and present cohabit here in what was the first Spanish capital of New Spain. San Juan Indians, though Roman Catholics, still practice traditional religious rituals; thus two rectangular *kivas* flank the church in the main plaza, and *caciques* (pueblo priests) share influence with civil authorities. Forget about photos here, though: no cameras or sketching are permitted in the pueblo, fee payment or no. That even goes for the San Juan Fiesta, June 23–24.

The **Eight Northern Indian Pueblos Council** (tel. 505/852-4265) is a sort of chamber of commerce and social-service agency for the Nambe, Picuris, Pojoaque, San Ildefonso, San Juan, Santa Clara, Taos, and Tesuque Pueblos. In part because of its presence here, crafts of all eight pueblos are sold in this pueblo's well-known multipurpose arts center.

The **O'ke Oweenge Arts and Crafts Cooperative** (tel. 852-2372) is a fine place to seek out San Juan's distinctive red pottery, a lustrous ceramic incised with traditional geometric symbols. Also exhibited and sold are seed, turquoise and silver jewelry, wood and stone carvings, indigenous clothing and weavings, embroidery, and paintings. Artisans often work in the center for visitors to watch. The co-op is open from 9 a.m. to 4:30 p.m. daily except Sunday and San Juan Feast Day.

Right on the main road through the pueblo is the **Tewa Indian Restaurant,** serving traditional pueblo chile stews, breads, blue-corn dishes, posole, teas, and desserts. It's open from 9 a.m. to 2 p.m. Monday through Friday, except holidays and feast days.

Fishing and picknicking are encouraged at the **San Juan Tribal Lakes,** open year round. Tribal licenses, priced at $3 for adults, $2 for seniors and $1.50 for children, can be obtained at the tribal office.

The commercial center of **Española** (pop. 7,000) no longer has the railroad that was responsible for its establishment in the 1880s, but it does have perhaps New Mexico's greatest concentration of "low-riders." Their owners give much loving attention to these late-model customized cars, so called because their suspension leaves them sitting exceedingly close to the ground. You can't miss them cruising the main streets of town, especially on weekend nights.

Significant sights in Española include the **Bond House Museum,** a Victorian-era adobe home displaying exhibits of local history and art; and the **Santa Cruz Church,** built in 1733 and renovated in 1979, which houses many fine examples of Spanish colonial religious art. Major events include the July **Fiesta de Onate,** commemorating the valley's founding in 1596; the **Tri-Cultural Art Festival** in October on the Northern New Mexico Community College campus; and the **Summer Solstice** celebration staged by the nearby, 200-strong Sikh Dharma New Mexico ashram.

Santa Feans sometimes take the half-hour drive to Española simply to dine at **Matilda's Café,** Corlett Road (tel. 753-3200). Open from 9 a.m. to 9 p.m. Tuesday through Sunday, it's noted for its Hispanic food, including vegetarian plates.

Full information on Española and vicinity can be obtained from the **Española Valley Chamber of Commerce,** 417 Big Rock Center, Española, NM 87532 (tel. 505/753-2831).

The **Santa Clara Pueblo** (tel. 505/753-7330) is just across the Rio Grande from Española on N.M. 5. With a population of about 1,200, it's one of the larger pueblos. Driving and walking tours are offered daily (9 a.m. to 4:30 p.m.) year round from the tribal office, and include visits to the pueblo's historic church and artists' studios. Its main crafts are highly polished red-and-black pottery and baskets. Cameras (fees from $5) are welcome on Santa Clara Feast Day (August 12) and other dance days, including buffalo and deer dances in early February and children's dances on December 28.

The Santa Clara people migrated to their home on the Rio Grande in the 13th century from a former home high on the Pajarito Plateau to the west. The ruins of that past life have been preserved in the **Puye Cliff Dwellings,** an 11-mile climb west of the pueblo on N.M. 5. Thought to have been settled more than 1,000 years ago, this site at the mouth of the Santa Clara Canyon is a national landmark. Visitors can descend via staircases and ladders from the 7,000-foot mesa top into the 740-room pueblo ruin, which includes a ceremonial chamber and community house. Petroglyphs are evident in many of the rocky cliff walls.

The Puye Cliff Dwellings are open daily from 9 a.m. to 6 p.m., year round. Fees are $4 for adults, $3 for children and seniors; there's a modest additional charge for guided tours, and a pueblo feast and dance can also be included for a package charge of $15 to $20.

Six miles farther west on N.M. 5 is the **Santa Clara Canyon Recreational Area,** a picturesque location open summers for camping and year round for picnicking, hiking, and fishing in ponds and Santa Clara Creek. Tribal license fees apply.

From Española, it's 24 miles back to Santa Fe on U.S. 84/285.

SANTA FE–LOS ALAMOS–CENTRAL PUEBLOS LOOP

Some 225 miles in distance, this route follows U.S. 84/285 as far as Pojoaque, then crosses to the west side of the Rio Grande for about 100 miles before reaching Interstate 25 and zigzagging off the main Albuquerque–Santa Fe highway.

Turn left on N.M. 4 at Pojoaque. It's about six miles to **San Ildefonso Pueblo** (tel. 505/455-3549), nationally famous for the matte-finish black-on-black pottery developed by tribeswoman Maria Martinez in the 1920s. The pottery-making process is explained at the San Ildefonso Pueblo Museum, where exhibits of pueblo history, arts, and crafts are presented April through October. Tours of the pueblo are offered at the Visitor and Information Center, open from 9 a.m. to 5 p.m. daily except holidays in summer, 9 a.m. to 4 p.m. weekdays only in winter. Camera fees start at $5.

San Ildefonso Feast Day, January 23, is a good time to observe the social and religious traditions of the pueblo, which has a population of about 450. There are also dances for St. Anthony's Day (June 13), Santiago's Day (July 25), and the Harvest Festival (early September), as well as Christmas.

The third full weekend in July, the pueblo is the site of the annual **Eight Northern Indian Pueblos Council Artist and Craftsman Show.** More than 600 artisans sell their work at 300 booths between 8 a.m. and 6 p.m. on Saturday and Sunday; traditional food is served continually, and tribal dances are performed between 11 a.m. and 4 p.m. each day.

The atomic bomb was born in **Los Alamos,** a city of 11,000 spread on the craggy, finger-like mesas of the Pajarito Plateau, between the Jemez Mountains and Rio Grande Valley, 18 miles west of Pojoaque. Although Pueblo Indians had lived in this rugged area for well over 1,000 years, and an exclusive boys' school had been operating atop the 7,300-foot plateau since 1928, it was only in 1943 that Los Alamos National Laboratory was founded in secrecy as Project Y of the Manhattan Engineer District, the hush-

hush wartime program to split the atom and develop the world's first nuclear weapons.

Project director J. Robert Oppenheimer, later succeeded by Norris E. Bradbury, worked with a team of 30 to 100 scientists in research, development, and production of the weapons. Today 3,000 scientists and another 4,000 support staff work at **Los Alamos National Laboratory,** making it the largest employer in northern New Mexico. Still operated by the University of California for the federal Department of Energy (which provides more than 80% of its $600-million annual budget), its 32 technical areas occupy 43 square miles of mesa-top land.

The laboratory is known today as one of the world's foremost scientific institutions. It's still geared heavily to the defense industry—the Trident and Minuteman strategic warheads were created here, for example—but it has many other research programs, including studies in nuclear fusion and fission, energy conservation, nuclear safety, the environment, and nuclear wastes. Its international resources include a genetic sequence data bank, with wide implications for medicine and agriculture, and an Institute for Geophysics and Planetary Physics and others.

The **Bradbury Science Museum,** on Diamond Drive (tel. 667-4444), is the lab's public showcase. This outstanding museum focuses on atomic research in a wide variety of scientific and historical displays, including more than 35 hands-on exhibits. Visitors, who pay no admission fee, can see films and peruse photographs and documents highlighting the earliest days of Project Y, including a 1939 letter from Albert Einstein to President Franklin D. Roosevelt suggesting research into uranium as a new and important source of energy. There are exhibits on weapons research, including an overview of the nation's nuclear arsenal; achievements in alternative energy research, from solar and geothermal and laser and magnetic-fusion energy; biomedical research and development; computer technology; and basic research into the nature of nuclei, atoms, and molecules. Visitors may peer through microscopes, align lasers, and monitor radiation. The museum theater continually shows short, locally produced features on subjects ranging from computer graphics to treatment of eye cancer in cattle. The museum is open from 9 a.m. to 5 p.m. Tuesday through Friday, 1 to 5 p.m. Saturday through Monday; closed holidays.

The log building at 2132 Central Ave. that housed the Los Alamos Ranch School for boys from 1928 to 1943 is now a national historic landmark known as the Fuller Lodge. Its current occupants include the **Los Alamos Historical Museum** (tel. 662-6272), which recounts area history from prehistoric cliff dwellers to the present; the **Fuller Lodge Art Center** (tel. 662-9331), with works of regional artists and visiting exhibitions; and the **Los Alamos County Chamber of Commerce,** P.O. Box 460B, Los Alamos, NM 87544 (tel. 505/662-8105 or 662-5595), which doubles as a visitor information center. The museum and art center are open from 10 a.m. to 4 p.m. Monday through Saturday and 1 to 4 p.m. on Sunday, with free admission.

Los Alamos's events schedule includes a Sports Skiesta in late March or early April; arts-and-crafts fairs in May and October; a bicycle race, golf tourney, and mini-marathon in July; a county fair, rodeo, and arts festival in August; and a triathlon in August/ September. A ski area—**Pajarito Mountain** (tel. 662-5725)— and public golf course (tel. 662-8139) are at the edges of town, and the **Larry R. Walkup Aquatic Center** (tel. 662-8035) is the highest-altitude indoor Olympic-size swimming pool in the United States. There's even an ice-skating rink.

If you choose to stay overnight, the recently renovated **Hilltop House Hotel,** Trinity at Central, Los Alamos, NM 87544 (tel. 505/662-2441), has 80 tastefully furnished rooms with prices starting at $54 for two. Each room has satellite TV, and guests have access to a swimming pool and coin-op laundry. The third-floor Trinity Sights Restaurant, which affords a stunning view across the Rio Grande to Santa Fe, has a lengthy dinner menu that includes the likes of Cajun-style prime rib ($13), chicken saltimbocca ($13), and scallops Portofino ($16).

Across town, with prices in the same $55 to $60 range, is the 115-room **Los Alamos Inn,** 2201 Trinity Dr., Los Alamos, NM 87544 (tel. 505/662-7211). The restaurant features dinner specials like teriyaki shrimp and scallops ($11) and steak Mexican ($10); it has a big salad bar and a comfortable lounge with frequent entertainment.

A budget lodging alternative is the **Cottage Inn,** a bed-and-breakfast at 1531 42nd St., Los Alamos, NM 87544 (tel. 505/ 662-4614). Doubles, which include a private entrance, pine-roofed patio, and private bath, are only $25 a night.

The **Chili Village,** 1743 Trinity Dr. (tel. 662-7591), is a popular choice for homemade Mexican food, including breakfast burritos ($2.25) and taco, tortilla, or enchilada plates (from $3.25). It's open in winter from 7 a.m. to 3:30 p.m. daily except Sunday; hours are extended to include dinner in summer.

The nearby town of **White Rock,** ten miles south of Los Alamos on Alternate N.M. 4, has a couple more popular restaurants. Many folks visit, however, simply to picnic at White Rock Overlook with its spectacular panoramas of the Rio Grande valley.

Bandelier National Monument (tel. 672-3861), fewer than 15 miles south of Los Alamos along N.M. 4, is the nearest major prehistoric site to Santa Fe, combining the extensive ruins of an ancient Anasazi pueblo culture with 46 square miles of canyon-and-mesa wilderness.

Most visitors, after an orientation stop in the visitor center and museum to learn about the culture that persisted here between A.D. 1100 and 1550, follow a cottonwood-shaded 1½-mile trail along Frijoles Creek to the principal ruins. The pueblo site, including a great underground *kiva*, has been partially reconstructed. The biggest thrill for most folks, though, is climbing hardy piñon ladders to explore the interiors of cliff dwellings carved into ancient volcanic rock 140 feet above the canyon floor. Tours are self-guided or led by a National Park Service ranger. Campfire talks and other interpretive programs are presented in summer.

Elsewhere in the monument, 60 miles of maintained trails lead to more Indian ruins and ceremonial sites, waterfalls, and wildlife habitats. The separate Tsankawi section of the monument, close to White Rock, contains a large unexcavated ruin on a high mesa overlooking the Rio Grande Valley.

Areas are set aside for picnicking and camping. Admission is $1 per person. The national monument—named after Swiss-American archeologist Adolph Bandelier, who explored here in the 1880s—is open year round daily except Christmas; hours are 8 a.m. to 7 p.m. in summer, 8 a.m. to 5 p.m. in winter.

Most people are surprised to learn that the largest volcanic caldera in the world is here in northern New Mexico. **Valle Grande,** a vast meadow 16 miles in diameter and 76 square miles in area, is all that remains of a massive volcano that erupted nearly a million years ago. When the mountain spewed ashes and dust as far as Kansas and Nebraska, its underground magma chambers collapsed, forming this great valley. Lava domes which pushed up after the collapse obstruct a full view across the expanse. New Mexico Hwy. 4 skirts the caldera beginning about 15 miles west of Los Alamos.

Outdoor lovers enjoy camping and fishing at **Fenton Lake State Park,** 35 miles west of Los Alamos on N.M. 126, and swimming at **Soda Dam,** a natural mineral deposit on the Jemez River 40 miles west of Los Alamos on N.M. 4.

The side-by-side ruins of a 12th-century Indian pueblo and a 17th-century Spanish mission provide the basis for **Jemez State Monument** (tel. 829-3530), 41 miles from Los Alamos on N.M. 4. The former site of the pueblo of Giusewa ("Place at the Boiling Waters") is demarcated, but more in evidence is the Church of San José de los Jemez, built in 1622. The unearthed walls are six to eight feet thick; an octagonal tower, containing a circular stairway, rises 42 feet above the altar and sanctuary. A small museum offers historical background and artifacts.

One more mile down the road is **Jemez Springs,** a hunting and fishing center more famous for its hot mineral spa. The 154° to 186° waters are cooled at the Jemez Springs Bath House, to which people from around the world throng to get therapy for arthritis, rheumatism, dermatitis, and other ailments. The water contains calcium, iron, magnesium, potassium, sodium, sulphate, phosphates, and other minerals in lesser quantities.

Jemez Pueblo (tel. 505/834-7359) is about 13 miles south of the hot springs, also on N.M. 4. Its 2,100 inhabitants, among whom are the descendants of those who fled the Pecos Pueblo east of Santa Fe in 1838, are the sole surviving speakers of the Towa language. Plaited yucca-leaf baskets, weaving, and pottery are sold by individual artisans. The pueblo is better known for its dances, staged in two rectangular *kivas* on the feast days of Our Lady of the Angels (August 12) and San Diego (St. James; November 12). There's no entrance fee—but then, cameras aren't allowed either. Permits are sold for fishing and camping at several springs and ponds.

Turn left three miles south in San Ysidro, at the junction of N.M. 44, and proceed another seven miles to the **Zia Pueblo** (tel. 867-3304). If you don't see it right away, look again: its soft-brown shades blend like camouflage into the desert around it. The sun symbol you've seen all over New Mexico—the circle with three straight lines coming out in each of the cardinal directions—is the traditional sun sign of the Zia people. You'll sometimes see it reproduced in the fine polychrome pottery or, rarely, in the pueblo's famous watercolors. Most of the 580 Zia people work in Albuquerque, 38 miles south. Their annual feast day, honoring St. Lawrence, is highlighted by a corn dance on August 15. Cameras are not permitted.

The **Santa Ana Pueblo** (tel. 505/867-3301) is eight miles closer to Albuquerque along the same highway. Its 500 citizens live mainly on irrigated farmlands surrounding the pueblo proper, and return to the village on special occasions. The Ta-Ma-Myia Cooperative Association markets the pueblo's woven belts and pottery. Except on feast days—January 1 and 6, Easter, June 24 and 29, July 26 (St. Anne's Day), and the Christmas holidays—the pueblo is closed to the public. No cameras are allowed.

Coronado State Monument (tel. 867-5351), near Bernalillo six miles from the Santa Ana Pueblo, preserves the ruins of the ancient Anasazi pueblo of Kuaua, including a restored underground *kiva* complete with entrance ladder. A village on this site was visited by Spanish explorer Francisco Vasquez de Coronado in 1540. There's an excellent small archeological museum here, and an interpretive trail through the ruins. It's open daily except holidays, from 9 a.m. to 6 p.m. May 1 to September 15, 8 a.m. to 5 p.m. the rest of the year; admission is $1 for adults, 50¢ for children. The adjacent Coronado State Park has full camping facilities.

At Bernalillo, an Albuquerque suburb, join Interstate 25 and head north about ten miles to the turnoff for the **San Felipe Pueblo** (tel. 505/867-3381). About three miles farther, on a mesa on the west bank of the Rio Grande, is this traditional village of 2,000. The pueblo is most famous for its ceremonial dances: countless thousands of dancing feet have worn its plaza into a virtual bowl shape. Hundreds of men, women, and children participate in the all-day corn dance during the Festival of San Felipe (St. Philip) on May 1. Other dance days include January 6, February 2, and Christmas.

Santo Domingo Pueblo (tel. 505/465-2214) is about eight miles north via Tribal Rte. 84, or 17 via I-25 and N.M. 22. The largest (pop. 3,300) of the Keresan-speaking pueblos, it is located on the east bank of the Rio Grande and is noted for its shell and turquoise jewelry, silverwork, weaving, and pottery. A lavish and dramatic corn dance is performed here on August 4, during the Fiesta de Santo Domingo; it features more than 500 traditionally clad dancers as well as clowns, singers, and drummers. Other festivals take place on January 6, February 2, Easter, June 29, and Christmas. There's no admission charge—and no cameras.

Cochiti Pueblo (tel. 505/465-2244) can be reached from Santo Domingo by taking N.M. 22 another nine miles north, away from the Interstate. Double-headed cottonwood drums, beadwork, moccasins, and pottery—especially the prized storyteller figures—are noted crafts. The pueblo's Church of San Buenaventura, though rebuilt and remodeled since, still contains sections of its original 1628 structure. Feast day for the saint is July 14, when a corn dance and rain dance are performed. Other dance events in this village of 900 are held January 1 and 6, Easter, May 3, and at Christmastime. There's no admission, and neither are cameras permitted.

To return to Santa Fe, take N.M. 22 and 16 back to I-25, a distance of about 10 miles. It's another 22 miles from there to the Plaza.

SANTA FE–TAOS, VIA LAS VEGAS

This 235-mile route, much of it following the old Santa Fe Trail on Interstate 25, includes two national monuments (Pecos and Fort Union) and two very different towns with distinct frontier atmosphere (Las Vegas and Cimarron).

About 15 miles east of I-25's Las Vegas Hwy. on-ramp at Santa Fe, the freeway meanders through **Glorieta Pass,** site of an important Civil War skirmish. In March 1862 volunteers from

Colorado and New Mexico, along with Fort Union regulars, defeated a Confederate force marching on Santa Fe, thereby turning the tide of Southern encroachment on New Mexico.

Take N.M. 50 east to **Pecos,** a distance of about seven miles. This quaint town, well off the beaten track since the interstate was built, is the site of a noted Benedictine monastery. North of here 26 miles on N.M. 63 is the village of **Cowles,** gateway to the natural wonderland of the Pecos Wilderness. There are many camping, picnicking, and fishing locales en route.

Pecos National Monument, two miles south of the town of Pecos off N.M. 63 (tel. 757-6414), contains the ruins of a 14th-century pueblo and 17th-century mission. The pueblo was well known to Coronado in 1540: "It is feared throughout the land," he wrote. With a population of about 2,000, the Indians farmed in irrigated fields and hunted wild game. Their pueblo had 660 rooms and many *kivas.* By 1620 Franciscan monks had established a church and convent. Military and natural disasters took their toll, however, and in 1838 the 20 surviving Pecos Indians abandoned their ancestral home and took up residence with relatives at the Jemez Pueblo.

The E. E. Fogelson Visitor Center tells the history of the Pecos people in a well-done, chronologically organized exhibit, complete with dioramas of pre-Hispanic lifestyles. A 1¼-mile loop trail departs from the center and leads through Pecos Pueblo and the Mission de Nuestra Señora de Los Angeles de Porciuncula, as the church was formally known. This excavated structure—170 feet long and 90 feet wide at the transept—was once the most magnificent church north of Mexico City.

Visitors to the national monument are asked to pay $1 admission, which goes to further preservation.

Rejoin I-25 at Rowe, 4 miles south of the national monument. Las Vegas is 38 miles northeast. En route, keep your eyes open for N.M. 3, which leads 12 miles to the picturesque Spanish colonial village of **Villanueva.** Nearby **Villanueva State Park** offers hiking, camping, and picnicking between high red sandstone bluffs in the Pecos River Valley.

Las Vegas, New Mexico, should never be confused with Las Vegas, Nevada. The gambling town was named after these urban meadows (*vegas*), founded in 1835 by a land grant. The Santa Fe Trail came through here beginning in the 1850s, and with the advent of the Atchison, Topeka & Santa Fe Railroad in 1879, Las Vegas boomed. The town's vast number of well-preserved Territorial-style buildings, and its Queen Anne and Victorian homes, date from the subsequent era of affluence. Some 90 buildings are on the National Register of Historic Places; the **Las Vegas Chamber of Commerce,** 727 Grand Ave. (P.O. Box 148), Las

Vegas, NM 87701 (tel. 505/425-8631), provides maps and brochures for self-guided walking and driving tours.

Today the town of 16,000 is primarily a ranching center. Among its points of interest is the **Rough Riders Memorial and City Museum** (tel. 454-1401), next door to the chamber of commerce. About 40% of Teddy Roosevelt's Spanish-American War campaigners in 1898 came from this frontier town, and this museum chronicles their contribution to U.S. history. It's open from 9 a.m. to 4 p.m. daily except Sunday and holidays. **New Mexico Highlands University** is located in Las Vegas, and another campus —the unique and highly acclaimed **Armand Hammer United World College**—is five miles west at Montezuma hot springs. **Las Vegas National Wildlife Refuge** (tel. 425-3581), about six miles southeast of town via Rtes. 104 and 281, boasts 220 species of birds and animals on 8,750 acres of wetland. Three state parks are reached via N.M. 518 north: **Storrie Lake,** four miles north, with fishing, swimming, waterskiing, camping, and a visitor center with historic exhibits about the Santa Fe Trail; **Morphy Lake,** a pristine primitive-use area 35 miles away near Mora; and **Coyote Creek,** a secluded stream with beaver ponds 14 miles north of Mora via N.M. 434.

Important annual events in Las Vegas include Cinco de Mayo, the Mexican independence day celebration, May 5; Rails and Trails Days, celebrating the town heritage with rodeos, music, and square dancing, the first full weekend of June; and a three-day Fourth of July Fiesta.

An overnight stay at the restored **Plaza Hotel,** 230 Old Town Plaza, Las Vegas, NM 87701 (tel. 505/425-3591), puts visitors in an immediate mood for historic and architectural exploring. Considered the finest hotel in the New Mexico Territory when it was built in Italianate bracketed style in 1882, it was renovated with a $2-million investment exactly 100 years later. Rates for the 37 guest rooms are $50 and $55 double, or $70 and up for suites. The hotel restaurant, looking out on the lush shaded Plaza, is the best in town (try the onion relleno: *bueno!*); Bryon T's bar has an interesting display of historic photographs of Las Vegas.

Fort Union National Monument (tel. 425-8025) is reached by traveling 18 miles north on I-25 and another 8 miles west on N.M. 161. The way is well marked. Established in 1851 to defend Santa Fe against attacks from the Plains Indians, it was expanded in 1861 in anticipation of a Confederate invasion, subsequently thwarted at Glorieta Pass. Its location on the Santa Fe Trail made it a welcome way station for travelers, but when the railroad replaced the trail, the fort was on its way out. It was abandoned in 1891.

Today the fort, the largest military installation in the 19th-century Southwest, is in ruins. There's little to see but adobe walls and chimneys, but the very scope of the fort is impressive. Santa Fe Trail wagon ruts are still visible nearby. The national monument visitor center has interpreted the fort's history through exhibits, booklets, and a walking trail. Special living-history events, with soldiers and traders in appropriate costumes, are held the last weekends of June, July, and August. The site is open daily from 8 a.m. to 6 p.m. Memorial Day to Labor Day, 8 a.m. to 4:30 p.m. the rest of the year; closed Christmas and New Year's Days.

In the little town of **Springer,** 68 miles north of Las Vegas via I-25, the **Santa Fe Trail Museum** (tel. 483-2394) is housed in the 1881 Colfax County Courthouse. It contains pioneer artifacts and memorabilia from trail travelers.

The junction of N.M. 58 is six miles north of Springer. Turn left here and drive 19 miles to **Cimarron.** Few towns in the American West have as much lore or legend attached to them. Nestled against the eastern slope of the Sangre de Cristo range, the town (its name is Spanish for "wild" or "unbroken") achieved its greatest fame as an outpost on the Santa Fe Trail between the 1850s and 1880s. Frontier personalities like Kit Carson and Wyatt Earp, Buffalo Bill Cody and Annie Oakley, painter Frederick Remington and novelist Zane Grey, Bat Masterson and Jesse James all passed through and stayed—most of them at the St. James Hotel—at one time or another.

The **St. James Hotel,** Route 1, Box 2, Cimarron, NM 87714 (tel. 505/376-2664), looks much the same today as it did in 1873, when it was built by Henri Lambert, a chef for Abraham Lincoln and Gen. Ulysses S. Grant. In its early years it was a place of some lawlessness: 26 men were said to have been killed within the two-foot-thick adobe walls, and current owners Ed and Pat Sitzberger can point out bullet holes in the pressed-tin ceiling of the dining room. The ghosts of some are believed to inhabit the hotel still.

Restored and reopened by the Sitzbergers in 1985, the St. James now has 15 guest rooms decorated with priceless antiques. Rates vary from $40 to $75 per night for one or two people. The finest meals in this part of the state are served in the St. James dining room, with poultry, beef, and seafood dinners priced $10 to $17.

A stone's throw from the St. James is the **Old Mill Museum,** built in 1864 by Lucien Maxwell, whose 1.7 million acres of land represented the largest holding by any single individual in U.S. history. The stone grist mill, built to supply flour to Fort Union, now houses an interesting collection of early photos and memorabilia. It's open from 9 a.m. to 5 p.m. daily except Thursday (1 to 5 p.m. on Sunday) from May to October. Admission is $2 for adults, $1 for seniors and children.

Cimarron is the gateway to the **Philmont Scout Ranch,** a 137,000-acre property donated to the Boy Scouts of America by Texas oilman Waite Phillips in 1938. Scouts from all over the world use it for backcountry camping and leadership training from June through August, and for conferences the remainder of the year.

There are three museums on the ranch, all open to the public. **Villa Philmonte,** Phillips's Mediterranean-style summer home, was built in 1927 and remains furnished with the family's European antiques from that era. Three miles south of Cimarron, it's open daily in summer for guided tours, other times by appointment. The **Ernest Thompson Seton Memorial Library and Museum** (tel. 376-2281) commemorates the art and taxidermy of the naturalist and author who founded the B.S.A., and has exhibits on the varied history of the Cimarron area. It's open year round, daily from June to August, closed Sunday the rest of the year. The **Kit Carson Museum,** seven miles south of Philmont headquarters in Rayado, is a period hacienda furnished in 1850s style. Staff in historic costumes lead tours daily June through August. Admission is free to all ranch museums.

The **Cimarron Chamber of Commerce,** P.O. Box 604, Cimarron, NM 87714 (tel. 505/376-2614), has complete information on the region.

New Mexico Hwy. 58 from Cimarron leads west 24 miles to Eagle Nest, passing en route **Cimarron Canyon State Park,** a designated state wildlife area at the foot of crenellated granite formations known as the Palisades. From Eagle Nest, it's a 31-mile drive to Taos on U.S. 64.

SANTA FE–CHAMA

This short (100-mile) spur follows U.S. 84 to the rail and outdoor-recreation center of Chama, passing en route through Georgia O'Keeffe country around Abiquiu and through the weaving center of Tierra Amarilla. A side trip leads into the Jicarilla Apache Indian Reservation.

The late Ansel Adams immortalized the village of **Hernandez,** six miles north of Española, in his famous photograph of a full moon rising. Three miles farther, a turnoff leads a short distance to **Medanales,** a small community famous for its weaving tradition. Cordelia Coronado's shop is especially well known. Ask directions locally to the **Dar al-Islam** community, with its circular adobe replica of a Middle Eastern mosque.

There's no museum to mark her former residence, but the celebrated artist Georgia O'Keeffe spent most of her adult life in **Abiquiu,** a tiny town in a bend of the Rio Chama 22 miles north of Española on U.S. 84. The inspiration for O'Keeffe's startling landscapes is clear in the surrounding terrain. Many dinosaur skeletons have been found in rocks along the base of cliffs near **Abiquiu Reservoir,** a popular fishing spot formed by the Abiquiu Dam.

The **Ghost Ranch Living Museum** (tel. 685-4312), 14 miles north of Abiquiu, is a U.S. Forest Service–operated exhibit of regional plant and animal life, geology, palentology, and ecology. Short trails lead past re-created marsh, grassland, canyon, and forest land, inhabited by 27 species of native New Mexican animals and birds, most of them brought here injured or orphaned. A miniature national forest, complete with a fire lookout tower, illustrates conservation techniques; a trail through a severely eroded arroyo affords an opportunity to study soil ecology. Temporary exhibits from the New Mexico Museum of Natural History are presented in an indoor display hall. The Ghost Ranch is open daily from 8 a.m. to 6 p.m. May to September, Tuesday through Sunday from 8 a.m. to 4:30 p.m. October through April. There's no admission, though donations are welcomed.

Some 13 miles west of the Ghost Ranch via a dirt road into the Chama River Canyon Wilderness is the isolated **Christ-in-the-Desert Monastery,** built in 1964 by Benedictine monks. The brothers produce crafts, sold at a small gift shop, and operate a guesthouse. Three miles north of the wildlife museum on U.S. 84 is **Echo Canyon Amphitheater,** with a campground and picnic area. A natural "theater," hollowed out of sandstone by thousands of years of erosion, is a ten-minute walk from the parking area.

The distinctive yellow earth in the area gave the town of **Tierra Amarilla** its name. Throughout New Mexico, its name is synonymous with a continuing controversy over the land-grant rights of the descendants of the original settlers. But the economy of this community of 1,000, 44 miles north of the Abiquiu at the junction of U.S. 84 and 64, is dyed in the wool, literally. A cooperative program is at work to save the long-haired Spanish churro sheep from extinction through breeding, introduce other unusual wool breeds to the valley, and perpetuate a 200-year-old tradition of shepherding, spinning, weaving, and dyeing. Many of the craftspeople work in conjunction with **Tierra Wools** (tel. 588-7231), which has a showroom and workshop in a century-old mercantile building in the Los Ojos historic district at the northern edge of Tierra Amarillo. One-of-a-kind blankets and men's and women's apparel are among the products displayed and sold.

Two state parks are a short drive from Tierra Amarilla. **El Vado Lake,** 14 miles west on N.M. 112, offers boating and waterskiing, fishing, and camping by summer; cross-country skiing and ice fishing by winter. **Heron Lake,** eight miles west on N.M. 95, has a 3-mph speed limit for motor vessels, adding to its appeal to fishermen and sailors. There's an interpretive center, and camping and picnic sites. The 5½-mile Rio Chama Trail connects Heron and El Vado Lakes.

Chama, 15 miles north of Tierra Amarilla on U.S. 84/64 and just nine miles south of the Colorado border, is an important summer and winter recreation center. Hunting and fishing, cross-country skiing, and snowmobiling are the sports of choice. Important annual events in this community of 1,250 are the Chama Chili Classic, New Mexico's biggest nordic ski races with 400 racers from eight states competing in 5-km and 10-km events in mid-February; the High Country Winter Carnival, featuring dog-sled races, also in February; and the Chama Days rodeo and parade in August. For details, write the **Chama Valley Chamber of Commerce,** P.O. Box 306, Chama, NM 87520 (tel. 505/756-2306).

Chama's No. 1 attraction is the **Cumbres & Toltec Scenic Railroad,** a historic narrow-gauge steam railroad that winds 64 miles through the San Juan Mountains to Antonito, Colorado. Built in 1880 to serve mining camps in these rugged highlands, it is considered the finest remaining example of a once-vast Rocky Mountain rail network. The track climbs a precipitous 4% grade out of Chama, crests at 10,015-foot Cumbres Pass, then descends through tunnels and trestles to the rail town of Osier, Colorado. Here the *New Mexico Express* from Chama and the *Colorado Limited* from Antonito stop to exchange engines. After a picnic or catered lunch, round-trip passengers return to their starting point; onward passengers continue a descent through spectacular Toltec Gorge on the Los Pinos River, past strange rock formations and groves of pine and aspen, to Antonito.

A through trip from Chama to Antonito (or vice versa), traveling one way by van, runs $41.50 for adults, or $20 for children 11 and under. A regular round trip, without transfers, is $27, but misses either the pass or the gorge. Either way, it's an all-day adventure, leaving between 8 and 10:30 a.m. and returning between 4:30 and 6:30 p.m. Write or phone ahead for reservations: P.O. Box 789, Chama, NM 87520 (tel. 505/756-2151). The train operates daily from mid-June to mid-October. Owned by the states of Colorado and New Mexico, it's a registered National Historic Site.

If time permits, consider a side trip to **Dulce,** 27 miles west of Chama on U.S. 64. Dulce, a town of 3,200, is the headquarters of the 768,000-acre **Jicarilla Apache Indian Reservation.** The word *jicarilla* (pronounced "hick-a-*ree*-yah") means "little basket," so it's no surprise that tribal craftspeople are noted for their basket weaving and beadwork. See their work, both contemporary and museum quality, at the **Jicarilla Apache Arts and Crafts Shop and Museum,** a lime-green building along the highway west of downtown (tel 759-3362). Tribe members guide fishermen and trophy hunters, most of whom seek elk and mule deer, into the reservation's wilderness backcountry. Highlights of the Jicarilla calendar are the Little Beaver Roundup the third weekend in July and the Stone Lake Fiesta on September 14 and 15 annually. The best accommodation in this part of state is the **Best Western Jicarilla Inn,** U.S. 64 at the east edge of town, Dulce, NM 87528 (tel. 505/759-3663, or toll free 800/528-1234), with rates in the $50 range double.

To return from Chama to Taos, backtrack to Tierra Amarilla, then turn east on U.S. 64. It's 49 miles to Tres Piedras and 31 more across the Rio Grande Gorge Bridge to Taos.

SANTA FE–ALBUQUERQUE, VIA THE TURQUOISE TRAIL

This famous 70-mile trip can take all day if you want it to. It follows N.M. 14, which essentially parallels I-25 but on the east side of the Sandia Mountains. En route, it skirts an ancient turquoise-mining area, passes through several virtual ghost towns in varying states of habitation, and offers an enticing side trip to Sandia Crest overlooking metropolitan Albuquerque.

Head out of Santa Fe on Cerrillos Road, continuing straight ahead on the underpass beneath I-25 until you find yourself on N.M. 14. About 15 miles on is **Cerrillos,** a village of dirt roads that sprawls along Galisteo Creek. It appears to have changed very little since it was founded during a lead strike in 1879: the old hotel, saloon, even sheriff's office have a flavor very much like an Old West movie set.

Madrid, three miles farther, seems to have progressed beyond the 1880s but stuck in the 1960s. Its funky, ramshackle houses have many counterculture residents—the "hippies" of yore—who operate several crafts stores and import shops. The **Old Coal Mine Museum** (tel. 473-0743) features a mine shaft and railroad repair yard where blacksmiths and metal and leather workers still ply their trades; it's open daily, with admission of $1. The adjacent Mine Shaft Tavern has buffalo steak and live music every day, attracting many folks from Santa Fe.

Golden, 11 miles south of Madrid near the foot of San Pedro Mountain, is more definitely a "ghost town" than its more northerly cousins. There are a general merchandise shop, a gift shop, and a "garden" of blue bottles here, but the community is more characterized by adobe ruins, patchwork wood houses, and mining relics strewn through the hills.

At San Antonito, 12 miles farther down N.M. 14, N.M. 536 begins a long uphill climb to **Sandia Crest,** elevation 10,678 feet. This is the drivers' route to the Sandia Peak Ski Area and High Finance Restaurant more directly reached via the Sandia Peak Tramway. The view from the top, across New Mexico's largest city to the Rio Grande and beyond, is spectacular. (See Chapter XIV "What to See and Do in Albuquerque," for details.)

New Mexico Hwy. 14 joins I-40 at Cedar Crest, six miles past San Antonito. It's just a few miles west from here to Albuquerque's eastern city limits.

CHAPTER XIII

SETTLING INTO ALBUQUERQUE

□ □ □

From the rocky crest of Sandia Peak, the lights of this city of almost half a million people spread out like needlepoint on an enormous quilt at sunset.

As the sun drops beyond the western horizon, it glints off the Rio Grande, flowing through Albuquerque more than a mile beneath the observation post to the top of the Sandia Peak aerial tramway.

The tram, said to be the world's longest at 2.7 miles, climbs from the northeastern outskirts of the city to the top of 10,378-foot Sandia Peak, passing high above cathedral-like crags and sparse ponderosa and aspen forest.

From the summit, with keen eyes and a little imagination, you can see the site where Spanish colonists established a villa on the Old Chihuahua Trail in 1706 and named it after regional governor Don Francisco Cuervo y Valdez, the 13th Duke of Alburquerque (the first "r" was later deleted from the city's name).

Reminders of the colonial past of the "Duke City" still abound, though Albuquerque has become a major metropolis that now sprawls 16 miles from the lava-crested mesas on the west side of the Rio Grande to the steep alluvial slopes of the Sandia Mountains on the east, and another 14 miles north-south through the Rio Grande valley. It boomed as a transportation center with the arrival of the railroad in 1880, but that economic explosion was nothing compared to what happened during World War II, when Albuquerque was designated as a major national center for military research and production. Its population has grown by more than ten times in four decades.

ORIENTATION

The sprawl of the city takes a bit of getting used to at first. A visitor's first impression is often that of a massive grid of main thoroughfares, all lined with shopping malls and fast-food establishments, while residential neighborhoods are tucked behind on side streets. Albuquerque does, in fact, have considerably more character than that first impression might suggest.

If you lay a map of Albuquerque before you, the first thing you'll notice is that it lies at the crossroads of **Interstate 25** north-south and **Interstate 40** east-west. Refocus your attention to the southwest quadrant of the X: this is where both downtown Albuquerque and **Old Town,** center of most of the tourist attractions, lie.

Lomas Boulevard and **Central Avenue,** the old "Route 66" (U.S. 66), flank downtown on the north and south. They come together two miles west near the **Old Town Plaza,** the historical and spiritual heart of the city thoroughly described in Chapter XIV, "What to See and Do in Albuquerque." Its 18th- and 19th-century adobe buildings contrast markedly with the tall steel-and-glass structures of downtown. The Rio Grande greenbelt lies about half a mile southwest of Old Town.

Lomas and Central continue east across I-25, staying half a mile apart as they pass by first the University of New Mexico, then the New Mexico State Fairgrounds. The **Albuquerque International Airport** is due south of campus about three miles via Yale Boulevard; **Kirtland Air Force Base**—containing Sandia National Laboratories and the National Atomic Museum—is an equal distance south of the fairgrounds via Louisiana Boulevard.

Roughly paralleling I-40 to the north is **Menaul Boulevard,** focus of the **"Uptown"** shopping and hotel district where it is crossed by Louisiana Boulevard 3½ miles east of I-25. There are more major hotels near the intersection of Menaul and University Boulevards, hard by the I-25/I-40 interchange. And as Albuquerque expands north, the **Journal Center business park** area, about 4½ miles north of the interchange on I-25, is getting more attention as a center for convention hotels. Broad San Mateo Boulevard connects Journal Center with Uptown.

For address purposes, Central Avenue divides the city into north and south and the railroad tracks split it into east and west. Street names are followed by a directional: NE, NW, SE, or SW.

TRANSPORTATION: Major construction and expansion continues at the airport in 1989, complicating the chore of arriving and departing. Its completion is anxiously awaited. The city is served by nine **national and regional airlines:** America West (tel. toll free 800/247-5692), American (tel. 505/242-9464), Continental (tel. 505/842-8220), Delta/Western (tel. toll free 800/221-1212), Mesa (tel. toll free 800/637-2247), PSA (tel. toll free 800/435-9772), Southwest (tel. 505/831-1221), TWA (tel. toll free 800/221-2000), and United (tel. 505/242-1411).

Amtrak trains arrive and depart daily from and to Los Angeles and Chicago. The station is on 1st Street SW, two blocks south of Central Avenue (tel. 842-9650 for information).

Greyhound (tel. 243-4435) buses serve the Albuquerque Bus Transportation Center adjacent to the train station on 2nd Street SW.

The city's official visitors guide lists 13 **car-rental agencies,** among them Alamo (tel. 842-4057), Avis (tel. 842-4080), Budget (tel. 884-2666), Hertz (tel. 842-4235), National (tel. 842-4222), and Thrifty (tel. 842-8733). All provide airport service.

For those without vehicles at their disposal, an excellent **city bus network** cloaks the main thoroughfares. Contact Sun Tran of Albuquerque (tel. 843-9200) for information on routes and fares. The **Albuquerque Trolley** (tel. 242-1407), better known as the "Molly Trolley," runs hourly service between Old Town and Uptown via Downtown from 9 a.m. to 5 p.m. on Monday, to 9 p.m. Tuesday through Saturday, and noon to 9 p.m. on Sunday, for a fare of $1.

The **Yellow-Checker Cab Co.** (tel. 247-8888), a joint effort of two old standbys, offers service 24 hours a day, 365 days a year (it is difficult to hail a taxi, so call).

USEFUL INFORMATION: Dial 911 for police, fire, or other **emergencies** in the Albuquerque area. For everyday business, contact Albuquerque Police (tel. 766-7700), the Bernalillo County Sheriff (tel. 766-4160), the New Mexico State Police (tel. 841-8066), or the Albuquerque Fire Department (tel. 243-6601). . . . The **ambulance** service number is 765-1100. . . . Leading hospitals include **Presbyterian Hospital,** 1100 Central Ave. SE (tel. 841-1234), with satellite UrgentCare Centers around the city, and **St. Joseph Hospital,** 400 Walter St. NE (tel. 848-8000). . . . The city offers everyday **medical referral** services for doctors (tel. 268-2446) and dentists (tel. 292-2620).

The main **post office** is on Mountain Road at Broadway, four blocks north of Lomas Boulevard near downtown. . . . There are recorded numbers for **road and weather conditions** (tel. 841-8066) and **time and temperature** (tel. 247-1611).

The **Albuquerque Convention and Visitors Bureau** maintains its head office at 625 6th St. SW, Suite 210, Albuquerque,

NM 87102 (tel. 505/243-3696, or toll free 800/321-6979, 800/843-3659 in New Mexico). Branch information centers are at Albuquerque International Airport, at the lower east end of the terminal, open from 9 a.m. to 8 p.m. weekdays and 1 to 4:30 p.m. on Saturday; and in Old Town at 305 Romero St. NW (tel. 243-3215), open from 10 a.m. to 5 p.m. Monday through Friday, from 11 a.m. on Saturday.

WHERE TO STAY

A hotel glut that looks grim to those in the Albuquerque hospitality business is good news to travelers looking for quality rooms at reasonable cost. Except during peak periods—specifically, the New Mexico Arts & Crafts Fair in late June, the New Mexico State Fair in September, and the Albuquerque International Hot Air Balloon Fiesta in early October—most of the 8,000 rooms in the city are vacant, so guests can frequently request and get a lower room rate than the one posted.

In the following listing, hotels are categorized first by the part of town in which they're located (Downtown/Old Town, Midtown/Freeway Loop, Airport or Journal Center) and second by price range—deluxe (over $100 per night double), upper bracket ($70 to $100), moderate ($40 to $70), and budget (under $40).

State tax is 5%. The city of Albuquerque charges an additional 5¼% bed tax, so every bill will be 10¼% higher than suggested by these rates.

DOWNTOWN/OLD TOWN: This area is best if you want to stay close to the major sights and attractions.

Deluxe

The nearest hotel to the Albuquerque Convention Center is the **Albuquerque Doubletree Hotel,** 201 Marquette St. NW, Albuquerque, NM 87102 (tel. 505/247-3344, or toll free 800/545-4444). Formerly the Regent Hotel, it was purchased by the Doubletree Corporation in November 1987, and a $6.2-million renovation was completed in late 1988.

The Doubletree has some 300 guest rooms, with year-round rates of $105, single or double. The new rooms feature a mauve or navy-blue color scheme, with cable TV hidden in an armoire, southwestern-motif prints on the walls, radio-alarm clocks, and full-size mirrors on the bathroom doors. The 15-story hotel now has a rooftop swimming pool and workout facility, a new gourmet restaurant and adjacent nightclub, and a ceiling-to-floor waterfall in the main lobby. And 24-hour courtesy van service is available.

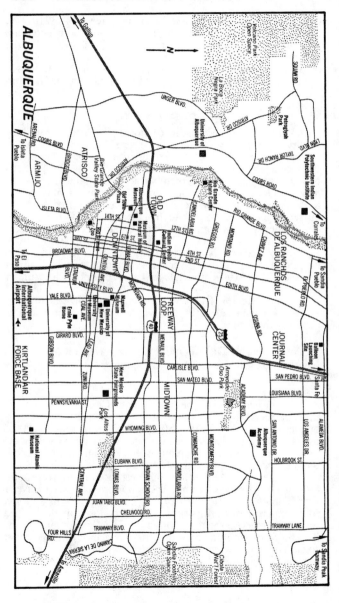

The Upper Bracket

No Albuquerque hotel is closer to the majority of tourist attractions than the **Sheraton Old Town,** 800 Rio Grande Blvd. NW, Albuquerque, NM 87104 (tel. 505/843-6300, or toll free 800/325-3535). Within five minutes' walk of the Old Town Plaza and overlooking two of the city's major museums, it's an ideal spot for visitors without their own vehicles who don't want to be at the mercy of taxis or rental cars.

Visitors get the red-carpet treatment right from the start, as they follow a crimson path through the double doors of the hotel from the 800-car parking lot. Mezzanine-level windows light the adobe-toned lobby, which is separated from the Fireside Lounge by a double-sided fireplace.

The hotel has 190 guest rooms, each one characterized by a Pueblo Indian craft on the wall over the beds. Pastel greens, blues, and mauves are the preferred shades of decoration. All furniture, including dressers, desks, and chairs, is handmade. There's cable TV/radio, alarm clocks, full-length closet mirrors, direct-dial phones (local calls are 50¢), and Pierre Cardin amenities (shampoo and lotion) in the bathrooms. The southside rooms, facing Old Town, have private balconies. Rates are $80 to $92 for singles with king-size beds, $76 to $88 for double rooms with two double beds with additional guests $8 and children free. The 20 suites are priced at $105 and $115 year round.

The hotel has a 24-hour courtesy car, an outdoor swimming pool and Jacuzzi, and an exercise room. The Sheraton owns and operates Old Town Place, a shopping center to which it is directly connected. Shops include arts and crafts dealers, a bookstore, beauty salon, and manicurist.

There are two restaurants and one separate lounge. The Customs House Restaurant, designed like an old warehouse, is the main dining room. It specializes in seafood, with such lunchtime offerings as Neptune's Delight (a seafood omelet with shrimp, crab, snapper, and sole in a cream sauce; $5.25) and the Main Sail (pan-fried rainbow trout topped with pecan butter; $7). The Café del Sol is the Sheraton's coffeehouse: for something different here, try the jalapeño chicken breast stuffed with goat cheese and topped with jalapeño glaze and black beans ($12).

The Customs House is open for lunch weekdays from 11:30 a.m. to 2 p.m.; for dinner, seven days from 5:30 to 10:30 p.m.; and for Sunday champagne brunch, from 11:30 a.m. to 2 p.m. Café del Sol is open seven days from 6 a.m. to 9 p.m. Taverna Don Alberto, serving drinks in a nook off the main lobby, features dance bands Wednesday through Saturday nights.

If it's traditional Hispanic atmosphere you see, the obvious choice is **La Posada de Albuquerque,** 125 2nd St. NW (at Copper Street), Albuquerque, NM 87102 (tel. 505/242-9090, or toll free 800/777-5732). Built in 1939 by Conrad Hilton as the famed hotelier's first inn in his home state of New Mexico, the twice-sold and reburbished hostelry is listed on the National Register of Historic Places.

As soon as you enter the hotel through one of two corridors, you feel as if you've just left New Mexico and entered Old Mexico. In the center of a tile floor is an elaborate Moorish brass-and-mosaic tile fountain, and beyond it, a piano bar surrounded by plush leather-upholstered seating. Old-fashioned tin chandeliers hang from the two-story-high ceiling, while behind the bannister of the mezzanine is a gallery of work by local abstract painters. Surrounded on all sides by high archways, the total effect is of a 19th-century hacienda courtyard.

The 114 guest rooms are equally charming, especially the corner rooms near the elevators with king-size beds set back in an alcove apart from the spacious living area. As in the lobby, all furniture is handcrafted, but here it's covered with cushions of stereotypically southwestern design. There are limited-edition lithographs by R. C. Gorman and Amado Pena on the white walls, adobe-toned ceramic lamps on the tables flanking the couch, and an ample desk opposite the wood-shuttered windows. The wardrobe closet is a little on the small side and the heating/air-conditioning unit outdated, but that might be expected in a hotel 50 years old. Each room has cable TV with built-in radio and direct-dial phones (local calls are 50¢). Rates vary from $62 to $96 single, $72 to $106 double, and $98 to $225 for suites. Some of the higher-priced rooms have their own fireplaces.

Eulalia's is one of Albuquerque's exclusive restaurants. Entering from the colonial-style lobby, you'll feel you're walking into a village in the Yucatán, with a replica of a six-foot Mayan sculpture shrouded in palms and other greenery. Intimate, semicircular booths upholstered in pastel patterns are candlelit at night. Diners might start with chilled gazpacho ($3) or hearts-of-palm salad ($5), then opt for a pepper steak ($16) or Cornish game hen ($13.25). Flambé dessert specials are $5. Dinner is served from 6 to 10 p.m. nightly. Eulalia's is also open from 7 a.m. to 2 p.m. Monday through Saturday for breakfast and lunch, and 11 a.m. to 2 p.m. on Sunday for brunch.

The Plaza Coffee Shop, attached to the hotel but privately owned, is open for breakfast and lunch from 6 a.m. to 3 p.m. Monday through Friday and 7 to 11 a.m. on Saturday. All-you-can-eat lobby buffets are served against an Aztec-style mural for $5 during weekday noon hours, and a bar menu is offered in the lobby until 11 p.m.

A Moderately Priced Choice

Comfortable bed-and-breakfast accommodation is offered at the **William E. Mauger Estate,** 292 Placitas Rd. NW, Albuquerque, NM 87107 (tel. 505/242-8755). Located about four miles north of downtown off 4th Street, the "estate" has six rooms and one suite priced $40 to $65 a night.

The Budget Range

Very centrally located, the **El Centro Plaza Hotel,** 717 Central Ave. NW, Albuquerque, NM 87102 (tel. 505/247-1561), has 145 units with year-round rates of $32 single, $36 double, plus $4 per additional person (children under 16 stay free with their parents). Rooms are decorated in earth tones and have all standard furnishings—dresser, nightstands, table, and chairs. Each room has cable TV/radio. Local phone calls are free, and portable refrigerators are available to guests planning long-term stays. There's a coin-operated guest laundry, a swimming pool, a 24-hour courtesy car, a coffeeshop (open from 5 a.m. to 10 p.m. daily), and a cocktail lounge.

For real wallet-watchers, the **Albuquerque International Hostel** is in this neighborhood at 1012 Central Ave. SW, Albuquerque, NM 87106 (tel. 505/243-6101), three blocks west of El Centro Plaza. Men's and women's dorm beds are $7 to $9 nightly; private rooms with double beds are $20 per night. As in all youth hostels, bathroom and kitchen facilities are shared.

MIDTOWN/FREEWAY LOOP: Accommodations in these areas may prove to be the most convenient for auto travelers.

A Deluxe Choice

The city's most elegant hotel is the **Albuquerque Marriott Hotel,** 2101 Louisiana Blvd. NE, Albuquerque, NM 87110 (tel. 505/881-6800, or toll free 800/228-9290). A classically beautiful lobby greets the visitor with plush red seating surrounding a player piano, beneath the ceiling of a two-story atrium.

The hotel has 412 rooms and suites in 16 stories looming high over I-40 as it enters Albuquerque from the east. Most rooms are decorated in pastel shades of green, peach, or lilac, with a palm or similar plant against the window. Many have an unusual Oriental motif, which extends from prints of Japanese cranes on the walls to patterns on the bedspreads. Furniture maintains the theme with cane and rattan construction. There's satellite TV/radio, alarm clocks, phones (50¢ for local calls), and big closets with full-size mirrors on the doors. Half-size refrigerators are provided on request. Two floors comprise the Concierge Level, catering to business travelers with a private lounge, complimentary continental breakfast, evening hors d'oeuvres, and a well-stocked honor bar. Rooms on these levels have hairdryers, robes, and shoeshines—for just $10 above the standard rates of $112 single, $122 double, year round.

Athletic facilities include an indoor/outdoor swimming pool; a health club featuring Nautilus equipment, free weights, exercise bikes, and aerobics videos; men's and women's saunas; a Jacuzzi . . . and a games room. The hotel has a 24-hour courtesy car and a gift shop specializing in southwestern crafts. Albuquerque's two largest shopping centers, Winrock and Coronado, are within easy walking distance.

Nicole's, which greets diners with a cactus garden, is widely considered one of the city's finest restaurants. The classical décor includes rich green upholstery on hand-carved chairs, with 19th-century oils hanging on the walls. The luncheon menu includes everything from tortellini Toscana ($8) to Cajun blackened filet mignon ($11). Popular dinner entrees include shrimp étoufée ($12.25) and eight-ounce prime rib with prawns ($17). The chocolate macadamia dessert ($3) is exquisite.

Nicole's Lounge, adjoining, has nightly entertainment with bands performing hits of the '50s and '60s. The Herbs & Roses restaurant, a coffeeshop, serves three meals daily.

The Upper Bracket

White stuccoed corridors with petroglyph-style paintings are a trademark of the **Albuquerque Hilton Hotel,** 1901 University Blvd. NE, Albuquerque, NM 87102 (tel. 505/884-2500, or toll free 800/821-1901). Located just south of Menaul Boulevard near the I-25/I-40 interchange, the hotel is operated by Hotels of Distinction, Inc., a Boston-based hotel company whose holdings include its hometown's Copley Plaza and Back Bay Hilton as well as Le Grand Hotel in Montréal.

Many of the 450 rooms are in a high-rise tower which underwent a multi-million-dollar renovation in 1987. Two floors of rooms are at concierge level for business travelers; cabaña rooms with 15-foot cathedral ceilings surround the outdoor pool, and outside villa rooms sit beside the tennis courts. Standard rooms, if there is such a thing, typically have maroon carpeting and peach walls with limited-edition prints by Susan Brooke. Furnishings include a queen-size bed, sofa bed, desk, satellite TV, dresser, full wall mirror, and radio/alarm clock. Direct-dial calls are 50¢ from any of the room's three telephones (desk, toilet, bedside). Year-round room rates run $65 to $95 single, $75 to $105 double; children stay free with their parents. In addition to the seasonal outdoor pool and two tennis courts, the Hilton has a year-round indoor pool complex with whirlpool and saunas open until 11 p.m. nightly.

The Ranchers Club restaurant sets a marvelous western mood with its polished wood décor, flagstone fireplace, and remarkable longhorn chandelier. But the food outdoes the atmosphere. Consider the "small" (14-ounce) New York sirloin, grilled over sassafras with wild mushroom sauce ($19.50); or the Norwegian salmon, grilled over mesquite with curried apple chutney ($18). All entrees are served with a choice of two vegetables. The "club" is open for lunch Monday through Friday from 11:30 a.m. to 2 p.m., and for dinner Monday through Thursday from 5:30 to 10 p.m. and on Friday and Saturday to 11 p.m.

The Hilton's more pedestrian mealtime option is Casa Choco, open daily until 10 p.m. for regional and traditional breakfasts, lunches, and dinners. The Cantina, with its *fajitas* grill and piano bar, serves as the hotel lounge.

The **Ramada Hotel Classic,** 6815 Menaul Blvd. NE (at Louisiana Boulevard), Albuquerque, NM 87100 (tel. 505/881-0000, or toll free 800/2-RAMADA), is called "classic" because one of its owners, local Coors Beer distributor Phil Maloof, is a collector of classic automobiles. In fact, one or another beauty is positioned just outside the hotel's main doors at all times.

Major room renovations are to be completed by mid-1989. At this inspection, most of the 300 rooms were decorated with southwestern abstracts and light wood décor. All had twin sinks, refrigerators, and cable TV/radios. Year-round rates are $70 to $85 single, $80 to $95 double, $125 and up for the 24 suites with wet bars and pullout sofas. The Ramada has an indoor swimming pool, Jacuzzi, and sauna, a gift shop and beauty shop, and a courtesy car available from 6 a.m. to midnight.

Chardonnay's, the fine-dining establishment, is open daily for lunch and dinner. It offers entrees like lamb chops Madagascar ($16) and prawns Chardonnay (stuffed with a crabmeat-and-scallop mousse; $15). Café Fennel, open daily for three meals, has southwestern specials and standard burgers, pastas, salads, and quiches, with nothing on the menu priced higher than $9. A lobby piano bar and the Quest Lounge, a disco, have happy hours from 4:30 to 7 p.m. daily.

One of Albuquerque's longest-established luxury hotels is the **Clarion Four Seasons,** 2500 Carlisle Blvd. NE (at I-40), Albuquerque, NM 87110 (tel. 505/888-3311, or toll free 800/545-8400). Originally built in 1971, it was completely overhauled in 1986. In 1988 the 358-room hotel's management was taken over by Dallas-based Wyndham Hotels, which has 19 other properties in the United States and Caribbean.

The hotel is spread across three buildings. The main lobby is in the Garden Building, which features a Japanese garden in its atrium, complete with footbridge and waterfall.

Two-thirds of the rooms, decorated in an evergreen theme, have twin double beds. Furnishings include satellite TV/radio (with pay in-house movies) in the armoire, a sofa and coffee table, and two sinks—one at a dressing table. Standard rates are $59 to $66 single, $69 to $76 double; suites cost $85 to $105, single or double. Weekend rates are $39 to $69.

The Clarion has two swimming pools: an indoor pool beneath a skylight surrounded by palms, and an outdoor pool in the center of the Lanai Building with a snack and cocktail bar. (It's no wonder the hotel sometimes calls itself the "inner city resort.") The Supreme Courts health club, free to guests, features 11 racquetball and four tennis courts, Nautilus equipment and weights, a sauna, whirlpool, and steamroom. The hotel has gift and jewelry shops, a hair salon, and 24-hour courtesy van service.

There are two restaurants. Delfino's, specializing in gourmet New Mexican cuisine in the $10 to $14 range for dinner, is open for lunch from 11:30 a.m. to 2 p.m. Monday through Friday, and for dinner from 6 to 10 p.m. Monday through Thursday, to 11 p.m. on Friday and Saturday. Sunday champagne brunch is served from 11 a.m. to 2 p.m. Maxie's coffeeshop, open from 6 a.m. to 2 p.m. and 5 to 11 p.m. daily, keeps its prices to a Max-imum of $9. The restaurant is named after Albuquerque balloonist Maxie Anderson, who made the first transatlantic balloon voyage in 1978 but was killed in a ballooning accident in West Germany in 1983. It has balloon décor, of course. The DQ (formerly Don Quixote) Lounge is a roomy, dimly lit bar with DJ dancing.

Spanish classical architecture dominates the all-suite **Best Western Barcelona Court**, 900 Louisiana Blvd. NE (at Lomas Boulevard), Albuquerque, NM 87110 (tel. 505/255-5566, or toll free 800/222-1122). Four wings radiate from the central two-story Fountain Court, so named because of its centerpiece, an impressive classical fountain whose sculpted fish spout water. The tile courtyard is lit by skylights and surrounded by potted plants, giving it a lush look. Two more stained-glass skylights tower above the three-story lobby atrium.

The hotel includes 164 suites, priced year round at $79 single, $89 double. (Weekend rates are $61.75, with up to two children under 12 free in their parents' room.) Enter from a garden plaza to a living room whose furnishings include a couch that converts to a bed, an easy chair with ottoman, a games table and chairs, and satellite TV. There's a second TV in the bedroom with remote bedside controls. A marble vanity sits outside each bathroom; the kitchenettes include a microwave and refrigerator/freezer. Each suite has phones in the living room, bedroom, and bathroom.

All guests are entitled to a complimentary full breakfast, and two hours (5:30 to 7:30 p.m.) of free cocktails, in the Fountain Court. Everyone has access to indoor and outdoor swimming pools, sauna, whirlpool bath, exercise room, and coin-operated laundromat. Best of all, signs declare: "No tipping, please."

The 367-room **Holiday Inn Midtown,** 2020 Menaul Blvd. NE, Albuquerque, NM 87107 (tel. 505/884-2511, or toll free 800/HOLIDAY), is the headquarters lodge for the city's annual International Hot Air Balloon Festival in October. Thus miniature balloons dangle high above a spacious, two-story atrium, and the rest of the hotel has a similarly airy appeal.

Nicely appointed rooms have all standard furnishings, including satellite television, radio/alarm clocks, and direct-dial phones (local calls are 40¢). They're priced at $69 to $80 single, $75 to $86 double, year round. The hotel has a swimming pool, an exercise room with Nautilus equipment, a sauna and whirlpool, and a variety of table and video games for kids young and old.

The Sandia Springs Restaurant, famous for its frequent all-you-can-eat buffets, is adjoined by the popular Sandia Springs Lounge, featuring live country-and-western music nightly except Sunday. The Springwater Deli serves sandwiches and snacks under the atrium roof, and the adjacent Conversations Lounge offers drinks and—you guessed it—conversation.

Moderately Priced Accommodations

The **Best Western Winrock Inn,** 18 Winrock Center NE (at I-40 and Louisiana Boulevard), Albuquerque, NM 87110 (tel. 505/883-5252, or toll free 800/528-1234), is attached to Albuquerque's second-largest shopping center. A hotel with prime appeal to international visitors, its two separate buildings are wrapped around a private lagoon and garden featuring Mandarin ducks, giant *koi* (carp), and an impressive waterfall.

The 174 rooms are priced at $52 single, $58 double, May through October, and $4 less during the off-season. Decorated in tones of beige and adobe, they have all standard furnishings plus remote-control satellite TV, direct-dial phones (local calls are 32¢), and full-mirror doors on the wardrobe closet. Many rooms have private patios overlooking the lagoon.

There's an outdoor swimming pool and 24-hour courtesy van service. An International Visitors Bureau is on the property.

The Winrock Inn's on-premises restaurant is the Japanese Kitchen, a hibachi-style steakhouse. It comes in two sections: five eight-seat hibachi grills, on which master chefs slice and cook steaks, seafood, and chicken before your eyes; and a separate full sushi bar. Grills are priced $5 to $8 for lunch; full dinners run $10 (teppan yaki chicken) to $25 (lobster and prawns). Don't miss the museum-quality samurai uniform just outside the entrance. The Japanese Kitchen is open daily from 11 a.m. to 2 p.m. and 5 to 10 p.m. A cocktail lounge is attached: ever try a banzai?

A stay at the **ClubHouse Inn,** 1315 Menaul Blvd. NE (at I-25), Albuquerque, NM 87107 (tel. 505/345-0010, or toll free 800/258-2466), is the next best thing to never leaving home. The lobby, first of all, sets the tone for the rest of the inn by looking just like your living room, complete with fireplace, sofas, and lush plants. Furnishings in each of the 137 brightly appointed rooms include a free-standing desk with phone (free local calls), a cable TV, and a sofa or easy chair with ottoman. The 17 suites include kitchenettes and numerous other special touches. There's a swimming pool, Jacuzzi, and laundry for guest use, and backyard barbecues for summer grills. Rates are $45 single, $51 double, $60 and $66 for suites, with children under 10 free with their parents. A complimentary buffet breakfast is served from 6:30 to 9 a.m., and drinks from 5 to 7 p.m., daily in the Club House.

Le Baron Inn, 2126 Menaul Blvd. NE, Albuquerque, NM 87107 (tel. 505/884-0250, or toll free 800/444-7378), has 215 motel rooms priced $37 to $40 single, $39 to $44 double. Over 50% of those rooms are set aside for nonsmokers. A rich navy-blue or maroon color scheme dominates the rooms, which have standard furnishings including satellite TV and two phones, one in the bath (free local calls). There's a swimming pool and hot tub and coin-op laundry on the premises, and 24-hour courtesy car service. A 24-hour restaurant, the Village Inn, is on adjoining property.

A Budget Choice

The **American Family Lodge,** next door to Le Baron at 2108 Menaul Blvd. NE, Albuquerque, NM 87101 (tel. 505/884-2480), is an adequate choice for budget-conscious travelers in this section of town. Rooms have two double beds, table and chairs, a credenza with satellite TV, and free local phone calls. They're priced at $25 single, $30 double, a night, with children under 6 free. In the small lobby are a game and snack room and a coffee maker next to an aquarium.

AIRPORT: There are some fine accommodations within minutes of your arriving and departing flights.

The Upper Bracket

No accommodation is closer to Albuquerque International Airport than the **AMFAC Hotel,** 2910 Yale Blvd. SE, Albuquerque, NM 87106 (tel. 505/843-7000, or toll free 800/227-1117). Its 266 rooms have a bright floral décor and are furnished with king-size beds, four-drawer dressers, leather easy chairs with ottomans, cable TV/radios, and phones (local calls are 50¢). There's an outdoor swimming pool, a coed sauna, and two all-weather tennis courts; room guests can show their keys for free admittance to The Club, an athletic facility with weights and racquetball courts a block away. Lil's is an exclusive Victorian restaurant serving continental cuisine beneath crystal chandeliers; the Harvey House Restaurant offers gourmet breakfasts, lunches, and dinners for much more reasonable prices.

The Spanish Colonial-style **Radisson Inn,** 1901 University Ave. SE, Albuquerque, NM 87106 (tel. 505/247-0512, or toll free 800/228-9822 or 800/333-3333), is a full mile from the airport, as opposed to the AMFAC's two blocks. But the extra distance is easily covered by a courtesy car, and it's nice to be away from the hubbub of the airport. The 148 rooms are decorated in emerald green, navy blue, or dusty rose, and are furnished with king-size beds, two-drawer credenzas, tables and chairs, cable TV/radios, and telephones. Rack rates run $72 to $95 single, $82 to $95 double. Facilities include a lobby art gallery, a year-round outdoor swimming pool and hot tub, free guest membership in The Club, and Rivera's restaurant, featuring international entrees —many priced under $10 for dinner.

A Moderately Priced Choice

The nicest of many nice things about the **Best Western Airport Inn,** 2400 Yale Blvd. SE, Albuquerque, NM 87106 (tel. 505/242-7022, or toll free 800/528-1234), is the landscaped garden courtyard behind it. It's a lovely place to relax on cloudless days. The 120 rooms, with dark-brown carpets and beige-checkered bedspreads, contain standard furnishings plus cable TV and free local phone calls. They're priced $49 to $54 single, $57 to $62 double. Deluxe units, with refrigerators and other special touches, are $7 to $8 more. The inn has an outdoor swimming pool and Jacuzzi, and a courtesy car on call from 6 a.m. to midnight. Breakfast is served free in rooms, or guests can get a coupon good for $3 off their morning meal at the adjacent Village Inn.

JOURNAL CENTER: This area offers accommodations ranging from the fantastic to the simple but comfortable.

The Upper Bracket

Driving north from Albuquerque toward Santa Fe, you can't help but be startled by the spectacular stepped Aztec pyramid that seems to rise from nowhere on the west side of the I-25 freeway. It's not there by accident: this is the **Holiday Inn Journal Center,** a major hotel and convention complex at 5151 San Francisco Rd.

NE, Albuquerque, NM 87109 (tel. 505/821-3333, or toll free 800/238-8000). Reached via the Paseo del Norte exit 232 from I-25, it's a monument to what modern-day hotel architecture can be like.

The nine guest floors, with 311 rooms, focus around a "hollow" skylit core. Vines drape from planter boxes on the balconies, and a fountain falls five stories to a pool between the two glass elevators. The Aztec theme pervades in the sand-and-cream color tones and the figures etched into the glass facing the fountain, opposite the entry.

The color scheme carries to the spacious rooms, furnished with king-size or queen-size beds, two easy chairs, a desk, four-drawer dresser, fully lit dressing table, cable TV with in-room movies, radio/alarm clock, and direct-dial phone (local calls are 50¢). They're priced at $70 to $86 single, $76 to $92 double. The hotel offers guests an indoor/outdoor swimming pool, health club, sauna, two whirlpools, 24-hour courtesy car, and full-service concierge. Jogging trails wind through 313-acre Journal Center business park, soon to be graced with the John Q. Hammons Trade Center—named for the owner of this hotel.

"The Pyramid," as it likes to be called, has two restaurants and two lounges. The Gallery is open for fine dining from 5 to 10 p.m. nightly except Sunday. Entrees include oysters Tasso in cream ($14), boneless duck breast Chambord ($13), and fresh salmon in raspberry and green-peppercorn sauce ($14.75). The Terrace, an atrium café surrounded by planter boxes, is open from 6 a.m. to 2 p.m. and 5 to 10 p.m. daily; dinner prices top out at $8, and even vegetarians are catered to with a tofu stir-fry ($5). The Palm Court, next to the Terrace, has a baby grand piano bar open until 10 p.m. every day. The Pyramid Club attracts the younger set with a disc jockey providing video music for dancing until 2 a.m. Monday through Saturday nights.

Moderately Priced Choices

The **Howard Johnson Plaza Hotel,** 6000 Pan American Frwy. NE (at San Mateo Boulevard), Albuquerque, NM 87109 (tel. 505/821-9451, or toll free 800/654-2000), doesn't try to be as grand as the Pyramid. But it does have a five-story lobby atrium with fountains of its own. A three-story-high tapestry reminds viewers of Albuquerque's obsession with hot-air ballooning, and there are old-fashioned flower-topped lampposts on the mezzanine deck.

Howard Johnson's has 150 rooms, priced at $48 single, $53 double ($20 extra during the balloon fest). Private balconies are an outstanding feature of every room. They've got all standard furnishings, including remote-control cable TV and phones. Pets are permitted with the manager's prior approval.

The hotel has an indoor/outdoor swimming pool, sauna and Jacuzzi, and exercise room with Nautilus equipment. It also has a coin-op guest laundry, gift shop, and 24-hour van service. Earl's Café, open from 6 a.m. to 2 p.m. and 5 to 9 p.m. daily, has good southwestern fare; the Atrium Lounge has a big-screen TV for watching sports events.

The **Amberley Suite Hotel,** 7620 Pan American Frwy. NE, Albuquerque, NM 87109 (tel. 505/823-1300, or toll free 800/228-5151), has 170—you guessed it—one- and two-bedroom suites. They're fully carpeted units, with a living room/kitchenette and bedroom (with six-drawer dresser!). Kitchen facilities include a refrigerator (with complimentary beverages), microwave oven, coffee maker, pots, pans, and utensils. Each living room has a swivel rocker with ottoman and a cable television. Every bathroom is provided with a built-in hairdryer. Rooms are $48 to $68 single, $56 to $76 double, with discounts for longer stays, weekend arrivals, or corporate or government travelers. (Prices are jacked up $15 for the balloon fiesta.)

A hotel health facility has a Universal gym, computerized treadmill, exercycles, sauna, and hot tub. There's an outdoor swimming pool, a coin-op laundry, and 24-hour courtesy car. Watson's Café and Deli serves an all-you-can-eat breakfast buffet from 6 to 10 a.m. daily ($4.50) and a luncheon buffet with soup and salad from 11 a.m. to 2 p.m. ($5.50).

The **Hampton Inn,** 7433 Pan American Frwy. NE, Albuquerque, NM 87109 (tel. 505/344-1555, or toll free 800/HAMPTON), has 125 rooms priced at $35 to $51 single, $45 to $56 double. The 125 sound-insulated rooms for cost-conscious travelers have all standard furnishings, plus remote-control cable TV and free local phone calls. A complimentary continental breakfast is served each morning to guests. The inn has an outdoor swimming pool, but no courtesy car or other exercise facilities.

WHERE TO EAT

As might be expected in any large city, Albuquerque has a seemingly limitless choice of places to eat. The following breakdown offers some of my suggestions, categorized according to cuisine.

REGIONAL CUISINE: The Old Town standout is **Maria Teresa,** 618 Rio Grande Blvd. NW (tel. 242-3900), certainly the city's most beautiful and classically elegant restaurant. Located in the 1840 Salvador Armijo House, this historic property is entirely furnished with Victorian antiques and paintings. Diners are seated in six separate rooms or on a patio. Dinner prices range from $9 to $21 for complete meals; suggestions include chicken Acapulco (with avocado and crab meat; $12) or the house special burrito ($11). The fully licensed restaurant, located adjacent to the Sheraton Old Town, is open from 11:30 a.m. to 2 p.m. for lunch and 5 to 9 p.m. for dinner daily.

Right in the heart of Old Town, set back in the rear of a courtyard in an old adobe home, is **Catalina's,** 400 San Felipe St. (tel. 842-6907). The white stuccoed interior, covered with Mexican handcrafts, still has its original log beams. All meals are homemade by Catalina Walsh; the chile rellenos are superb, as are the tacos, tostadas, enchiladas, and so forth. All meals run $3.50 to $6. Breakfast is served from 8 to 11 a.m. daily, lunch is 11 a.m. to 4 p.m., and dinner (summers only), from 4 to 9 p.m. The owners often take vacation from mid-January through March.

The **Cervantes** restaurant, Gibson Boulevard and San Pedro Drive near Kirtland Air Force Base (tel. 262-2253), has an impressive classical Spanish décor within a rather unimpressive exterior. Miguel Cervantes, author of the classic *Don Quixote,* has a portrait in a place of honor, though he only shares a name with the owners. New Mexican dinners with all the trimmings are extremely reasonably priced: a combination plate of a taco, tamale, enchilada, and carne adovada, for instance, is just $5.75, including beans, rice, chili, and sopaipillas. Open from 11 a.m. to 2 p.m. and 4:30 to 10 p.m. daily.

NOUVELLE CUISINE: The **Monte Vista Fire Station Restaurant and Bar,** 3201 Central Ave. NE, at Bryn Mawr Street (tel. 255-2424), has been a city landmark since it was built in pure Pueblo Revival style in 1936. Its occupants no longer make house calls, however, concentrating instead on serving a unique menu within an art deco interior. You might start with shrimp wonton ($3.50) or eggplant and spinach rollitino ($5), then move on to grilled swordfish (market price), char-broiled chicken with crabmeat and béarnaise ($14), or veal and shrimp Marengo ($15). Open from 5 to 10:30 p.m. Sunday through Thursday, to 11 p.m. on Friday and Saturday. A popular singles bar on the fourth-story landing hops until 1:30 a.m. most nights.

Sara's Fresh Fabulous Foods, 3109 Central Ave. NE (tel. 256-7272), is an exercise in elegant simplicity: candlelit white linen service on a hardwood floor, with gallery prints on the walls and a classical pianist playing softly in one corner of the room. The eclectic menu sticks to vegetarian and seafood dishes—like spinach lasagne ($9), cioppino (Italian fish stew; $10), and an Oriental sampler built around vegetable tempura and miso soup ($9). You can have fine wine here, but there's no smoking. Open Monday through Friday from 11:30 a.m. to 5 p.m. for lunch, and Monday through Thursday from 5 to 9:30 p.m., on Friday and Saturday to midnight, for dinner or after-the-show supper.

The **2nd Street Grill** is actually at 44 First Plaza, downtown (tel. 242-5451). In a subtle art deco atmosphere, a reasonably priced menu of salads, fresh pastas, grills, and sandwiches are served daily from 11 a.m. to 7 p.m. Manager Greg Atkin recommends the egg linguine, with sautéed chicken and roasted green chile in a Parmesan cream sauce ($6). Breakfast, served daily from 7 to 10 a.m., includes outstanding blue-corn waffles with honey lime butter ($3.75).

STEAKS AND SEAFOOD: High Noon, 425 San Felipe St. NW (tel. 765-1455), offers crêpes and regional food for lunch ($5.50 to $7.95), fine steaks, seafood, and continental cuisine for dinner ($12 to $21). It's done in a 19th-century saloon atmosphere with stuccoed walls, high and low ceiling beams, and historical photos on the walls. Open Monday through Saturday from 1 a.m. to 3 p.m. and 5 to 10 p.m. and on Sunday from noon to 9:30 p.m.

The **Cooperage,** 7220 Lomas Blvd. NE (tel. 255-1657), is shaped to feel as if you're within a gigantic barrel. It's circular and wood paneled, with 19th-century painting and reproductions of coopers at work making barrels. The dinner menu is priced from $7 to $18 for entrees, and includes trout Parmesan ($10) and prime rib ($15). Open for lunch from 11 a.m. to 2:30 p.m. Monday through Friday and noon to 2:30 p.m. on Saturday; and for dinner, from 5 to 10 p.m. Monday through Friday, to midnight on Saturday, and noon to 9 p.m. on Sunday.

Café Oceania, 1414 Central Ave. SE (tel. 247-2233), is built on several levels. A curved skylight connects two sections, with basement seating below and an oyster bar in a rear courtyard. The raw-wood atmosphere is almost saloon style, but art deco posters are framed on the walls. Lunch offerings, served from 11 a.m. to 3 p.m. Monday through Friday, include a seafood Louie tostada ($5) and a mako shark teriyaki sandwich ($6). Dinner entrees, offered from 5 to 11 p.m. Monday through Thursday, a half hour later on Friday and Saturday, start at $8 and feature barbecued shrimp ($10). Oyster hour specials are available between 3 and 6:30 p.m. weekdays.

CAJUN: The Courtyard Kitchen, 412 San Pedro Blvd. SE, at Zuñi Road (tel. 255-6882), is a local curiosity—a New Orleans–style restaurant with world-famous food but less satisfactory service. Chef Françoise Auclair le Vison previously ran the

acclaimed Café le Cabotin in Dallas, Texas; Washington, D.C.; Montserrat, West Indies; and London, England. But she stopped wandering in Albuquerque, where she now whips up meals like crayfish étouffée ($8.75) and black roux gumbo ($6.75) in an atmosphere of Dixieland jazz, posters, and photographs. Service is less than spectacular, however: the only waiter is Françoise's partner ("The Waiter"), and he must rely on a couple of busboys to assist him with taking orders and bringing food to the hundreds who throng here for lunch Tuesday through Friday and dinner on alternate Saturdays.

CONTINENTAL: The **Artichoke Café,** 424 Central Ave. SE, at Edith Street (tel. 842-8740), has established a reputation for fine food and service since its establishment in 1983. The no-frills décor is clean and tasteful, with modern-art prints on azure walls, white linens on tables shaded by standing plants, and classical music playing in the background. Be sure to start your meal with an artichoke appetizer ($4.50 to $6.25), then go on to an entree like veal scallopine with Duxelle mushrooms ($16.75). Crêpes, pastas, and the like are priced in the $5 to $10.75 range for lunch. The café has an excellent list of California and French wines. Open from 11 a.m. to 2 p.m. Monday through Saturday for lunch, 5:30 to 10 p.m. Tuesday through Saturday for dinner.

The famous **Prairie Star,** Jemez Dam Road, off N.M. 44 near Bernalillo (tel. 876-3327), is open for dinner from 5 to 10 p.m. Monday through Thursday, to 11 p.m. on Friday and Saturday. You'll need reservations to dine on meals like shrimp Mariposa, Cajun pork Wellington, and chateaubriand bouguetierra for prices starting in the $16 range. Private parties often reserve the patio and tiled swimming pool.

Ask directions locally to **Casa Vieja,** in Corrales (tel. 898-7489). It's strange to get fine French and northern Italian cuisine served in an ancient adobe house by waiters dressed in black coats and ties. Pastas run $6 to $9; entrees, $10 to $15. Open for dinner only Tuesday through Saturday, 6 to 10 p.m., Sunday 5 to 9 p.m.

FRENCH: The best in Albuquerque is offered up at **Le Marmiton,** 5415 Academy Blvd. NE (tel. 821-6279), not far from Journal Center. The name means "the apprentice," but there's nothing novice about the food or presentation. The 12 tables seat 30 people in a romantic French provincial atmosphere. Recommended entrees include fantaisie aux fruits de mer, a mixture of shrimp, scallops, and crab in a mushroom-cream sauce on pastry ($16) and cailles et New York steak, whole quail finished with a sherry-cream sauce and served with a rolled steak ($18). There's a long wine list, and great cinnamon-apple crêpes for dessert. Open from 11 a.m. to 2:30 p.m. Monday through Friday for lunch, 5:30 to 9:30 p.m. Monday through Saturday for dinner; on Sunday, by reservation only.

ITALIAN: Between downtown and Old Town, **The Villa** (formerly Villa di Capo) is at 722 Central Ave. SW (tel. 242-2006). Roman-style porticos overlook an elegant décor of polished-wood tables and hanging chandeliers. There's also a Roman fountain in a lovely garden, but you must book ahead to sit there. Lasagne's a great bargain anytime at $6.25. Lunches are priced $3.75 to $6.75 for sandwiches, salads, and pastas; dinner entrees include pasta marinara with stuffed mushrooms ($6) and chicken manicotti ($7.25). Blackboard specials also include a catch of the day. Fully licensed. Open from 11 a.m. to 9 p.m. Monday through Thursday, to 10 p.m. on Friday, 4 to 10 p.m. on Saturday, and 4 to 8 p.m. on Sunday.

ASIAN: The spicy cuisines of Hunan and Peking are the fare at the **Hunan Chinese Restaurant,** 1218 San Pedro Blvd. SE (tel. 266-3300). In this garish red-and-gold décor you can start with hot-and-sour soup ($3.25), then try sizzling beef (sautéed with peanuts, water chestnuts, and green onions; $8) or whole fish with hot bean sauce ($14). Usually open from 11:30 a.m. to 9:30 p.m. daily, but hours may vary, so call ahead to confirm.

   India Kitchen, 6910 Montgomery Blvd. NE, in a shopping strip near Louisiana Boulevard (tel. 884-2333), is the pride and joy of Ajay Gupta, an 18-year U.S. resident who left his job as a Chicago engineer to start cooking. He does it well! Entrees, all served with pullao (rice), puri (wheat bread), and bhujia (mixed vegetables), include the likes of korma (beef with almonds, pecans, and sour cream; $8) and shrimp curry in coconut-cream sauce ($8). There are also vegetarian dishes like jackfruit vindaloo ($8) or lobhia dhal (black-eyed pea stew; $6). Wash your meal down with a yogurt lassi ($1). Raga music from sitars plays continuously in the background as you dine, and there are Mughal-style paintings and batiks on the walls. Open from 11 a.m. to 2:30 p.m. Monday through Saturday for lunch, and 5 to 9:30 p.m. Sunday through Thursday and 5 to 10:30 p.m. on Friday and Saturday for dinner.

BUDGET CHOICES: With two city locations, **Souper Salads,** 1606 Central Ave. SE (tel. 243-9751) and 5001 Montgomery Blvd. NE in the Montgomery Plaza (tel. 883-9534), advertises a "1930s atmosphere serving 1980s appetites." Indeed, early-20th-century photographs line the walls above tile floors, and the soup and salad options are superb. There's a 50-item salad bar, including 13 fresh vegetables (like okra) and such not-often-seen additions like watermelon and hard-boiled eggs. Soup specials vary by day, but may include cream of zucchini, seafood gumbo, or red beans, rice, and sausage. All you can eat from salad bar and soup stove will run you $4.25. Sandwiches, beer, and wine are also available. Open from 11 a.m. to 9 p.m. Monday through Saturday at both locations, plus noon to 8 p.m. on Sunday at Montgomery Plaza.

The Soup Tureen, 215 Central Ave. NW (tel. 247-2417) and 2813 San Mateo Blvd. NE (tel. 883-1806), makes soup specialties daily ($2.50 a bowl), and you'll never go wrong with one. It also has sandwiches ($4 to $5, including vegetarian varieties) and salads ($2 to $4.75). Open from 7 a.m. to 2:30 p.m. weekdays, plus Saturday at the Midtown location.

Weekdays, 520 Central Ave. SW (tel. 247-2312), offers solid soup, salad, and sandwich lunches in comfortable downtown décor. You can get a turkey-and-avocado sandwich for $4, a bowl of homemade green chile stew for $2.25, or a shrimp-and-pasta chef salad for $4.25. Breakfast, including the 99¢ egg, potato, and biscuit special, is served until 11 a.m. Open Monday through Friday from 7 a.m. to 2 p.m.

CHAPTER XIV

WHAT TO SEE AND DO IN ALBUQUERQUE

□ □ □

Albuquerque's original town site, today known as Old Town, is the central point of interest for visitors to the city today. Here, centered around the Plaza, are the venerable Church of San Felipe de Neri and numerous restaurants, art galleries, and crafts shops. Several important museums stand nearby.

But don't get stuck in Old Town. Elsewhere in the city are the Sandia Peak Tramway, Kirtland Air Force Base and the National Atomic Museum, the University of New Mexico with its museums, and a number of natural attractions. Within day-trip range are several Indian pueblos, two national monuments, and Chaco Canyon National Historic Park.

OLD TOWN

A maze of cobbled courtyard walkways lead to hidden patios and gardens where many of the district's 150 galleries and shops are located. Old adobe buildings, many refurbished in Pueblo Revival style in the 1950s, focus around the tree-shaded **Plaza,** created in 1780. Pueblo and Navajo Indian artisans often display their pottery, blankets, and turquoise-and-silver jewelry on the sidewalks lining the Plaza.

The buildings of Old Town once served as mercantile shops, grocery stores, and government offices; but the importance of Old Town as Albuquerque's commercial center declined after 1880, when the railroad came through 1¼ miles east of the Plaza and businesses relocated nearer the tracks. Old Town clung to its historical and sentimental roots, but the quarter was disintegrating until it was rediscovered in the 1930s and 1940s by artisans and other shop owners, and tourism burgeoned as an industry.

The first structure built when colonists established Albuquerque in 1706 was the **Church of San Felipe de Neri,** facing the Plaza on its north side. The house of worship has been in almost continuous use for 282 years. When the original building collapsed about 1790, it was reconstructed and subsequently expanded several times, all the while remaining the spiritual heart of the city. The annual parish fiesta, held the first weekend in June, brings food and game booths and traditional Mexican dancing to the Plaza area.

The Albuquerque Museum conducts guided **walking tours** of Old Town's historic buildings during the summer at 11 a.m. Wednesday through Friday and at 1:30 p.m. on Saturday and Sunday. The $2-per-person price includes museum admission. For visitors who don't find those times convenient, the museum publishes a brochure for a self-guided walking tour of Old Town.

Try to visit Old Town on a Sunday, when costumed actors re-create **Wild West shootouts** on Romero Street throughout the year. On weekends, there are also regular puppet plays at the **Old Town Puppet Theatre** (tel. 243-0208).

For suggestions on shops and galleries to visit in Old Town, see this chapter's subsequent section on "Fine Arts" or obtain a shopping guide from the **Old Town Association,** P.O. Box 7483, Albuquerque, NM 87194 (tel. 505/842-9100).

Easter and Christmas bring gaiety to the quarter. The Old Town Easter Parade, held annually on the Saturday preceding Easter, brings the Easter Bunny to the streets of Old Town along with a variety of floats and marching bands. On Christmas Eve, thousands of *luminarias* or *farolitos*—brown paper bags filled with sand and lighted candles—line the narrow streets and flat-roofed buildings surrounding the Plaza.

West of Old Town on the Rio Grande, **San Gabriel State Park** offers camping, picnicking, playgrounds, a baseball diamond, and a scenic loop drive through the cottonwoods along the riverbank.

ALBUQUERQUE MUSEUM: The largest collection of Spanish colonial artifacts in the United States is featured in the Albuquerque Museum (formerly the Albuquerque Museum of Art, History, and Science), 2000 Mountain Rd. NW (tel. 243-7255 or 242-4600). A permanent exhibit, "Four Centuries: A History of Albuquerque," chronicles the city's evolution from the earliest 16th-century forays of Coronado's *conquistadores* to its present-day status as a center of military research and high-technology industries.

Among objects held in the museum's collection are arms and armor used during the Hispanic conquest, a 17th-century family tapestry once belonging to the Duke of Alburquerque, medieval religious artifacts and weavings, maps from the 16th to 18th century, and coins and domestic goods traded during that same period. A multimedia audio-visual presentation, *Albuquerque: The Crossroads,* depicts the development of the city since 1875. There's also a gallery of early and modern New Mexico art, with permanent and changing exhibits; and a major photo archive. Lectures are offered and workshops staged in an auditorium and classroom.

The museum is open from 10 a.m. to 5 p.m. Tuesday through Friday and 1 to 5 p.m. on Saturday and Sunday. Admission is $2 for adults, $1 for seniors and children under 12. A gift shop offers a variety of souvenirs and other wares.

NEW MEXICO MUSEUM OF NATURAL HISTORY:

Two life-size bronze dinosaurs stand outside the entrance to the New Mexico Museum of Natural History, 1801 Mountain Rd. NW (tel. 841-8836 or 841-8837), opposite the Albuquerque Museum. The pentaceratops and albertosaur are indicative of the schoolchild thrust of this modern museum, which contains permanent and changing exhibits on zoology, botany, geology, and paleontology. High-tech exhibits enable visitors to take a walk through geologic time, explore an Ice Age cave, or stand inside a volcano complete with simulated magma flow. Hands-on exhibits in the Naturalist Center permit use of a video microscope, viewing of an active beehive, and participation in a wide variety of other activities.

The museum is open daily except Christmas from 10 a.m. to 5 p.m., in summer to 6 p.m. Admission is $2 for adults, $1.50 for seniors, $1 for children 3 to 11. There's a gift shop on the premises.

OTHER ALBUQUERQUE SIGHTS

INDIAN PUEBLO CULTURAL CENTER: Owned and operated by the 19 pueblos of northern New Mexico, the Indian Pueblo Cultural Center, 2401 12th St. NW (tel. 843-7270), is a fine place to begin an exploration of native culture. Located about a mile northeast of Old Town, this museum—modeled after Pueblo Bonito, a spectacular ruin in Chaco Culture National Historic Park—consists of several parts.

In the basement, a permanent exhibit depicts the evolution from prehistory to present of the various pueblos, including displays of the distinctive handcrafts of each community. Upstairs is an enormous (7,000-square-foot) gift shop—a fine place to price the Pueblo peoples' colorful ceramics, weavings, and paintings before bartering with private artisans. A gallery displays a variety of ancient and modern works from different pueblos, with exhibits changing monthly. From Mother's Day in May through the Balloon Fiesta in October, native dancers perform and artisans demonstrate their crafts expertise in an outdoor arena surrounded by original murals. An annual craft fair is held on July 4.

The center's exhibits are open Monday through Saturday from 9 a.m. to 5:15 p.m., plus Sunday in summer. Photography is welcome. Admission is $2.50 for adults, $1.50 for seniors, $1 for students.

A restaurant, open for breakfast and lunch from 7:30 a.m. to 3:15 p.m., emphasizes the cornmeal-based foods of the Pueblo people. Daily specials are priced at $4, although an ample meal is posole, treated dried corn with beef, chili, and oven-fried bread.

SANDIA PEAK: The world's longest tramway extends 2.7 miles from Albuquerque's northeastern city limits to the summit of 10,360-foot Sandia Peak. A ride up the **Sandia Peak Tramway,** 10 Tramway Loop NE (tel. 298-8518 or 296-9585), is a memorable experience, rising from urban desert at its base to lush mountain foliage in the Cibola National Forest at its peak. The view from the observation deck encompasses more than 11,000 square miles, well beyond Santa Fe and Los Alamos to the north.

Winter skiers often take the tram to the **Sandia Peak Ski Area,** where visitors can couple their trip with a ride on the resort's 7,500-foot double-chair lift through the spruce and ponderosa pine forests on the mountain's eastern slope. (A single ride costs $4; the chair operates from 10 a.m. to 3 p.m. in summer, 9 a.m. to 4 p.m. in winter.)

The Sandia Peak tram is a "jigback"; in other words, as one car approaches the top, the other nears the bottom. The two pass halfway through the trip, in the midst of a 1.5-mile "clear span" of unsupported cable between the second tower and the upper terminal.

The tramway is open daily from 9 a.m. to 10 p.m., Memorial Day through Labor Day; the remainder of the year it's open from 9 a.m. to 9 p.m. on Monday, Tuesday, Thursday and Sunday; 9 a.m. to 10 p.m. on Friday and Saturday; and 5 to 9 p.m. on Wednesday. Admission is $9 for adults, $8 for seniors, $7 for children ages 5 to 12.

There are popular and high-priced restaurants at the tramway's summit—**High Finance** (tel. 243-9742)—and base—**The Firehouse** (tel. 292-3473). Special tram rates apply with dinner reservations.

To reach the base of the tram, take I-25 north to the Tramway Road/Alameda exit, then proceed east about 5 miles on Tramway Road (N.M. 556); or take Tramway Road (N.M. 541) north of I-40 approximately 8.5 miles. Turn east the last half mile on Sandia Heights Road to Tramway Loop.

For those who prefer their own transportation, 10,678-foot **Sandia Crest** can be reached by driving east on I-40 to the Tijeras/Cedar Crest exit, north on N.M. 14 (the Turquoise Trail), then west at Sandia Park on N.M. 165 to N.M. 536. The road is paved and well maintained, and there is parking at the summit overlook.

Sandia Crest is the high point of the Sandia Mountains and, like Sandia Peak, offers a spectacular panoramic view in all directions. Many miles of Cibola National Forest trails, including the popular north-south Sandia Crest Trail, run through here; box lunches can be provided for day hikers by the **Sandia Crest House Restaurant & Gift Shop** (tel. 243-0605). The restaurant is open daily from 10 a.m. to 9 p.m. May to October, 10 a.m. to one hour after sunset the rest of the year.

En route to the summit in Sandia Park is the **Tinkertown Museum** (tel. 281-5233), a miniature wood-carved western village with more than 6,000 objects on display, including 500 animations. It's open daily from 9 a.m. to 6 p.m. June through August, with special hours during spring and fall. Admission is $1 for adults, 50¢ for children.

UNIVERSITY OF NEW MEXICO: The state's largest institution of higher learning stretches across a 700-acre campus about two miles east of downtown Albuquerque, north of Central Avenue and east of University Boulevard. There are six museums on the university campus, all of which plan special exhibits during 1989 as the school observes the centennial of its founding. It's an attractive campus, with all buildings constructed in a modified pueblo style. Popejoy Hall, in the south-central part of campus opposite Yale Park, hosts many performing arts presentations, including those of the New Mexico Symphony Orchestra; other public events are held in nearby Keller Hall and Woodward Hall.

Maxwell Museum of Anthropology

This internationally acclaimed repository of southwestern anthropological finds is situated on the west side of campus on Redondo Drive (University Boulevard) at Ash Street NE (tel. 277-4404). Mimbres and Pueblo pottery, Hopi *kachina* dolls, Navajo weavings, and a variety of regional jewelry, basketry, and textiles are on display. The collections support education and research in anthropology, archeology, and ethnology. Native arts and books about the state's cultural heritage are on sale in the museum's gift shop. It is open Monday through Friday from 9 a.m. to 4 p.m. and on Saturday from 10 a.m. to 4 p.m.; closed Sunday and holidays. Admission is free.

University of New Mexico Art Museum

Adjoining Popejoy Hall in the Fine Arts Center (tel. 277-4001) on Cornell Street, just north of Central Avenue, the multi-level University Museum focuses on 19th- and 20th-century American and European art. The prides of its permanent collection are an exhibit of early modernist work, and exhibitions covering the history of photograph and prints. It's open fall and spring semesters Tuesday through Friday from 10 a.m. to 5 p.m. and 7 to 10 p.m., on weekends from 1 to 5 p.m.; in summer, Tuesday through Friday from 10 a.m. to 4 p.m. and on weekends from 1 to 4 p.m.; closed Monday and holidays. Admission is free. A gift shop offers reproductions of many of the works displayed.

Jonson Gallery

This small gallery at 1909 Las Lomas Blvd. NE (tel. 277-4967), on the north side of the central campus, features more than 2,000 works by the late Raymond Jonson, a leading modernist painter in early-20th-century New Mexico. Its hours are the same as the University Museum; admission is free.

Geology and Meteoritic Museums

Located in Northrop Hall (tel. 277-4204), about halfway between the Maxwell Museum and Popejoy Hall in the southern part of campus, these adjacent facilities cover the gamut of recorded time from dinosaur bones to moon rocks. The 3,000 meteorite specimens held here comprise the sixth-largest collection in the United States. The museums are open Monday through Friday from 8 a.m. to 4 p.m.; the Meteoritic Museum is closed from noon to 1 p.m. daily. Admission is free.

Museum of Southwest Biology

This display in the Biology Annex (tel. 277-5340), adjacent to Northrop Hall, presents fauna and flora specimens from the Southwest, Mexico, and Central America. Call for times and other information.

NATIONAL ATOMIC MUSEUM: On the grounds of Kirtland Air Force Base, the National Atomic Museum (tel. 844-8443) is the next best introduction to the nuclear age after the Bradbury Science Museum in Los Alamos. It traces the history of the top-secret Manhattan Project of the 1940s, starting with a copy of the letter written to President Franklin D. Roosevelt by

Albert Einstein suggesting the possible development of an atomic bomb. A 53-minute film, *The Ten Seconds That Shook the World,* is shown three times daily, at 10:30 a.m., 2 p.m., and 3:30 p.m. There are full-scale models of missiles and wartime bombers, as well as exhibits and films on peaceful applications of nuclear technology and other alternative energy sources.

Visitors can obtain a pass to the museum at Kirtland AFB's Wyoming Gate, south of Central Avenue on Wyoming Boulevard SE, about six miles east of downtown. The museum is open from 9 a.m. to 5 p.m. daily except Christmas Day, New Year's Day, Easter, and Thanksgiving Day. Admission is free.

ERNIE PYLE HOME: The 1939 home of America's favorite war correspondent is now the **Ernie Pyle Memorial Branch Library,** 900 Girard Blvd. NE (tel. 766-7921). Memorabilia and poignant exhibits recalling the Pulitzer Prize–winning journalist, killed in action during World War II, stand in display shelves between the book racks. It is open on Tuesday and Thursday from 9 a.m. to 8 p.m.; on Wednesday, Friday, and Saturday to 5:30 p.m.; closed Sunday and Monday. There is no admission charge.

NATURAL ATTRACTIONS

In an area of many great natural wonders, three stand out: the Rio Grande Zoo and Rio Grande Nature Center, both spread along the riverbank; and Indian Petroglyph State Park in the volcanic mesas on the west side of the city.

RIO GRANDE ZOOLOGICAL PARK: Open motif exhibits, including an African savanna and Amazon rain forest, are the earmarks of this fine zoo a short distance south of downtown at 903 10th St. SW (tel. 843-7413). More than 1,200 animals of 300 species live on 60 acres of riverside *bosque* among ancient cottonwoods. The zoo has an especially fine collection of endangered African hoofed animals, including bongo, gerenuk, and sable, as well as the requisite apes, big cats, elephants, giraffes, and native southwestern species. A children's petting zoo is open during the summer.

The zoo is open from 9 a.m. to 5 p.m. daily except Thanksgiving, Christmas, and New Year's Days. Hours may be extended in summer. Admission is $4 for adults, $1.50 for seniors and accompanied children ages 3 to 11. Parking is free. There are numerous snackbars on the zoo grounds; the La Ventana Gift Shop carries film, gifts, and souvenirs.

RIO GRANDE NATURE CENTER STATE PARK: Located on the Rio Grande Flyway, an important migratory route for many birds, this wildlife refuge extends for nearly a mile along the east bank of the Rio Grande at 2901 Candelaria Rd. NW (tel. 344-7240). Numerous nature trails wind through the cottonwood *bosque,* where a great variety of native and migratory species can be seen at any time of year; the center publishes a checklist to help visitors identify them, as well as several self-guiding trail brochures.

Housed in a unique building constructed half above ground and half below, the visitor's center contains classrooms, laboratory space, a library, and exhibits describing the history, geology, and ecology of the Rio Grande valley. Films and interpreted hikes are scheduled every weekend.

The nature center is open from 10 a.m. to 5 p.m. daily except Thanksgiving, Christmas, and New Year's Days. Admission is free.

INDIAN PETROGLYPH STATE PARK: Albuquerque's western city limits are marked by five extinct volcanoes. The ancient lava flows were a hunting ground for prehistoric Indians, who camped among the rocks and left a cryptic chronicle of their lifestyle etched and chipped in the dark basalt. Some 10,500 of these petroglyphs have been found in several concentrated groups at this archeological preserve on Unser Boulevard NW, west of Coors Road (tel. 823-4016).

Plaques interpret the rock drawings—animal, human, and ceremonial forms—to visitors, who may take four hiking trails, ranging from easy to moderately difficult, winding through the lava. The 45-minute Mesa Point trail is the most strenuous but also the most rewarding.

Camping is not permitted in the park; it is strictly for day use, with picnic areas, drinking water, and rest rooms. The park is open daily except Tuesday, Wednesday, and state holidays. It closes at 4:30 p.m. in winter, often later in summer. Admission is $1 per vehicle.

NEARBY PUEBLOS

Ten Indian pueblos are located within an hour's drive of central Albuquerque. Six of them—Cochiti, Jemez, San Felipe, Santa Ana, Santo Domingo, and Zia—are described in Chapter XII. The other four are Sandia, Isleta, Laguna, and Acoma.

SANDIA PUEBLO: The pueblo (tel. 867-3317), whose most visible aspects are its Bingo parlor and **Bien Mur Indian Market,** is located 14 miles north of Albuquerque off I-25 or U.S. 85. Established about 1300, it was one of the few pueblos visited by Coronado's contingent in 1540 when it was known as Nafiat. Remains of that village are still visible near the present church. The Sandia people temporarily fled to Hopi country after the Pueblo Rebellion of 1680, but later returned to the Rio Grande.

Many of today's 300 Tiwa-speaking inhabitants work in Albuquerque or at pueblo-run farms or a sand-and-gravel company. They also run the Bingo hall (sessions Monday through Thursday at 12:30 and 6:30 p.m.) and the market on Tramway Road (tel. 867-2876), an outlet for pottery, jewelry, and other crafts.

The pueblo celebrates its feast day on June 13 with a midmorning mass, procession, and afternoon corn dance. No sketching, recording, or picture taking is allowed at any time.

ISLETA PUEBLO: Just 14 miles south of Albuquerque off I-25 or U.S. 85, this largest of the Tiwa-speaking pueblos (tel. 869-3111) comprises several settlements on the west side of the Rio Grande. The largest village, Shiaw-iba, contains one of the few mission churches not destroyed in the 17th-century Pueblo Rebellion.

There is no admission fee to enter the pueblo, though cameras are not allowed. Seek out local women potters whose distinctive red wares feature red-and-black designs on a white background.

The annual feast day, honoring St. Augustine, is September 4. It begins with a midmorning mass and procession, followed by an afternoon harvest dance. The feast day is preceded by one weekend by a Spanish Fiesta at the pueblo.

Most of Isleta Pueblo's 3,000 residents work in Albuquerque; others are employed in farming and ranching, private business, a Bingo hall, or at the Isleta Lakes fishing and camping areas. (Permits can be purchased at the recreation area.)

LAGUNA PUEBLO: The major Keresan-speaking pueblo (tel. 552-6654) consists of a central settlement and five smaller villages some 45 miles west of Albuquerque along I-40 and U.S. 66. Many of the population of 6,000 are engaged in uranium mining as employees of Laguna Enterprises, which has a contract with the U.S. Defense Department. Others are in agriculture or private business, including a tribal-operated residential center for Indian elderly. Permits for fishing in **Paguate Reservoir** can be obtained in the village of Paguate.

Pueblo and Navajo people from throughout the region attend the September 19 Fiesta de San José at the Laguna mission. The fair kicks off with a mass and procession, followed by a harvest dance, sports events, and carnival. New Year's Day (January 1) and Three Kings Day (January 6) are also celebrated at the pueblo with processions and dances. Each smaller village has its own feast day between August 28 and October 17; call the pueblo office for details.

Admission to the pueblo is free, but camera regulations vary from village to village. Visitors should check with officials to see whether photographs are allowed.

ACOMA PUEBLO: The spectacular **"Sky City,"** a walled adobe village perched high atop a sheer rock mesa 365 feet above the 6,600-foot valley floor, is said to have been lived in since the 11th century—the longest continuously occupied community in the United States. As such, both the pueblo (tel. 552-6604) and its mission church of **San Estevan del Rey** are National Historic Landmarks. When Coronado visited in 1540 he suggested that Acoma was "the greatest stronghold in the world"; those who attempt to follow the cliffside footpath to the top, rather than take the modern road, might agree.

The Keresan-speaking Acoma (pronounced "*Ack*-uh-mah") pueblo boasts about 4,000 inhabitants, but only about 50 reside year round on the 70-acre mesa top. Many others maintain ancestral homes and occupy them during ceremonial periods. The terraced three-story buildings face south for maximum exposure to the winter sun. Most of Sky City's permanent residents make livings from tourists who throng here to see the magnificent church, built in 1639 and containing numerous masterpieces of Spanish colonial art, and to purchase the thin-walled white pottery, with brown-and-black designs, for which the pueblo is famous.

Visitors start their tours of Acoma at the visitor center at the base of the mesa. Adults pay $4 (admission is $2.50 for students 12 to 18, $2 for children 6 to 11) to board a 13-seat tour bus, which climbs through a rock garden of 50-foot sandstone monoliths and past precipitously dangling outhouses to the mesa's summit. There's no running water or electricity in this medieval-looking village; a small reservoir collects rainwater for most uses, and drinking water is transported up from below. Wood-hole ladders and mica windows are prevalent among the 300-odd adobe structures.

One-hour tours begin at the visitor center every 20 minutes from 8 a.m. to 5 p.m. in fall and winter, to 6 p.m. in spring, and to 7 p.m. in summer. No tours are offered Easter weekend, the long weekend following the Fourth of July, or the first weekend of October. In addition to tour fees, a charge of $4 is made for still photography and $40 for sketching or painting. While waiting for tours to begin, visitors can peruse the excellent little museum of Acoma history and crafts at the visitor center, or dine on native food in an adjoining café.

The annual San Esteban del Rey feast day at old Acoma (Sky

City) is September 2, when the pueblo's patron saint is honored with a midmorning mass, a procession, an afternoon corn dance, and an arts-and-crafts fair. Traditional "rooster pulls" take place on June 24 and 29 and July 25; a Governor's Feast is held annually in February; and four days of Christmas festivals run from December 25 to 28. Cameras are not allowed on the mesa during feast days.

Other celebrations are held in low-lying pueblo villages at Easter (in **Acomita**,) early May (Santa Maria feast at **McCartys**) and August 10 (San Lorenzo Day in Acomita). Many Acomas work in Grants, 15 miles west of the pueblo, or in Albuquerque; others are cattle ranchers or operate a tribal Bingo parlor. There's also fishing and camping at **Acomita Lake;** permits are available from the pueblo office in Acomita.

To reach old Acoma, drive west 52 miles from Albuquerque on I-40 to the Acoma–Sky City exit, then 13 miles south on paved tribal roads to the visitor center.

SALINAS NATIONAL MONUMENT

The Spanish conquerors' Salinas Province, on the east side of the Manzano Mountains southeast of Albuquerque, was an important trade center in the 17th century because of the salt diligently extracted by colonists from its alkaline beds. Franciscan priests, seeking spiritual and physical protection from raids by Plains Indians, constructed missions of adobe, sandstone, and limestone for their hundreds of native converts. The ruins of some of the most durable—along with evidence of preexisting Anasazi and Mogollon cultures—are highlights of a visit to Salinas National Monument, P.O. Box 496, Mountainair, NM 87036 (tel. 505/847-2585).

The 645-acre monument consists of three separate parcels—the ruins of Abo, Quarai, and Gran Quivira. They are centered around the quiet town of Mountainair, 75 miles southeast of Albuquerque at the junction of U.S. 60 and N.M. 14.

Abo (tel. 847-2400), nine miles west of Mountainair on U.S. 60 and half a mile north on N.M. 513, boasts the 40-foot-high ruins of the Mission of San Gregorio de Abo, a rare example of medieval architecture in the United States.

Quarai, eight miles north of Mountainair on N.M. 14 and one mile west at Punta, preserves the largely intact remains of the Mission of La Purisma Concepción de Cuarac; a small museum in the contact station has a scale model of the original church and samples of artifacts found at the site.

Gran Quivira, 26 miles south of Mountainair on N.M. 14, is still under excavation. More than 1,500 natives once lived on this site in Las Humanas pueblo; 300 rooms and six *kivas,* some as early as 1300, can be seen here. There are indications that an older village, dating to 800, may have previously stood here. Ruins of two churches and a convent have also been preserved.

All three pueblos, and the churches that rose above them, are believed to have been abandoned by the 1670s. Self-guided tour pamphlets can be obtained at the parcels' respective contact stations and at the national monument visitor center in Mountainair's Shaffer Hotel, a block south of U.S. 60 on N.M. 14. The visitor center, which offers films and audio-visual presentations on the region's history, artifacts displays, and an art exhibit, is open daily from 8 a.m. to 5 p.m.

The three sites are open daily from 9 a.m. to 6 p.m. in summer, 8 a.m. to 5 p.m. the rest of the year. A one-time entrance fee of $1 per person or $3 per vehicle is charged from May to September at Quarai and Gran Quivira.

Picnicking is permitted at all sites. Would-be campers might consider **Manzano Mountains State Park,** in wooded foothills 13 miles northwest of Mountainair on N.M. 55, or **Sen. Willie M. Chavez State Park,** on the Rio Grande near Belen, 45 miles west of Mountainair and 30 miles south of Albuquerque on U.S. 85. Both have drinking water and modern rest rooms, and are recommended spots for birdwatchers.

SIGHTS ALONG INTERSTATE 40 WEST

Travelers heading west along I-40 from Albuquerque to Arizona and southern California pass by or near numerous intriguing attractions.

Grants, a uranium-mining town of 10,000 people 76 miles west of Albuquerque, is of particular interest for its **New Mexico Museum of Mining,** 100 Iron St. (tel. 287-4802). Former miners conduct underground tours of a simulated (but very realistic) uranium mine. Admission is $2; the museum is open from 10 a.m. to 4 p.m. Monday through Saturday (closed from noon to 1 p.m.) and 1 to 4 p.m. on Sunday. Lodging and meals are available in Grants at Best Western's **The Inn,** East Spur Hwy. (P.O. Drawer T), Grants, NM 87020 (tel. 505/287-7901).

El Malpais National Monument, dedicated in 1988, comprises 114,000 acres of lava badlands, threaded with lava tubes and ice caves, south of Grants. Major points of interest include the Sandstone Bluffs overlook and La Ventana Natural Arch on N.M. 117 and the Bandera Crater and Ice Cave (tel. 783-4303) along N.M. 53. Several waterless hiking trails weave across the badlands terrain.

El Morro National Monument (tel. 783-5132), 43 miles west of Grants along N.M. 53, has been called "Inscription

Rock." Passersby for three centuries—beginning with Don Juan de Onate in 1605, 15 years before the Pilgrims landed at Plymouth Rock—carved their names and messages into the sandstone. It was preserved by the National Park Service in 1906. Conquistadors and missionaries, U.S. Army officers, and pioneer emigrants left their own notes in passing; Indian petroglyphs show that they were not the first. Self-guided trail booklets to the inscriptions and to pueblo ruins atop the rock are available at the visitor center, open from 8 a.m. to 8 p.m. in summer and 8 a.m. to 5 p.m. in winter. A campground is open year round.

Zuñi Pueblo (tel. 782-4481), 30 miles south of Gallup, is the largest of New Mexico's 19 pueblos with 6,600 citizens. In many regards it's the most unusual of all pueblos. The language spoken by the Zuñi is different from any other dialect, and the religion, which has persisted despite missionary influence, is likewise unique.

Though traditionally farmers, the Zuñi are best known for their turquoise-and-silver inlay jewelry and other handcrafts, including stone animal fetishes. Zuñi needlepoint is an elaborate art form in its own right, finely cut turquoise set in intricate patterns of silver.

The largest number of Zuñi live at the old pueblo, ten miles west of the intersection of N.M. 32 and 53. Others live in nearby Black Rock, Pescado, and similar outlying settlements. Many Zuñi work in Gallup, but a majority are employed in diverse local occupations, including the Zuñi School District and a private radio station. Camping, fishing (at Nutria Lake), and hunting permits can be obtained from the tribal Game and Fish Department. Guide service can also be arranged.

The Zuñi Fair and Rodeo attracts large crowds each year during Labor Day weekend, but those interested in traditional culture and religion are more likely to be drawn to the Shalako ceremony over an early December weekend. The celebration lasts all night long with dances and chants. The exact date is not decided until mid-November.

No cameras are allowed on the pueblo on ceremonial days; at other times, there's a small fee.

There's more to **Gallup** than the town's seemingly endless U.S. Rte. 66 neon strip, extending for several miles east and west of downtown, might at first indicate. A frontier atmosphere lingers among the late-19th- and early-20th-century buildings, and Gallup's proliferation of Indian trading posts/pawnbrokers offers opportunities for shopping and bargaining not found elsewhere in New Mexico.

Recommended accommodation is at Best Western's **The Inn,**

3009 W. 66th Ave., Gallup, NM 87301 (tel. 505/722-2221), or at the historic **El Rancho Hotel,** 1000 E. 66th Ave., Gallup, NM 87301 (tel. 505/863-4408). The **Gallup Convention and Visitors Bureau,** 103 W. 66th Ave., Gallup, NM 87301 (tel. 505/722-2227), is a valuable resource for visitors to the town.

Red Rock State Park, six miles east of downtown Gallup in a natural amphitheater of red sandstone buttes, features an auditorium/convention center, historical museum, post office, stables, and modern campgrounds. Its 8,000-seat arena is the site of the annual Inter-Tribal Indian Ceremonial, a four-day mid-August spectacle which has incorporated rodeo, dancing, and arts-and-crafts competition since 1922.

Chaco Culture National Historic Park, Star Route 4, Box 6500, Bloomfield, NM 87413 (tel. 505/988-6727 or 988-6716), represents the high point of pre-Columbian pueblo civilization. A must-see attraction for any visitor even vaguely interested in ancient Indians, it includes more than a dozen large Anasazi ruins and hundreds of smaller sites in the wide streambed of the normally dry Chaco Wash. **Pueblo Bonito,** constructed over three acres of land in the 11th century A.D., may have been the largest apartment house built anywhere in the world prior to 1887; it probably housed as many as 1,200 people.

Many artifacts found during excavations, including those like sea shells and macaw feathers indicating a strong system of trade, are displayed in the museum at the visitor center. Self-guiding trail brochures are obtained here, as well as overnight camping permits.

New Mexico Hwy. 57 is unpaved for some 20 miles before it enters the park 95 miles northeast of Gallup. It is passable for standard vehicles in most weather, but suggested only for four-wheel-drives when conditions are rainy and muddy.

OUTDOOR ACTIVITIES

Despite its urban sprawl, Albuquerque is easy to get away from—and residents frequently do, to participate in a wide variety of sporting pursuits within and beyond the city limits.

SKIING: The **Sandia Peak Ski Area** has twin base-to-summit chair lifts to its upper slopes at 10,360 feet, and a 1,700-foot vertical drop. There are 22 trails, 14 of them geared to intermediates, and a short beginner hill above the day lodge and ski-rental shop. All-day lift tickets are $21 for adults, $15 for children; rental packages are $11 for adults, $9 for kids. For full information, contact the ski area's general offices at 10 Tramway Loop NE, Albuquerque, NM 87122 (tel. 505/296-9585).

RIVER RAFTING: Check out the offerings of **Wolf Whitewater Rafting Co.,** P.O. Box 666, Sandia Park, NM 87047 (tel. 505/836-0008, or toll free 800/552-0070).

HORSE TRIPS: Two outfitters cater to equestrians with daily schedules: **Los Amigos Round-Up,** P.O. Box 10359, Alameda, NM 87184 (tel. 898-8173); and **Tramway Riding,** 25 Tramway Rd., Albuquerque, NM 87133 (tel. 293-1270).

HORSE RACING: On the State Fairgrounds at Lomas and Louisiana Boulevards NE, **The Downs at Albuquerque** (tel. 265-0943) has racing and betting from January 30 to April 27.

HIKING AND BACKPACKING: The 1.6-million-acre **Cibola National Forest** offers ample opportunities. In the Sandia Mountain section alone are 18 recreation sites, though only one—Cedro Peak, four miles southeast of Tijeras—allows overnight camping. For details, contact national forest headquarters at 10308 Candelaria Rd. NE, Albuquerque, NM 87112 (tel. 505/275-5207).

GOLF AND TENNIS: There are a dozen public and private golf courses in and near the city, and some 130 public tennis courts. Contact the visitors bureau at 243-3696 for information.

BALLOONING: Visitors not content to watch the colorful craft rise into the clear blue skies have a choice of several hot-air balloon operators from whom to get a ride. They include **Beautiful Balloons Co.,** 4801 Ellison St. NE, Suite O (tel. 344-7334); **Tours of Enchantment,** 5801 Jones Pl. NW (tel. 831-4285); and **World Balloon Corporation,** 4800 Eubank Blvd. NE (tel. 293-6800).

SPECTATOR SPORTS: The Albuquerque Dukes of the Class AAA Pacific Coast League are the No. 1 farm team of the 1988 world-champion Los Angeles Dodgers. They play 72 baseball games from April to September in the city-owned **Albuquerque Sports Stadium,** 1601 Stadium Blvd. SE at University Boulevard (tel. 243-1791). On the south side of Stadium Boulevard are the 30,000-seat **University of New Mexico Stadium,** home of the Lobos football team, and the 17,000-seat **University Arena,** where capacity crowds cheer the UNM basketball team.

SPECIAL EVENTS

There's a full calendar of events throughout the year in Albuquerque. The following listing touches on a few major occasions. **Gem and Mineral Show,** March 15–16, Old Airport Terminal Building, Albuquerque International Airport (tel. 265-3711, ext. 250). Geologists, mineralogists, and rockhounds engage in competitive displays, demonstrations of gold-panning and mining techniques, and identifications of ore samples.

Gathering of Nations Pow-Wow, mid-April, State Fairgrounds (tel. 831-1820). Dance competitions, arts, and crafts.

The Great Race, mid-May, 14-mile stretch of the Rio Grande (tel. 768-3490). Eleven categories of craft, including rafts, kayaks, and canoes, race down the river.

Spring Arts New Mexico, May 23 to June 30, many locations (tel. toll free 800/732-8267). A statewide exposure to the visual, performing, and literary arts, focusing on Albuquerque, Santa Fe, and Taos, with many events daily.

Summerfest, first Saturday of June through early August, Civic Plaza (tel. 768-3550). Arts and crafts, food, and entertainment from 5 to 10 p.m., each week featuring a different one of Albuquerque's many ethnic communities.

New Mexico Arts and Crafts Fair, last weekend of June, State Fairgrounds (tel. 884-9043). The second-largest event of its type in the United States presents more than 200 artisans demonstrating and selling their crafts, plus nonstop entertainment from 10 a.m. to 10 p.m. on Friday and Saturday and 10 a.m. to 6 p.m. on Sunday. Admission is charged.

Fireworks displays, July 3–5, various locations throughout the city. The biggest is the Optimists display in Old Town.

Feria Artesana, last weekend of August, Convention Center and Civic Plaza (tel. 848-1334) or 766-7660). Four centuries of Hispanic heritage are celebrated with music, dancing, food, and an outdoor folk mass, plus juried competitions of more than 250 artisans from all over the state.

New Mexico State Fair, 17 days in September, State Fairgrounds (tel. 265-1791). One of America's top ten fairs, it features parimutel horse racing, a nationally acclaimed rodeo, entertainment by top C&W artists, Indian and Spanish villages, and the requisite midway and livestock shows.

Albuquerque International Hot Air Balloon Fiesta, first through second weekends of October (tel. 344-3501). The world's largest balloon rally brings together 500 colorful aerialists in races and contests. Mass ascensions leave at 7 a.m. on Saturday and Sunday from the Balloon Fiesta Launch Site at Alameda Boulevard and Washington Street NE, near Albuquerque's northern city limits. Various special events are staged throughout the city all week long.

Southwest Arts and Crafts Festival, mid-November, Exhibit Hall, State Fairgrounds (tel. 881-2777 or 265-1791). More than 150 artisans in mixed media from throughout the United States attend this invitational juried competition with an emphasis on southwestern art. Works are shown on Friday and Saturday from 10 a.m. to 10 p.m. and on Sunday from 10 a.m. to 6 p.m.

CULTURE AND NIGHTLIFE

Santa Fe may be known as the cultural capital of the American Southwest, but Albuquerque—ten times the size of the state capital—has its share of artisans and milieus. These listings are selective; pick up the monthly *Albuquerque Living* magazine or *Route 66* tabloid, or check the Friday *Albuquerque Journal* or *Tribune,* for current listings of performances.

PERFORMING ARTS: The **Albuquerque Civic Light Opera Association** (tel. 345-6577) produces five major Broadway shows per year in March, June, July, September, and December at Popejoy Hall on the University of New Mexico campus.

The **Albuquerque Little Theatre** (tel. 242-4750) presents six plays annually during a September-to-June season. The 57-year-old company has a 626-seat theater at 224 San Pasquale Ave. SW.

The **Albuquerque Opera Theatre** (tel. 296-3564 or 248-8492) has an October-to-May season at the historic KiMo Theatre, 423 Central Ave. NW (tel. 848-1374).

La Compañia de Teatro de Albuquerque (tel. 242-7929), one of only ten major professional Hispanic companies in the U.S. and Puerto Rico, presents four productions at the KiMo Theatre during a September-to-May season.

The **New Mexico Repertory Theatre** has its headquarters at the KiMo Theatre (tel. 243-4500). The state's only resident professional theater company, its annual program varies from classical drama to contemporary comedy.

The **New Mexico Symphony Orchestra** (tel. 843-7657 or 842-8565) performs classical, chamber, pops, and ensemble concerts all over the state throughout the year. Local performances are usually given in the UNM's 2,100-seat Popejoy Hall.

The **Southwest Ballet Company** (tel. 294-1423) offers a variety of productions during a November-to-April season.

The Cultural Affairs Division of the City of Albuquerque hosts major international dance, music, and theatrical troupes year round at the **KiMo Theatre** and the **South Broadway Cultural Center,** 1025 Broadway SE (tel. 848-1320). Call the KiMo Theatre (tel. 848-1374) for details.

THE FINE ARTS: Several publications recommend Albuquerque arts and crafts galleries. Take a look at the brochure published by the Albuquerque Gallery Association, "A Select Guide to Albuquerque Galleries," or Wingspread Communications' annual "The Collector's Guide to Albuquerque," widely distributed at shops.

The greatest concentration by far of city galleries is in Old Town; others are spread around the city, with smaller groupings in the university district and in the more affluent suburbs of Albuquerque's eastern foothills.

Traditional Old Town favorites include the **Adobe Gallery,** 413 Romero St. NW (tel. 243-8485), specializing in native art and watercolors; the **Galeria de Artesanos,** 110 San Felipe St. NW (tel. 243-9711), a local cooperative gallery; the **Andrews Pueblo Pottery & Art Gallery,** 400 San Felipe St. NW (tel. 243-0414), with contemporary and pre-Columbian Indian pottery; the **Mariposa Gallery,** 113 Romero St. NW, with five rooms of contemporary crafts; and **Nizhoni Moses Ltd.,** 326 San Felipe St. NW (tel. 842-1808), featuring Pueblo pottery, Navajo weavings, Taos furnishings, and a variety of jewelry.

Top-quality products can also be obtained elsewhere in Albuquerque. Try the **J. B. Tanner Trading Company,** 3600D Menaul Blvd. NE (tel. 884-1056), for Navajo rugs, jewelry, and sand paintings; **The Palms,** 1504 Lomas Blvd. NW (tel. 247-8504), for pottery and turquoise jewelry; and **Andrew Nagan Old Navajo Rugs,** 14 Corrales Rd. in Corrales (tel. 898-5058), for sales and appraisals of historic weavings, by appointment.

NIGHTLIFE: As might be expected in a city of half a million people, there's no shortage of spots to play after dark.

Caravan East, 7605 Central Ave. NE (tel. 265-7877), calls itself America's largest country-and-western club—a claim that may be justified. Two bands play nightly from 5 p.m. to 2 a.m., and there are occasional national acts. There's a cover of $2 for women, $3 for men, only on weekends.

Cheers, 2100 Eubank Blvd. NE (tel. 291-8282), is a casual disco that attracts a college crowd. Weekend cover is $3.

Confetti, in a shopping mall at 9800 Montgomery Blvd. NE (tel. 298-2113), is a big hard-rock club with a sunken dance floor and pool tables for a younger crowd. The cover is $3; closed Sunday.

El Madrid, 421 First Ave. SW (tel. 242-0829), books blues bands to a beside-the-railroad-tracks venue near downtown. The clientele here is less concerned about looks than sounds.

The **Fat Chance Bar and Grille,** 2216 Central Ave. NE (tel. 265-7601), is a campus watering hole with live music Wednesday through Sunday.

L'Parc, 9500 Montgomery Blvd. NE (tel. 293-9500), an up-scale dress-to-kill disco, has dance floors on several levels, seven bars, and a DJ who plays nonstop except during "best legs" and similar contests. Cover charge is $4.

Shooters, 6601 Uptown Blvd. NE (tel. 883-0600), is a popular new C&W club with blackjack and roulette tables.

Index

NOW, SAVE MONEY ON ALL YOUR TRAVELS!
Join Frommer's™ Dollarwise® Travel Club

Saving money while traveling is never a simple matter, which is why the **Dollarwise Travel Club** was formed 31 years ago. Developed in response to requests from Frommer Travel Guide readers, the Club provides cost-cutting travel strategies, up-to-date travel information, and a sense of community for value-conscious travelers from all over the world.

In keeping with the money-saving concept, the annual membership fee is low —$18 (U.S. residents) or $20 (residents of Canada, Mexico, and other countries)—and is immediately exceeded by the value of your benefits, which include:

1. Any TWO books listed on the following pages.
2. Plus any ONE Frommer City Guide.
3. A subscription to our quarterly newspaper, *The Dollarwise Traveler*.
4. A membership card that entitles you to purchase through the Club all Frommer publications for 33% to 50% off their retail price.

The eight-page *Dollarwise Traveler* tells you about the latest developments in good-value travel worldwide and includes the following columns: **Hospitality Exchange** (for those offering and seeking hospitality in cities all over the world); **Share-a-Trip** (for those looking for travel companions to share costs); and **Readers Ask . . . Readers Reply** (for those with travel questions that other members can answer).

Aside from the Frommer Guides, the Serious Shopper Guides, and the Gault Millau Guides, you can also choose from our Special Editions. These include such titles as **California with Kids** (a compendium of the best of California's accommodations, restaurants, and sightseeing attractions appropriate for those traveling with toddlers through teens); **Candy Apple: New York with Kids** (a spirited guide to the Big Apple by a savvy New York grandmother that's perfect for both visitors and residents); **Caribbean Hideaways** (the 100 most romantic places to stay in the Islands, all rated on ambience, food, sport opportunities, and price); **Honeymoon Destinations** (a guide to planning and choosing just the right destination from hundreds of possibilities in the U.S., Mexico, and the Caribbean); **Marilyn Wood's Wonderful Weekends** (a selection of the best mini-vacations within a 200-mile radius of New York City, including descriptions of country inns and other accommodations, restaurants, picnic spots, sights, and activities); and **Paris Rendez-Vous** (a delightful guide to the best places to meet in Paris whether for power breakfasts or dancing till dawn).

To join this Club, simply send the appropriate membership fee with your name and address to: Frommer's Dollarwise Travel Club, 15 Columbus Circle, New York, NY 10023. Remember to specify which single city guide and which two other guides you wish to receive in your initial package of member's benefits. Or tear out the next page, check off your choices, and send the page to us with your membership fee.

FROMMER BOOKS   **Date**_____
PRENTICE HALL TRAVEL
15 COLUMBUS CIRCLE
NEW YORK, NY 10023
212-373-8125

Friends:
Please send me the books checked below:

FROMMER™ GUIDES

(Guides to sightseeing and tourist accommodations and facilities from budget to deluxe, with emphasis
on the medium-priced.)

☐ Alaska	$14.95	☐ Germany	$14.95
☐ Australia	$14.95	☐ Italy	$14.95
☐ Austria & Hungary	$14.95	☐ Japan & Hong Kong	$14.95
☐ Belgium, Holland & Luxembourg	$14.95	☐ Mid-Atlantic States	$14.95
☐ Bermuda & The Bahamas	$14.95	☐ New England	$14.95
☐ Brazil	$14.95	☐ New York State	$14.95
☐ Canada	$14.95	☐ Northwest	$14.95
☐ Caribbean	$14.95	☐ Portugal, Madeira & the Azores	$14.95
☐ Cruises (incl. Alaska, Carib, Mex, Hawaii,		☐ Skiing Europe	$14.95
Panama, Canada & US)	$14.95	☐ South Pacific	$14.95
☐ California & Las Vegas	$14.95	☐ Southeast Asia	$14.95
☐ Egypt	$14.95	☐ Southern Atlantic States	$14.95
☐ England & Scotland	$14.95	☐ Southwest	$14.95
☐ Florida	$14.95	☐ Switzerland & Liechtenstein	$14.95
☐ France	$14.95	☐ USA	$15.95

FROMMER $-A-DAY® GUIDES

(In-depth guides to sightseeing and low-cost tourist accommodations and facilities.)

☐ Europe on $40 a Day	$15.95	☐ New York on $60 a Day	$13.95
☐ Australia on $30 a Day	$12.95	☐ New Zealand on $45 a Day	$13.95
☐ Eastern Europe on $25 a Day	$13.95	☐ Scandinavia on $60 a Day	$13.95
☐ England on $50 a Day	$13.95	☐ Scotland & Wales on $40 a Day	$13.95
☐ Greece on $35 a Day	$13.95	☐ South America on $35 a Day	$13.95
☐ Hawaii on $60 a Day	$13.95	☐ Spain & Morocco on $40 a Day	$13.95
☐ India on $25 a Day	$12.95	☐ Turkey on $30 a Day	$13.95
☐ Ireland on $35 a Day	$13.95	☐ Washington, D.C. & Historic Va. on	
☐ Israel on $40 a Day	$13.95	$40 a Day	$13.95
☐ Mexico on $35 a Day	$13.95		

FROMMER TOURING GUIDES

(Color illustrated guides that include walking tours, cultural and historic sites, and other
vital travel information.)

☐ Australia	$9.95	☐ Paris	$8.95
☐ Egypt	$8.95	☐ Scotland	$9.95
☐ Florence	$8.95	☐ Thailand	$9.95
☐ London	$8.95	☐ Venice	$8.95

TURN PAGE FOR ADDITONAL BOOKS AND ORDER FORM.

FROMMER CITY GUIDES

(Pocket-size guides to sightseeing and tourist accommodations and facilities in all price ranges.)

☐ Amsterdam/Holland $7.95	☐ Minneapolis/St. Paul $7.95
☐ Athens $7.95	☐ Montréal/Québec City $7.95
☐ Atlantic City/Cape May $7.95	☐ New Orleans $7.95
☐ Barcelona* $7.95	☐ New York $7.95
☐ Belgium $7.95	☐ Orlando/Disney World/EPCOT $7.95
☐ Boston $7.95	☐ Paris $7.95
☐ Cancún/Cozumel/Yucatán $7.95	☐ Philadelphia $7.95
☐ Chicago $7.95	☐ Rio $7.95
☐ Denver/Boulder* $7.95	☐ Rome $7.95
☐ Dublin/Ireland $7.95	☐ San Francisco $7.95
☐ Hawaii $7.95	☐ Santa Fe/Taos/Albuquerque $7.95
☐ Hong Kong* $7.95	☐ Seattle/Portland* $7.95
☐ Las Vegas $7.95	☐ Sydney $7.95
☐ Lisbon/Madrid/Costa del Sol $7.95	☐ Tokyo* $7.95
☐ London $7.95	☐ Vancouver/Victoria* $7.95
☐ Los Angeles $7.95	☐ Washington, D.C. $7.95
☐ Mexico City/Acapulco $7.95	*Available June 1990

SPECIAL EDITIONS

☐ A Shopper's Guide to the Caribbean $12.95	☐ Manhattan's Outdoor Sculpture $15.95
☐ Beat the High Cost of Travel $6.95	☐ Motorist's Phrase Book (Fr/Ger/Sp) $4.95
☐ Bed & Breakfast—N. America $11.95	☐ Paris Rendez-Vous $10.95
☐ California with Kids $14.95	☐ Swap and Go (Home Exchanging) $10.95
☐ Caribbean Hideaways $14.95	☐ The Candy Apple (NY with Kids) $12.95
☐ Honeymoon Destinations (US, Mex & Carib) . . $12.95	☐ Travel Diary and Record Book $5.95

☐ Where to Stay USA (Lodging from $3 to $30 a night) $10.95
☐ Marilyn Wood's Wonderful Weekends (Conn, Del, Mass, NH, NJ, NY, Pa, RI, VT) $11.95
☐ The New World of Travel (Annual sourcebook by Arthur Frommer for savvy travelers) $16.95

SERIOUS SHOPPER'S GUIDES

(Illustrated guides listing hundreds of stores, conveniently organized alphabetically by category.)

☐ Italy $15.95	☐ Los Angeles $14.95
☐ London $15.95	☐ Paris $15.95

GAULT MILLAU

(The only guides that distinguish the truly superlative from the merely overrated.)

☐ The Best of Chicago $15.95	☐ The Best of Los Angeles $14.95
☐ The Best of France $16.95	☐ The Best of New England $15.95
☐ The Best of Hong Kong $16.95	☐ The Best of New York $14.95
☐ The Best of Italy $16.95	☐ The Best of Paris $16.95
☐ The Best of London $16.95	☐ The Best of San Francisco $14.95

☐ The Best of Washington, D.C. $14.95

ORDER NOW!

In U.S. include $2 shipping UPS for 1st book; $1 ea. add'l book. Outside U.S. $3 and $1, respectively.
Allow four to six weeks for delivery in U.S., longer outside U.S.
Enclosed is my check or money order for $_____

NAME _____

ADDRESS _____

CITY _____ STATE _____ ZIP _____

0190